Jonathan Okinaga is to be congratulated for putting together this marvelous resource, which includes well-researched biblical materials and helpful commentary to help followers of Christ address more than fifty different heart issues, spiritual matters, relationship challenges, and health concerns. The book is designed particularly for students, but also for church leaders, especially counselors. *A Biblical Handbook* lives up to its name by providing a thoughtful, biblical, hermeneutical, and theological foundation to engage these real-life issues. It is a joy to recommend this accessible and well-designed volume.

David S. Dockery
President, Southwestern Baptist Theological Seminary

Theory and practice are vital in any discipline. Here is a book that is solidly based on Scripture but is thoroughly practical. It is full of practical help and advice for the biblical counselor to utilize in a variety of counseling situations. Okinaga includes more than 150 discussion starters and 400 practical advice snippets, along with homework assignments. This book is one of the best "how to" guides for biblical counseling. Every pastor and biblical counselor needs this excellent volume!

David L. Allen Ph.D.
Distinguished Professor of Practical Theology and
Dean of the Adrian Rogers Center for Biblical Preaching,
Mid-America Baptist Theological Seminary

We all need help—just at different times of our lives. In truth, we each need different types of help in different seasons of our lives. So, here comes Dr. O to the rescue...with a handbook of help! While offering counsel on 48 "Heart Issues," even more so, this book presents biblical hope with practical help. Yes, the scriptural support from this book can benefit us all.

June Hunt
Founder, Hope for the Heart
Author of Counseling Through Your Bible Handbook *and*
The Biblical Counseling Reference Guide

Is there an answer in the Bible for every issue of human existence? Certainly not – but unequivocally, yes! There are no answers in the Scriptures about whether a person should vote Democrat or Republican. There is no information about whether one should move to California or Papua, Indonesia. Neither does the Bible suggest what one should decide about entering the bull-riding competition in the local rodeo. But there are clearly revealed in Scripture "heart principles" that provide the parameters for every decision in life. Jonathan Okinaga demonstrates that reality in his life, teaching, and writing.

Okinaga recognizes that "as a man thinks in his heart, so is he" (Prov 23:7). As a matter of fact, "a man's heart reveals the man" (Prov 27:19). Consequently, to experience the blessings of God you must "keep your heart with all diligence, for out of it springs the issues of life" (Prov 4:23). Okinaga's own life in a wonderful Christian home was shattered when he was deceived in his heart by the lure of drugs but regained when his heart yearned for the presence of the resurrected Christ. Jon Okinaga learned to follow the yearnings of his heart.

Subsequent to years of testing this hypothesis, Okinaga brings to his rich experience a fully developed grasp of God's Word. Thus, the professor introduces to counselees answers to the challenges of life with an amazing ability to find appropriate passages that reflect the heart of God and comfort the hearts of men and women. To comprehend how to use the Bible effectively in counseling, you will find this perspective volume to be an index to the heart. Read this book, and counsel with humility and confidence.

Paige Patterson
President, Sandy Creek Foundation

Having compassion for hurting people is a valuable trait. But compassion alone may not be adequate to bring healing. Believing biblical counseling can be part of the healing process is also valuable. But again, just believing in biblical counseling may not be adequate. Fortunately, Jonathan Okinaga has provided the missing elements that can result in help for hurting people.

In his book, *A Biblical Handbook for Counseling Heart Issues*, Okinaga (Ph.D.) has provided the hands-on tools biblical counselors need to lead people toward change and healing. He gives at least three Scripture passages for almost fifty heart issues, explains why each passage is applicable, provides practical advice, and suggests homework. He also includes discussion starters. Biblical counselors now have the tools they need to spark conversations about God, faith, and overcoming life struggles. This is one book that should be in every counselor's library.

Richard Ross, Ph.D.
Senior Professor of Student Ministry, Southwestern Baptist Theological Seminary

A Biblical Handbook for Counseling Heart Issues will walk individuals through resolving the heart of our problems, not just the symptoms. This book is not a handbook of how-tos for a better life, but a handbook for walking through heart-change in our life. Rather than avoiding or numbing the problems, this book addresses the sin in our hearts. I pray that this book is a blessing for you and those you counsel throughout life.

Jim DiLavore
Pastor, Grace Point Church Gallatin

Dr. Okinaga's vision and passion for counseling that overcomes even the darkest strongholds of sin through the power of Scripture is reflected as thoroughly in this work as in the rest of his ministry. His intensely practical and straightforward approach here is ideal for pastors in small and rural churches who often have limited time and resources for extensive research and training. I am thankful that this resource will be available to Brothers and Sisters around the globe as they seek to mend broken hearts and minds for the glory of God.

Jacob Lloyd Smith
Pastor, Urban Baptist Church

A Biblical Handbook
for Counseling

Heart
Issues

A Biblical Handbook
for Counseling

Heart
Issues

Jonathan Okinaga

NEBP
ACADEMIC

BENNINGTON, VT

TABLE OF CONTENTS

FOREWORD

Over 50 years ago, Jay Adams wrote a book called *Competent to Counsel*. In this book (which is still in print!) he provides encouragement for counselors to use the Word of God to help people deal with the challenges they face in life. *Competent to Counsel* kicked off the modern biblical counseling movement (what Jay Adams called Nouthetic Counseling) and presented the idea that the Bible is sufficient for counseling and that Christians can and should counsel others using God's Word.

In *Competent to Counsel*, Adams introduced the Personal Data Inventory (PDI), which provides a means to get information from prospective counselees. There are many variations of the form in use today, but commonly included on the form is a checklist of challenges, or heart issues, that the counselee may be facing. The instructions in the PDI tell the counselee to put a checkmark by any of these issues with which they struggle. This can be a great way for the counselor to plan out what topics to address with the counselee.

In this book, Jon Okinaga has developed an amazing resource to help counselors prepare to provide counseling for each of these heart issues listed on the PDI. He addresses forty-eight heart issues, and for each one, he provides three biblical passages that can be used in counseling the heart issue as well as an explanation of how the passages are applicable. Additionally, he provides a definition for each of the heart issues as well as practical advice for the counselor and homework assignments suggestions.

A Biblical Handbook for Counseling Heart Issues

This book will be very beneficial and can be utilized in at least three ways. First, for the counselor who uses a PDI and wants direction and assistance in preparing to counsel one or more of the heart issues, the material Dr. Okinaga presents on the issue can be of great help. Second, the book can be a great resource for any Christian who wants to learn more about one or more heart issues that they are interested in studying. Third, one can study through all of the topics as a way to learn about the issues as well as to proactively prepare to counsel someone they may encounter.

In Ephesians 4:15 we read, "but speaking the truth in love, we are to grow up in all aspects into Him who is the head, even Christ." It is my prayer that God uses this resource to help you be more effective speaking the Truth in love, and that you grow through doing so.

Minister the Word!

John Babler, Ph.D.
Chairman and Professor, Department of Biblical Counseling,
Mid-America Baptist Theological Seminary
Board Member and Fellow, Association of Certified Biblical Counselors

ACKNOWLEDGEMENTS

For the last four years, I have been teaching as a professor at Southwestern Baptist Theological Seminary. Though students often ask, I have never provided them the Scripture verses that I use in counseling sessions. I've told them, "I won't do it; the last thing I need is for you to use a passage I suggest, and then when your counselee asks why you used that scripture, all you can say is, 'Because Dr. O said so.'" This challenged my students to do their work, utilize the library's commentaries, or purchase what they needed from Logos. There was no reason for me to share or put the effort into writing everything out (or, I have to be honest, I did not want to spend all the time needed to do it formally).

Everything changed when I went to Japan. The students made me stop my lecture and re-share any passage I mentioned. It started to annoy me. The same thing happened again when I delivered my lectures on case studies. I would share my answers but would have to stop my lecture due to questions about the Bible verses I would use. Annoyed, I flippantly said, "Just look up the passages in a commentary so you are using the right passage!" One of the translators informed me that they don't have commentaries in Japanese, at least not to the extent that we do in America. I should have known when I had mentioned my Top Ten Biblical Counseling books...none were translated into Japanese, and only a few into Portuguese. I told the group, "I will provide three passages per heart issue on the Personal Data Inventory (PDI) + why the passage is applicable + Practical Advice + Homework."

A Biblical Handbook for Counseling Heart Issues

Me and my big mouth. Well, here it is almost a year later. I am forever grateful to Dr. Gady Youmans for his invaluable contributions to the passages, exposition, practical advice, and homework assignments, to Dr. Cheryl Bell, who helped with the homework and practical application, and to Dr. John Hofecker, who provided the chapter on how to interpret the Bible. Special thanks to Derrick Bledsoe for his theological edits. I want to thank the others who assisted in this work: Andrew Blackwell, Ricci Chen, Christian Delaney, Ubile Jenkins, Kelly Rich, Megan Tanner, Abigail Yarnell, and Matthew Wilbanks. This volume contains more than 360 Bible verses; each explained with relevance as to how it applied to overcoming struggles with the Bible as the foundation. Additionally, readers will find just under 400 practical advice/homework assignments and over 150 Discussion Starters to spark in-depth conversations about God, faith, and overcoming life struggles.

Jonathan Okinaga, Ph.D.
Assistant Professor of Biblical Counseling and
Hope for the Heart Chair of Biblical Counseling,
Southwestern Baptist Theological Seminary

HOW TO
USE THE BOOK

Always remember that biblical counselors do not try to "fix" anyone. The goal of biblical counseling is to lead our counselees to the feet of Christ and have them open up the Bible. The Holy Spirit will transform your counselees from the inside out.

This *Heart Issues* book is based on the PDI that I use in my counseling sessions.[1] Those I counsel complete the PDI. It identifies their struggles and helps determine what to discuss in our counseling sessions. Granted, I'm leaning on the Holy Spirit for wisdom and discernment concerning what we discuss, what passages we will examine, and what homework I will assign.

These passages, practical advice, and homework have been provided to give newer biblical counselors a framework and idea of what to do in their counseling settings. Many books have been written on why we need to practice biblical counseling in the church (that is, the philosophy of counseling); however, very little, if any, time has been spent sharing *how* to do biblical counseling. My hope and prayer are that this book can help fill this void.

Step One: Instruct your counselee to complete the PDI and ask them to clarify what they answered that you need help understanding.

Step Two: Consult the *Heart Issues* section of the PDI and identify the counselee's struggle.

---

1   This form, "Soul-Care Network Fillable PDI 2023," is available to download for free at https://soulcare.io/downloads.

A Biblical Handbook for Counseling Heart Issues

Step Three: Use the material in this book to provide you a springboard into the topics you will be facing.

Step Four: This book is NOT perfect so you **must** rely on the Holy Spirit to lead your counseling sessions. This book only intends to help point you in the right direction as you counsel.

HOW TO INTERPRET THE BIBLE

In the Acknowledgements, I expressed concern about producing a Handbook; I worried about biblical counselors who might not have access to necessary commentaries and counseling resources. To address this issue, I enlisted Dr. John Hofecker's assistance. He guides those who lack resources needed to exegete Scripture properly and accurately. Once again, use this Handbook as a guide, not a final resource. Spend time in God's Word and develop your own passages to use, reflections to share, practical advice to offer, homework to give, and Discussion Starters to begin conversations.

PREPARING THE HEART

Do your best to present yourself to God as one approved, a worker
who has no need to be ashamed, rightly handling the word of truth.
2 Tim 2:15, ESV

In his second Epistle to Timothy, Paul delivers some final instructions to his son in the faith. Because Paul understands that his time on earth is drawing to a close (2 Tim 4:6), he delivers some final words to his protégé, thus imparting to Timothy wisdom that he must pass on to others (2 Tim 2:2). Within those final instructions, Paul includes the following exhortation to Timothy: *to rightly handle the word of truth.* This task will take some effort on Timothy's part. This responsibility will prove demanding, yet it belongs to the high calling of all who walk faithfully with God.

However, an implication can be drawn from the exhortation that gives me pause. If we need to work at handling the word correctly, then by implication, we can *mishandle* it if we do not take great care in our task. I remember when I was a young boy, I received a gift—my first knife. My father spent some time showing me how to handle it well. He explained that if I did not treat the blade with a certain level of respect and handle it correctly, I could do significant harm to myself or others. Sadly, I have a few scars that demonstrate I learned some of those lessons the hard way. If I can harm myself with a simple knife, what harm might I do with something as powerful as the sword of the Spirit handled incorrectly?

Indeed, Paul provides a few examples of the harm that can be done by mishandling the Word. He speaks of *"ruining the hearers"* (v. 14), *"lead[ing] people into ungodliness"* (v. 16), and *"upsetting the faith of some"* (v. 18). These are terrible things—things that any biblical counselor, pastor, or teacher certainly wants to avoid. They are certainly not things of which I would want to be guilty when I stand before the Lord.

Peter also echoes this warning. Referencing the writings of Paul, he writes, *"There are some things in them that are hard to understand, which the ignorant and unstable twist to their own destruction, as they do the other Scriptures"* (2 Pet 3:16). Here, again, we read that some who have attempted to interpret the Bible have misunderstood and misused what they read, leading to dire consequences.

In Paul's writings, we read that humanity has a tendency to misunderstand God inherently. In Romans 1, Paul clarifies that God has made Himself plain to humanity and revealed Himself in clear ways. And yet, our sinful nature encourages us to "suppress the truth." Granted, the context of this passage is speaking of the unrighteous, but in chapter 2, Paul clarifies that no one is without excuse because "you practice the very same things" (Rom 2:1).

We are weak and limited creatures. Beyond that, we are rebellious and sinful. Indeed, the words of Isaiah ring true, *"You will indeed hear but never understand, and you indeed see but never perceive. For this people's heart has grown dull and with their ears they can barely hear, and their eyes they have closed"* (Isa 6:9-10). If we are going to learn to handle the Word of truth, then we will need some help. We need to have our eyes, ears, hearts, and minds opened to the Word and the Spirit.

Clearly, King David understood this aim very well. His most lengthy Psalm is one extolling the wonders of the word of God (Ps 119). Throughout it, one finds many requests from the psalmist: *"Teach me your statutes"* (v. 12), *"Deal bountifully with your servant...Open my eyes...Hide not your commandments from me"* (vv. 17-19), *"Give me life ... make me understand ... graciously teach me your law"* (vv. 25-29). He continues to repeat these petitions to the Lord throughout the Psalm, asking the Lord to help him understand the wisdom and truth of the Scripture that brings life, light, salvation, comfort, and love to the one who delights in the Law of the Lord.[2]

We should follow David's example, approaching the Scripture with a prayer and asking its Author to help us both understand and comprehend what we read in it. In humility, we should first acknowledge our weaknesses, needs, dull hearts, stopped ears, and closed eyes. We should come to the Bible hungry and thirsty for the life-giving hope of the Word of God, pleading for the Lord to fill us. Only with His grace and help can we interpret and rightly handle His Word.

ABOUT THE AUTHOR

All Scripture is breathed out by God and profitable for teaching, for reproof, for correction, and for training in righteousness, that the man of God may be complete, equipped for every good work.
2 Tim 3:16-17, ESV

In this passage, Paul says that every bit of the Scripture is *"breathed out by God"* (ESV and NIV). Other translations render this term *"inspired"* (NASB,

---

2   Nearly every verse of Psalm 119 contains one of eight words for God's revelation—specifically "instruction," "decree," "precept," "statute," "command," "judgment," "promise," and "word."

CSB, KJV). The term in the original Greek can be rendered "*God-breathed.*" Paul is reminding his young protégé that God Himself is the author of the Bible. Though penned by men, the Scripture is the Word of God.

Peter also reminds us of this fact. He writes, "*For no prophecy was ever produced by the will of man, but men spoke from God as they were carried along by the Holy Spirit.*" (2 Pet 1:21). The Bible has a divine Source. Men spoke (and wrote), each in their own unique way, but they were all "*carried along,*" as Peter puts it, by the Holy Spirit. Inasmuch, they were all inspired by the Lord to deliver His Word.

Understanding this truth should give anyone who reads the Word great hope. Because God is the author of the Scripture, we can be convinced about certain things being true about the Bible. For example, God cannot lie (Titus 1:2; Heb 6:18). Therefore, we can know that the Bible is also true (John 17:17). God is also eternal and unchanging (John 1:1; Rom 1:20; 1 Tim 1:17; Heb 6:18). In like manner, His Word is also constant and sure (Ps 119:89-91).

God desires to reveal Himself to us (Matt 13:10-16). God's self-revelation is the very reason the Bible exists in the first place. He wants us to know Him and to love Him. Therefore, He also helps us to understand His Word. Paul reminds us that the Holy Spirit, the same Holy Spirit that inspired the human authors, helps us to understand the Word (1 Cor 2:6-16). The Author of the Scriptures indwells us. He reveals to us God's wisdom and helps us to discern and interpret spiritual truths. No better person exists to ask for help interpreting a text than the Author who wrote that text.

ABOUT THE BOOK

... And that from childhood you have known the sacred writings which are able to give you the wisdom that leads to salvation through faith which is in Christ Jesus.
2 Tim 3:15, ESV

The book that we call the Bible could perhaps be better described as a "literary anthology." The Bible consists of sixty-six books, written by about forty different men, over one thousand five hundred years. Nothing else like it exists in the world. It is a collection of different voices, writing styles, and genres. And yet, even though this text had so many diverse contributors over such an extended period, a common theme unites the different narratives, prophecies, poems, and letters, linking them into a grand narrative of salvation and redemption.

As mentioned above, God is the ultimate author of Scripture. He is the One telling the story. An important thing to remember is that its story is not primarily about us. The Bible is not primarily a book of wisdom to help us understand how to live a good life (though it does). It is not primarily a history text chronicling the story of Israel and the Church (though it does). It is not primarily a book instructing us in ethics and moral values (though it does). It is not primarily a book about our problems and how to wisely counsel one another (though it does). The Bible is God's revelation of Himself to us. The Bible is about Jesus Christ. He is the central figure that the entire narrative revolves around. He is the climax of the greatest plot ever written.

Jesus Himself puts it this way to the religious scholars of His day: "*You pour over the Scriptures because you think you have eternal life in them, and yet they testify about me. But you are not willing to come to me so that you may have life*" (John 5:39-40). This point proves crucial. In this passage, Jesus was speaking to Pharisees. They were not negligent in their study of the Scriptures, but diligently sought to understand and interpret the sacred texts. They were the most precious possession, and they devoted themselves to studying these ancient words. However, according to Jesus, they had missed the true treasure contained within. They had missed *Him*. "They testify about *me*," he rebuked them. The Scriptures are designed to testify about Christ and to bring us face-to-face with Him. Unless we are willing to meet Christ, to come to Him, and to know Him as we read the Bible, we will miss the salvation they offer.

Once we have come to Christ, Peter reminds us in his second Epistle that He gives us everything required for life and godliness. To His own glory and from His goodness, He has given us great and precious promises that begin to change us from the corrupt into the divine (2 Pet 1:3-4).

Peter is describing the process of sanctification. This spiritual benefit is the goal of the Holy Spirit as He works in our lives to refine us and make us more like Christ (Rom 8:29). The Spirit uses the Word of God to bring about this transformation (John 17:17; Ps 119:9-16; 19:7-14; 2 Tim 3:15-17; Heb 4:12-13; 2 Cor 2:2-5). This transformation is not simply one of outward behavior but of the full person, including the desires and thoughts of the heart (2 Cor 5:17; John 3:3-6; Col 3:3; Eph 4:22-24). Isaiah promises that this transformation is as inevitable as rain and snow producing crops in the field. His Word will not return void, but will accomplish His desire (Isa 55:10-11).

This truth should also give anyone who reads it great hope and encouragement. The Holy Spirit and the Word of God opens blind eyes and deaf ears, as well as softens and pricks hardened hearts. We will be changed, shaped, and refined. Together, the Spirit and the Word display the glory and beauty of the Lord God. They will reveal the Way, the Truth, and the Life. They will accomplish the Lord's purpose, that we can know Him, love Him, and become like Him. Praise the Lord for His word that gives wisdom that leads to salvation through faith in Jesus Christ!

INTERPRETATION

Now that we have covered some elementary aspects of Bible interpretation, we now move to the more technical interpretation of the Scriptures, that is—hermeneutics. How do we come to comprehend what a text means? How do we understand it, and perhaps more importantly, how do we apply its relevancy for today? Can the story of Joshua and the conquest of Canaan help us today? What about the Proverbs written so long ago? Do they still apply today after so much in the world has changed? Do they mean the same thing regardless of differing cultures? What can we learn from Obadiah, Esther, or Philemon? While we cannot answer all those questions in a short chapter like this one, we can look at some essential tools that will help equip us to answer them. In fact, we already possess and utilize many of these tools daily.

We all practice hermeneutics—the science and art of interpretation. Any time we interact with another person, we must interpret or translate what we hear or see into something that means something to us. This skill is a basic aspect of the essence of communication. Some people are better at it than others, but we all interpret and discover meaning as part of interacting with others. In general, many of the same skills are utilized to understand the meaning of God's communication with us. God has chosen to communicate with us through the written Word, and He has done so in a way we can understand. He wants us to know Him, and He has graciously lowered Himself to our level to speak to us so we can grasp the original intent of His message to us. He has done so by accommodating Himself to our creaturely limitations. Therefore, we can utilize the same essential tools we usually use with one another as we read His words to us.

For example, when I come home from work at the end of the day, if my wife tells me she is *dead tired,* I do not call for an ambulance. I understand that she is using hyperbole, an extreme exaggeration, to help me understand the degree of tiredness she is feeling. I interpret her words in a different way than their literal meaning, and I understand that she wants me to know that she is exhausted, not that she is about to die. From previous experience, I also interpret this expression to mean that she probably wants my help cooking supper. This example is just one way of how we all use interpretive tools to understand the meaning of words and phrases. There are many others, again more than could be covered in a few pages, but let us consider a few that apply specifically to the written Word.

FORM

Writing comes in different forms and genres. Examples from Scripture would include stories, poems, and letters. We also find proverbs, parables, and prophecy. Different genres employ different tools to convey meaning. We do not read a narrative in the same way that we would analyze a haiku. We do not read a letter in the same way that we read a history book. In a similar manner, we need to be aware of and identify the specific genre of the particular Scripture we are reading.

A large part of the Bible was written in narrative form. God chose to reveal Himself and provide us with truths whereby we are to live in the form of stories. These stories are not fictional, but truthful and historical ones that involve real people, events, and places. The Bible should be considered an overarching, grand story, beginning at creation, ending at the consummation, and all the while telling God's plan of redemption. The Bible and the smaller narratives contained within possess all the common elements of a good story: the characters, setting, scenes, plot, conflict, resolution, and conclusion. Thus, we can use the same methods we use with secular literature to interpret the narratives of Scripture.

People have always used stories as a captivating and powerful way to do more than simply pass along facts or information; they utilize them to exemplify virtues, expose evil, provide perspective, pose questions, and/ or propose answers. From the *Odyssey* to *The Lord of the Rings*, from the *Seven Samurai* to *Star Wars*, stories assist us understanding ourselves and examining who we are and who we want to be. They help us describe our view of the world—what is true and right and what is wrong and evil. They give us perspective, and they should inspire us to act. If this assessment is the case, and it is, how much more so should this apply to the story that has been authored by the greatest Author Himself?

For much of the Bible, we can interpret in the same way we interpret secular stories, following the plot to its climax, identifying heroes and villains, and discovering sources of conflict, pain, and strife as we long for the resolution. We can identify with the characters within, real men and women who have real problems and respond to them in foolish or wise ways. We can sympathize with their questions when things seem to be going wrong. We can be inspired by the hope they find in God, placing their faith in Him even when they do not live to see the results. We can learn from how they related to God, how they obeyed, and how they rebelled.

Most importantly, we can see how God related to them by offering them grace, pursuing them when they fled, bringing judgment upon them when needed, and ultimately entering the story, Himself, as the God-Man to bring salvation to mankind. He even included some spoilers about how things will end. Like other stories, we can pull out life principles, wisdom, morals, and ideals that the author conveys through each narrative.

Other sections of the Bible are composed as poetry. Some estimate that about a third of Scripture presents itself in poetic form. Certain books are composed entirely of poetry, while others use this literary form to enhance the narrative. The writing of poetry varies from culture to culture and interpreting it correctly requires the ability to understand the forms and language of the culture from which it originates. For example, English poetry often emphasizes rhythm and the rhyming of words. The same rules would not apply to creating a haiku, a Japanese form of poetry that emphasizes syllabic structure and subject matter. However, some commonalities exist in all poetry. Poetry often uses figurative language and is used by the author to help put words to things that are difficult to describe, such as emotions, ideas, wonder, and beauty.

Most of the poetry in the Bible is found in the Old Testament and is written in Hebrew. Hebrew poetry also uses figurative language and form to communicate God's message to readers. For example, the Psalm to which we referred to earlier, Psalm 119, is written as an "acrostic," that is it is composed of sections of eight verses each. Within each section, the first word in each line begins with the same letter of the Hebrew alphabet, and all the sections are arranged in a Hebraic alphabetical order. It is visually striking when observed in the original language.[3] While the use of acrostics is common in Hebrew, the dominant feature of Hebrew poetry is parallelism.

Parallelism is sometimes like rhyming; it can be seen as rhyming ideas or thoughts instead of rhyming sounds. Two thoughts are placed side by side that bear some relation to one another. The resulting relationship may be synonymous to demonstrate a similarity, or antithetical

---

3   Unfortunately, no one knows exactly why the Hebrew writers used this form. Some suggest that it was a way to help with memorization, others propose it was a way to provide literary structure, and a few commentators believe it was a way for the author to convey a sense of completeness or wholeness, and yet some scholars argue that the use of this form conveyed that a person's faith was rational as well as emotional.

to show contrast. At other times, parallelism is utilized to reveal a cause-and-effect relationship. By doing so, the author provides assistance to the reader. If one line of the poetry is unclear or unfamiliar to the reader, the other line will offer clarification. Understanding this concept will help readers to understand and interpret Hebrew poetry.

Twenty-one books of the New Testament are written as letters (or Epistles). These letters express thanks, impart instructions, and sometimes issue an apostolic rebuke to church(es). As one might imagine, given the genre, they are like listening in on one side of a conversation. Sometimes, we can deduce from a letter's content the circumstances that may have prompted the letter to have been written. Sometimes, a letter contains general instructions.

The form of New Testament Epistles resembles the kind of letters we might send today. They typically include an opening, a greeting, the main body, and a closing or salutation. They are theologically rich and provide practical wisdom concerning Christian living. To comprehend them requires knowing (1) when the letter was written; (2) events the author had experienced; and (3) as much as you can about the church receiving the letter.

The first four books of the New Testament comprise what biblical scholars call the Gospels. These books were written by four men from different backgrounds, for slightly different purposes, and to varied audiences. Each of them offers a first-hand account of the life and ministry of Jesus Christ. They appear in narrative form, and inasmuch tell the story of Jesus' life, death, burial, and resurrection. However, each author presents particular aspects of Jesus' character to their audience in order to present a rich, multi-dimensional portrait of Christ. They also present His teachings, which often take the form of parables. Parables are short stories that illustrate a poignant spiritual truth. Someone once described them as earthly stories that have heavenly meanings. Generally, each parable is designed to reveal one truth—the "meat" of the story, you might say. Many times, Jesus Himself interprets the parables for His disciples to help them, as well as us, to understand the essential concepts He wants us to learn and embrace.

HISTORICAL/CULTURAL CONTEXT

Some time ago, I lived in another country. The town where I lived happened to be on a river that served as a national border. Just across that river was another nation. The people on the far side spoke a different language and used a different alphabet. On one side of the river, the people enjoyed the benefits of paved roads and automobiles, while on the other, they walked dirt paths and rode donkeys. At night, one side was lit by electric lights, and the other was draped in pitch blackness. While the people on both sides had much in common, they did live somewhat different lives. This is an excellent example to remind us as we read the Bible that things were slightly different when it was written.

Therefore, in addition to the genre, a reader should keep in mind and strive for an awareness of the culture and history of the author and the audience. The truth is that the most recent portions of the Bible were written nearly two thousand years ago, and some of it is much older. It was written by and for people in a culture quite different from today's life. When considering this reality, it is wise to remember that there are things we do not know about those times and how people lived. This lack of knowledge does not inhibit us from understanding the essential things we need to know. But as we learn more about the historical context, our understanding of the Bible can become deeper and richer. Gaining this knowledge comes with diligent study. But we must also be careful that we do not get hung up on insignificant details, get caught up in "*endless genealogies*," controversies, and promote speculations (Titus 3:9).

More importantly, we must realize some things we assume we know about certain passages we read may be uninformed opinions and thus, wrong. Also, we may import our own contemporary context for certain words and ideas that may distort the correct interpretation of a portion of Scripture. For example, often when we hear the word "church" today, we might think of an ornate building lined with chairs or pews. When we read the same word in the Bible, we should understand that "church" meant something vastly different to the audience at the time, referring to a group of people—a congregation. One thing we do not want to do is to carry our own interpretative "baggage" into the texts we read and miss the truth. A careful Bible reader will try to understand the text as the original audience would have understood it.

CONTEXT AND MEANING

Another crucial aspect of interpretation is the importance of context. I mean not only the surrounding circumstances and setting, as I mentioned above, but also the surrounding words and ideas of the text itself. Words are strung together to compose sentences that form paragraphs, which are parts of a discourse that ultimately becomes a book. Lifting a single sentence from the surrounding context is almost guaranteed to introduce some form of distortion to the meaning. For example, consider the phrase, "I can do all things through Him who strengthens me" (Phil 4:13). When we lift this phrase out of the conclusion of Philippians, we lose essential information that helps us to determine what Paul really means. What does "all things" include? Does it mean that Paul can do anything he wants? Maybe Paul is now capable of superhuman feats? Who is the "Him" that he is referring to? We can only accurately ascertain the author's meaning by considering the surrounding context and not inserting something of our own. By reading the text within the context, we understand that Paul speaks of the contentment he has found in Christ. His circumstances may change, but he remains content.

This brings up an important point. The meaning of the text is determined by the author, not the reader. The reader's goal is to try to understand what the author means, not to determine what the text means to the reader. Consider the example above. Perhaps I take Paul's words, "I can do all things through Him," to mean that if I believe in Christ enough and have enough faith, I can "power through" any adverse or unpleasant circumstance. In doing so, I have assigned my own meaning to the text. I have made it mean what I want it to mean, or what I think it should mean, rather than listening to what Paul, under the inspiration of the Holy

Spirit, meant. It may sound great and inspirational, but it has *become a lie*. It is not true, but it will lead me and others astray. I do not know about you, but I want to hear what God says to me in His word, not what I think He should say.

SOME GUIDELINES

I want to provide some general "rules of thumb" concerning Bible interpretation in this section. These guidelines will help us to read the text faithfully. First, let Scripture interpret Scripture. Some portions of Scripture are less clear than others. As we come across these, we must remember to take other, more transparent Scripture portions to help guide our interpretation. We also want to understand the parts as part of the whole. For example, some of the laws and regulations found in the Old Testament may be superseded by the events of the New Testament.

Read and study the Bible in the community. Reading the Bible together will help us to filter out our poor interpretations. If others in your community cannot see the same meaning in the text, you may need to look again. This helps us narrow in on the author's meaning instead of importing our own. Also, others may have gained insights into the text that we have overlooked. Do not forget the testimony of those who have come before as well. Compare your interpretation with the traditions and writings of the Church. We should not disregard what the Holy Spirit has shown to others, even though many years may separate us.

Start small. Pick a short book, or maybe a Gospel, and begin there. It takes time and practice to develop the skills of interpretation. Focusing on a specific book will help hone those skills instead of being overwhelmed by the task.

Meditate on the meaning. To be honest, it is a bit prideful to expect that we would instantly understand the meaning of the text with a simple cursory reading. The Bible is not a book meant for superficial reading. Take some time to "soak" in it. Ruminate on the words and the meaning of the text. Memorize a verse and consider it over days or weeks when you can. This practice helps us to understand and to make it a part of us. "I have treasured your word in my heart so that I may not sin against you" (Ps 119:11).

Be disciplined and patient. As they say, Rome was not built in a day. It takes time to do almost anything worthwhile. Keep at it, day by day and week by week. Realize that you will make mistakes. Do not let them keep you from pressing on. And remember that it is worth your time. "*The law from your lips is more precious to me than thousands of pieces of gold or silver*" (Ps 119:72).

Remember humility. As you gain skills, do not forget that you still have blind spots. Remember to ask the Spirit to help you to understand. Ask other Christians to seek meaning with you. Remember the prayers of David in Psalm 119 as he petitions the Lord to teach him His Word. Also, "*Do your best to present yourself to God as one approved, a worker who has no need to be ashamed, rightly handling the word of truth*" (2 Tim 2:15).

APPLICATION

In his Epistle, James helps us to understand the final step in biblical interpretation. He writes, "*But be doers of the word, and not hearers only, deceiving yourselves....The one who looks intently into the perfect law of freedom and perseveres in it, and is not a forgetful hearer but a doer who works—this person will be blessed in what he does*" (James 1:22, 25). James' point is simple. We cannot say that we fully understand the Word of God if it does not change how we live.

An Anglican pastor and scholar, John Stott, points out at least five ways the Word should change our lifestyle.[4] First, as we learn more about the true and living God, who He is, and what He has done for us, we *are compelled to* worship Him. We cannot help but worship His majesty. The Word of God reveals His character and His beauty and it inspires us to give glory and honor to our great God.

---

4   John R.W. Stott, *Understanding the Bible* (Grand Rapids, MI: Zondervan, 1980).

Second, Stott marks repentance as a facet of this change in our lives. As we understand more of God's holiness, our own unholiness will become more evident and egregious to us. The Word of God will act like a mirror showing us who we are and giving us a glimpse of who we should be (James 1:22-23). As we understand the Word, we should seek to repent of our sin. As those who first heard the Word preached it in the power of the Spirit, we should be cut to the heart and seek His forgiveness (Acts 2:37-38). Consider the words of Job after hearing from the Lord: "*I had heard of you by the hearing of the ear, but now my eye sees you; therefore, I despise myself, and repent in dust and ashes*" (Job 42:5-6).

Third, our faith will grow. Faith is based on knowledge. As we read and understand the Scriptures while the Holy Spirit reveals God's truth, our knowledge of God's trustworthiness and faithfulness will become deeper and richer. Stott keenly notes that we have no cause to envy others who have "greater" faith, "as if our lack of faith were like our temperament, a congenital condition which cannot be changed. God Himself has given us the means to increase our faith: 'Faith comes by hearing, and hearing comes from the word of God.'"[5]

Of course, an obvious way we become "doers" of the Word is to obey. We have understood the truth by submitting ourselves to the authority of Scripture and making fundamental changes in our everyday lives. Jesus clarifies this: "*If you love me, you will keep my commandments....He who has my commandments and keeps them, he it is who loves me....If a man loves me, he will keep my word...he who does not love me does not keep my words*" (John 14:15, 21, 23-24). As we come to know God and understand Him more, we cannot help but love Him. Our love for Him will overflow into our everyday lives, producing obedient and holy lives. As David reminds us, "*Your testimonies are wonderful; therefore, my soul keeps them*" (Ps 119:129).

Finally, Stott argues that one who understands the Word will want to share it with others. As we know the Lord more intimately, we want to introduce Him to others. We know that we cannot keep this precious treasure to ourselves—we are stewards of it. We see how it can help others in their struggles and reveal to them their need to know Christ. By sharing

---

5   Stott, *Understanding the Bible*, 248-249.

the gospel with others, we seek to help them understand and know Him. Like David, we will *"speak of your testimonies before kings and shall not be put to shame,"* our *"lips will pour forth praise,"* and our *"tongue will sing of your word"* (Ps 119:46, 171-172).

SUMMING UP

In conclusion, God has chosen to reveal Himself in the written Word of the Bible. To understand the Bible well, we must realize our limitations and seek the Author's assistance as we come to the word in humility. Only He can help us to understand the true meaning of the text. Thankfully, He has promised to do so.

First, He accommodated Himself to our lowly state by revealing Himself so that we can understand Him, through human language. Then He has indwelt us to illuminate the Scripture, to prick our hearts, to help us to appreciate the beauty and glory of His nature, and to find *Him* in the reading of the Scriptures.

He has revealed Himself to us through the writings of men like ourselves, and therefore, we can use the same tools of interpretation that we usually use in daily interactions with one another to grasp the meaning of their words. However, we also know that we likely have blind spots as we read the words of men who lived in a different time and place. Yet, they were men as we are and have written with plain meaning. With the help of the Holy Spirit, we can understand and apply the principles contained therein. We have been provided with everything that we need for life and godliness.

After interpreting the passage we read and study, we must place ourselves back under the authority of the text and live it out in our own lives. The Word should change, mold, and refine us to make us more like the Author. Let us take Paul's exhortation to Timothy to heart and seek to handle correctly the Word of truth. Let us seek to see the commandments and teachings of the Lord with the same love as David, building our lives on the precious promises contained therein.

THE #1 HEART ISSUE EVERY BIBLICAL COUNSELOR MUST ADDRESS: SALVATION

One of the primary, if not most important, differences between biblical counseling and secular psychology lies in the understanding of the spiritual nature of man. While the secular counselor will not see the need for evangelism in the counseling session, the believer in Christ practicing soul care in the counseling session recognizes that without salvation, nothing else matters in eternity. Helping people with physical needs, managing emotions, and transforming their thinking is good, but at best can only result in a behavioristic change. Without addressing the universal human need to be regenerated by the Holy Spirit through placing one's faith and trust in Christ, the counselor has done nothing more than help the counselee "white wash" the tomb.

Every biblical counselor must engage the counselee with discerning, evangelistic questions, regardless of his/her claim regarding his/her salvation. Unfortunately, many people misunderstand either what it means to be saved or to be born again; of upmost importance, this issue must be addressed quickly in course of the counseling setting. Some professing believers think they are saved, but their spiritual issues in counseling never get resolved because they are not genuinely saved. Others believe they are saved, yet because they seek counseling to better themselves, all they are seeking to achieve is behavioral/cognitive modification, not biblical soul transformation. Outside the misunderstanding of these individuals concerning their salvation, vastly more people are lost, and the biblical counselor must understand that the lost cannot claim the promises of Scripture because most, if not all, of its truths only apply to those who have surrendered their lives to Jesus. Biblical counselors can use Scripture to help a person feel, act, or even think better, but "better" does not equate to being born again. The subject of salvation can be raised with a counselee by asking him/her a simple question:

"ARE YOU SAVED?"

"Are you saved?" This question is a generic, yet loaded, question that can be explained simply. A biblical counselor might ask this question by replacing "saved" with words/phrases like "born again," "Christian," "surrendered to Jesus," and/or "right with God," but the counselee's answer significantly impacts the type of biblical counseling action to be taken. In the following few pages, we will offer a simple evangelistic approach to use with unbelieving counselees and/or those who claim Christ to solidify a genuine conversion experience. Consider utilizing the suggested Scriptures and answers when your counselee responds to your question with his/her own questions about salvation:

"HOW DO I GET SAVED, AND HOW CAN I BE SURE IT WAS REAL?"

All have sinned and fall short of the glory of God.
Rom 3:23

Every person who has ever lived (*i.e.*, all) has disobeyed God through his/her thoughts, words, and/or actions (*i.e.*, sinned). Not only has he/she sinned, but he/she has missed the standard (*i.e.*, fallen short) of the quality of His character (*i.e.*, glory of God). This means that everyone's track record is less than perfect, and because of such imperfections brought about by our sins, every person has a problem.

The #1 Heart Issue

For the wages of sin is death, but the gift of God
is eternal life in Christ Jesus our Lord.
Rom 6:23

The compensation we have earned and deserve (*i.e.*, wages) for our disobedience to God (*i.e.*, sin) is, first, the reality of physical death and, second, the reality of spiritual separation from God now and forever in eternity (*i.e.*, death). This reality means that we have done what it takes rightfully to deserve to spend eternity in Hell apart from God. However, God offers us the opportunity to have the right relationship with Him (*i.e.*, eternal life) to avoid death and separation from Him. This eternal life is only through Jesus being *our* Savior (*i.e.*, Christ) and Lord; there is no other way to receive eternal life. The most significant part about this is that we "earned" death, but life is only received as a "free gift." Eternal life, in the here and the hereafter, cannot be earned; it must be freely received.

But God proves his own love for us in that
while we were still sinners, Christ died for us.
Rom 5:8

Why would God offer us a free gift of life, especially after we have committed sins and deserve death? Simply, God loves us unconditionally and proves that to us (*i.e.*, demonstrates) by sending His Son Jesus to receive our "wage" of sin for us by dying on the cross. He did this not after we got our lives together but while we were still living actively in our rebellion and disobedience against His purposes for our lives. Imagine someone killing your entire family and the judge sentencing the murderer to death. You might say, "That is justice," and you would be right. However, what if, instead of wanting justice, the judge offered the murderer a chance at being pardoned that day? The only way the murderer could be freed is for someone to take his place and be sentenced to death. Out of love for his soul and wanting that murderer to be saved before he dies, you take his place. Such love would be a type of compassion that few could understand, but one that proves that you see his eternal life as more important than your own. That's what Jesus did for us. He and God the Father planned to offer us life even though we deserve to die. Jesus died to take our place, and the Father gives us life if and when we receive it through repentance and belief.

> *If you confess with your mouth, "Jesus is Lord,"*
> *and believe in your heart that God raised him*
> *from the dead, you will be saved*
> **Rom 10:9**

So how are we to receive this eternal life and be saved from the penalty of death that we so justly have earned and deserve? If we admit to God that Jesus is the only One who is righteous and deserves to be in control of our lives, and we do so with (1) a genuine understanding that He really is our Lord and Master and (2) an sure trust as absolute fact that the resurrection of Jesus happened as a proof that He has defeated death and can give us life, too, then we will be given eternal life. We will be saved! It's that simple. Anyone who will ask God to forgive him/her of his/her sin and ask Him to credit Jesus' payment to his/her account, he/she can have eternal life. Such a conversation could sound like this; "God, my way is sinful; teach me YOUR ways so that I can learn to not sin and instead follow Jesus as my Master obediently and immediately."

"HOW CAN I BE SURE THAT I AM SAVED?"

> *I have written these things to you who believe in the name of*
> *the Son of God so that you may know that you have eternal life.*
> **1 John 5:13**

John assures believers of the complete confidence they have to KNOW that in Christ they possess eternal life. The Christian faith is not a guessing game regarding believers' eternal destination and present status with God. Unlike many works-based religions worldwide whose adherents have no idea if their god has accepted them until they stand before it, the Bible wants believers to be confident from day one! Utilize the following three questions with your counselee to determine the validity of his/her salvation and/or the presence of God's salvation in his/her life.

When the Counselor comes, the one I will send to you from the Father— the Spirit of truth who proceeds from the Father—he will testify about me... If anyone loves me, he will keep my word. My Father will love him, and we will come to him and make our home with him. The one who doesn't love me will not keep my words. The word that you hear is not mine but is from the Father who sent me.... But the Counselor, the Holy Spirit, whom the Father will send in my name, will teach you all things and remind you of everything I have told you.
John 14:16-17, 23-26

First, does the Holy Spirit dwell within you? Jesus teaches His disciples that the Holy Spirit will dwell within a Christian at his/her salvation, and the role of the Spirit is to be a Helper to all believers. No blood test or medical exam can confirm the existence of the Holy Spirit within us, but the Holy Spirit does have a role that can be identified. He teaches us what Scripture means and how it applies to our lives. He helps us to recall, literally reminding us of things we need to know in the moments we need to know them. Finally, He empowers us, giving us supernatural strength and endurance to obey God's will and fulfill His purpose for our lives. Inquire of your counselee if he/she has ever heard the voice of the Holy Spirit leading, guiding, teaching, or reminding him/her of God's will and ways?

Ask your counselee whether or not he/she has ever experienced God's help in his/her life, knowing that the successful outcome of the situation in which he/she found himself/herself could not be attributed to their own ability but instead the help of Another? If he/she answers, "No," then he/she may not be saved, and you should further evangelize him/her. However, if he/she responds, "Yes," then continue the session by appealing to the following content from Romans 8:5-6:

For those who live according to the flesh have
their minds set on the things of the flesh, but those
who live according to the Spirit have their minds set
on the things of the Spirit. Now the mindset of the flesh
is death, but the mindset of the Spirit is life and peace .
Rom 8:5-6

Second, as your counselee if he/she has ever experienced his/her desires being changed? Paul tells us that once a person is saved, the Spirit Who now dwells within him/her changes his/her mindset, transforming the desires of the inner person—the heart—to desire the pursuit of God and His righteousness instead of the sinful actions of his/her past lostness. Even if his/her behavior has not changed overnight, does your counselee recognize a difference from the moment he/she was saved—a moment when his/her heart no longer is pleased with his/her sin, but seeks to please God? Yet when he/she engages in God-honoring activities or ways of thinking, he/she finds joy and peace? Is there a desire to do right, even if he/she struggles to do so, because he/she knows it pleases God, or does he/she lack any conviction over his/her sins even though he/she claims to have been saved and indwelt by the Holy Spirit? If he/she admits he/she has never felt this type of conviction, your counselee may not be saved; however, if he/she does experience the Spirit's conviction of his/her sin, then advance to the next Scripture.

I say, then, walk by the Spirit and you will certainly not carry out the desire of the flesh. For the flesh desires what is against the Spirit, and the Spirit desires what is against the flesh; these are opposed to each other, so that you don't do what you want. But if you are led by the Spirit, you are not under the law.

Now the works of the flesh are obvious: sexual immorality, moral impurity, promiscuity, idolatry, sorcery, hatreds, strife, jealousy, outbursts of anger, selfish ambitions, dissensions, factions, envy, drunkenness, carousing, and anything similar. I am warning you about these things—as I warned you before—that those who practice such things will not inherit the kingdom of

The #1 Heart Issue

God. But the fruit of the Spirit is love, joy, peace, patience, kindness, goodness, faithfulness, gentleness, and self-control. The law is not against such things.
Gal 5:16-23

Third, does your counselee's life provide evidence of the fruit of godliness? Many people, including the Pharisees in Jesus' day, attempted to determine from people's outward actions and deeds whether or not they were saved. If someone looks the part, talks the talk, and makes decisions like a Christian, maybe he/she is. However, he/she could be presenting a façade, meaning he/she is nothing more than a white-washed tomb and dead inside the heart. Someone sinning does not mean that he/she is lost any more than someone else doing something godly means he/she is genuinely saved. Yet, if a person claims to be saved, yet habitually practices the sinful things of this world, and his/her life is described by those who know him/her as one that appears to be a lost person, maybe he/she really is lost (or at a very minimum, has never been discipled in the Word). A Christian will walk in obedience to God, even if it is a struggle and even if he/she fails at times. Does your counselee have a life desiring to exemplify the fruits of the Spirit? Or does your counselee have a life habitually described by the sins of the flesh, with no conviction, especially after confronting their deeds with Scripture?

Go through these passages and solidify to both yourself as the counselor and to the other person as the counselee that he/she truly is saved and can confidently move forward with growing in Christ, or share the gospel with him/her, inviting him/her to turn from his/her sins and receive the gift of Jesus, which gives eternal life!

HEART ISSUE

DEFINITIONS

A **"Heart Issue"** *refers to the inner man's desires, thinking, intents, and emotions that direct our actions.* Proverbs 4:23 cautions, *"Guard your heart above all else, for it is the source of life."* This verse highlights the heart as the center of our spiritual life, the source of our emotions, thoughts, and will, which then control our perceptions, decisions, and behaviors.

DEFINITIONS OF HEART ISSUES
LISTED ON PDI

Adultery: Adultery signifies the breach of marital fidelity through engaging in sexual relationships outside the marriage covenant. Beyond the spiritual ramifications, committing adultery can yield emotional and relational distress for all parties involved. Within the biblical context, it is a grave sin that both disrupts the sacred bond between spouses and fractures one's relationship with God (Ex 20:14; 1 Pet 1:14-16; Prov 6:32; 28:13; Matt 5:27-28).

Anger: An intense emotional response characterized by displeasure and antagonism, typically brought about by a perceived wrong or offense. While the Bible does acknowledge the legitimacy of God's just anger towards sin, it also cautions believers against uncontrolled or prolonged human anger, advising instead for self-restraint and reflection. The Word of God further encourages followers to pursue peace, forgiveness, and understanding in the face of conflict (Eph 4:26-27; James 1:19-20; Prov 15:1-3; 19:11-12).

Anorexia and Bulimia: Chronic disorders where individuals severely restrict their food intake or engage in binge eating followed by purging. Grounded in an intense fear of weight gain and accompanied by a distorted perception of one's body, these conditions often mirror spiritual distress, highlighting deep-seated emotional pain and a desire for control. The Word of God reminds His people of God's love and affirms that their bodies are not mere physical entities but temples of the Holy Spirit, crafted with purpose and care. (1 Cor 6:19-20; Rom 12:1-2; Ps 139:14; 1 Pet 5:7; Jer 50:18-20; 1 Sam 16:7)

Anxiety/Worry: A condition of the immaterial heart characterized by unease or apprehension about potential outcomes or the well-being of others. This sentiment can range from a valid unease related to life's demands to intense and consuming fears arising from a skewed viewpoint of life's challenges. While Jesus understood and acknowledged the natural human inclination towards concern for necessities such as sustenance or shelter, He urged His followers to maintain a godly perspective. By prioritizing God's kingdom and righteousness, believers are reminded that other concerns will be addressed in God's providence and perfect timing (Ps 4:4-5; 139:23-24; Prov 3:5-8; Isa 26:3; Phil 4:6-9).

Apathy: Derived from the Greek term *apathēs*, meaning "without passion," apathy refers to indifference or lack of emotional investment in one's surroundings, relationships, and/or responsibilities. Within biblical counseling, apathy can be perceived as spiritual inaction, where believers neglect God's calling and His divine purpose for their lives (Prov 22:3; Isa 49:4; Zeph 1:12-13; Col 3:17, 23-24).

Bitterness: Grounded in Hebrews 12:15, bitterness can be described as a long-lasting animosity that festers within an individual's heart. This emotion can often stem from an unresolved conflict or offense, leading to persistent anger, resentment, and even thoughts of revenge. Such a disposition affects one's relationship with others and can impede one's relationship with God. It is imperative to address bitterness through the lens of Scripture, emphasizing the need for genuine forgiveness, as modeled by Christ, to restore the soul and foster spiritual growth (Lam 3:5, 22; Eph 4:31; Rom 8:31-34; Acts 8:23; Heb 12:15).

Children: Beyond the practicalities of day-to-day routines, a biblical vision for parenting encompasses a reflective responsibility entrusted by God. It signifies the intentional guardianship parents undertake, not just for their children's physical well-being but also for their spiritual growth. Anchored in God's Word, this perspective views children not merely as offspring but as eternal souls given by God into the care of parents. Parenting becomes a holy task, where guidance, discipline, and love cultivate a child's heart in preparation for a relationship with the Creator. This immense responsibility underscores the significance of each parent's role in shepherding their child into the path of righteousness for His name's sake (Deut 6:5-7; Prov 22:6; 29:17; Eph 6:1-4).

Childhood Sexual Abuse: In the light of Scripture, which underscores the sanctity and dignity of every individual, sexual abuse is a grievous sin and violation. It is a traumatic experience where a child is used for the sexual gratification of an adult or older child. Such abuse can disrupt a person's understanding of his or her God-given value and sense of self-worth, leading to challenges in trust, intimacy, and emotional and relational well-being (Ps 18:2; 56:8; 147:3; Isa 1:16-17; Rom 8:28-29).

Communication: A God-ordained mechanism by which one soul's inner reflections and intents are faithfully conveyed through speech to another, ensuring clarity and mutual understanding. Drawing upon the Word, effective communication seeks to transmit information and foster connection, edification, and unity in alignment with God's design for relationships (Prov 15:1; 25:11; Eph 4:29; James 1:19).

A Biblical Handbook for Counseling Heart Issues

Conflict: Interpersonal conflict is fundamentally anchored in the sinfulness of human nature. In the book of James, God articulates that the core of disputes and contentions arises from unchecked passions and yearnings within man. Delving deeper, the wisdom of Proverbs identifies individuals who propagate discord as being dominated by emotions and attitudes such as anger, greediness, and animosity. It is paramount in biblical counseling to address these sinful dispositions with the transformative power of God's Word, guiding individuals toward understanding reconciliation and a heart aligned with God's will (Prov 15:18; Matt 18:15-16; Rom 12:18; James 4:1-3; 1 Pet 4:8).

Control: Biblically understood as the capacity given by God to humans to influence and guide behaviors, choices, and the progression of situations. It reflects humanity's God-given dominion over creation while emphasizing the need for self-restraint and discipline. In interpersonal interactions, control is supposed to be an exercise of love, guidance, and stewardship, always aligned with God's will and directives, rather than a mere imposition of one's desires or dominance over others (Ex 14:14; Isa 41:10; Jer 10:23; Prov 16:9; Rom 6:11-13).

Critical Spirit: A disposition characterized by persistent, harsh judgments towards others, often magnifying their shortcomings while overlooking their virtues. Rooted in a lack of grace and mercy, this mindset can strain relationships, cause disunity within the body of Christ, and foster inner unrest. The address of a critical spirit requires a heart examination, repentance, and seeking God's transformative love to cultivate a spirit of humility and grace (Job 42:7; Matt 7:1; Rom 2:1-3; 1 Pet 4:8).

Deception: An act whereby individuals mislead or misrepresent the truth, often driven by their own desires, fear, or pride. The Bible unequivocally denounces such dishonesty, urging believers to embody truthfulness in their thoughts, words, and actions. Sincerity and transparency should be paramount in Christian relationships and interactions, reflecting Christ's character (Prov 12:22; Eph 4:25; Neh 6:8-9; Col 3:9).

Decision Making: A multifaceted process grounded in discernment and informed by Scripture. It encompasses the formation of judgments grounded in biblical wisdom and understanding. This process often necessitates demonstrating resoluteness and determination in one's choices, aligning actions with the will and teachings of God. In circumstances of conflict or ambiguity, decision making can signify a resolution guided by prayer, Scripture, and godly counsel, leading to a choice that upholds righteousness and justice (Ex 33:13a; Prov 3:5-6; Phil 4:6; James 1:5).

Depression: An emotional state marked by despondency, discouragement, and sorrow. This condition often aligns with feelings of personal powerlessness and a diminished zest for life. Scriptural narratives depict several individuals who demonstrate signs of depression stemming from varied circumstances. As believers turn to the Scriptures, they find solace and guidance in navigating this complex emotional terrain, recognizing that God's presence and promises offer hope that counters their despair (Ps 34:17-18; 42:11; Lam 3:18, 24; Matt 11:28).

Disciplined Living: The intentional and faithful stewardship of God-given resources, particularly time and money. Drawing inspiration from Scripture, believers recognize that true godliness stems from a life ordered by spiritual discipline. Central to this spiritual formation are the disciplines of time and money, which, when managed in alignment with God's will, pave the way to a life that reflects the character of Christ. Just as Jesus exemplified a life of purpose and sacrifice, disciplined living challenges believers to utilize their resources purposefully, ultimately bringing praise, glory, and honor to the Lord (Prov 25:28; Prov 21:5; 1 Cor 9:24-27; 2 Tim 1:7).

Disorganization: The lack of structure or order in one's life can diminish an individual's capacity to fulfill God's purpose and commands. Godly discipline enables believers to function by godly principles rather than transient desires. Believers establish dominion over fleshly appetites by consciously rejecting impulsive behaviors, ensuring that actions line up with God's will. This deliberate choice, grounded in self-control and the Fruit of the Spirit, allows truth, virtue, and integrity to govern thoughts and actions, bring them closer to the image of Christ, and equip them for every good work (1 Cor 14:40; 1 Cor 14:33; Prov 21:5; Prov 24:30-34).

Discouraged/Downcast: A state in which one experiences a diminishment of confidence or enthusiasm, often rooted in various life challenges or unmet expectations. In such moments, believers are reminded to hope in God and to seek His face, recognizing that the ultimate encouragement and strength come not from circumstances but from the sovereign Lord's unchanging nature and promises (Josh 1:9; Ps 63:6-8; 34:17-18; 2 Cor 4:8-9).

Drunkenness: A state of diminished cognitive and physical faculties induced by the excessive intake of alcoholic substances. Throughout the Word, drunkenness is denounced as a detrimental behavior incompatible with a life of righteousness and spiritual maturity. The Bible often underscores the virtues of sobriety, alertness, and self-mastery, placing these traits in sharp contrast with the traits of overindulgence in alcohol. A biblical portrait of a person overcome by alcohol is a metaphorical depiction of the despair those who oppose God's will and authority face (Eph 5:18; Prov 31:6-7; Prov 20:1; 1 Cor 6:10).

Dysfunctional Family: This term denotes a disordered family pattern that is characterized by consistent abnormal behaviors and conflicts, frequently resulting in deep emotional scars with damaging consequences. While the wounds from such an environment can be troubling, the Bible provides hope and direction. Restoration and reconciliation can be attained through biblical wisdom, understanding, genuine forgiveness, and deliberate behavioral shifts. The Bible underscores the significance of family unity and offers inspired counsel for repairing familial bonds (Ex 20:12; Prov 15:1; Col 3:13; Eph 6:1-4).

Envy: This sinful heart issue is one that Christians are explicitly warned against, as it mirrors the very transgressions of the devil. His envy precipitated his fall from grace, and similarly, this envy led to humanity's estrangement from God. Envy starkly contrasts the biblical mandate to love even those who oppose Believers. When one succumbs to envy, he or she is not only emulating the devil's sin but also rejecting the call to love others unconditionally—even when they possess what they desire (Prov 14:30; Phil 4:11; James 3:16; Gal 5:26; Prov 23:17).

Fear: In the intricate tapestry of human emotions, fear stands out as a complex response to perceived threats, encompassing feelings of anxiety, dread, and a momentary loss of courage. Both tangible dangers and intangible concerns can trigger this emotion. In the biblical context, the term "fear of God" has a dual significance. On one hand, it refers to a sense of awe, reverence, and respect, acknowledging God's sovereignty and majesty. This reverence is foundational to a right relationship with the Creator and is a guiding principle for righteous living. On the other hand, it can also describe the overwhelming dread and trepidation experienced when confronted with God's manifest presence or the judicious execution of His divine wrath (Isa 41:10; Prov 28:1; 2 Tim 1:7; Ps 23:4; 27:1; Matt 6:34).

Finances: As delineated in Scripture, financial stewardship encompasses more than the mere accumulation of wealth. It is a threefold principle that balances enjoyment, investment, and generosity. There is joy in the blessings God provides. Yet, above all, a heart inclined towards generosity reflects the nature of a giving God. An unwillingness to give can lead to spiritual deprivation, akin to a monkey trapped by its own greed and unwilling to release its hold on food to free its hand from the jar (Prov 22:7; Matt 6:24; 1 Tim 6:10; Matt 25:26-27; Prov 13:11; 21:5).

Gluttony: An overindulgence that extends beyond food and is synonymous with a heart that is unsatisfied with God's provisions and seeks to consume all excess on one's self. The Scriptures link gluttony with sinful behaviors, including stubbornness, rebellion, disobedience, drunkenness, and wastefulness. The Hebrew term, often translated as "glutton," can also encompass the characteristics of a wastrel, profligate, or one given to riotous and excessive living. The accusation against Jesus of being "a glutton and a drunkard" was rooted in this broader understanding, implying a life led without restraint or respect for divine boundaries. Beyond its spiritual implications, the vice of gluttony has tangible consequences. It dulls the spirit, brings about lethargy, fosters laziness, and can lead to poverty. As believers, it's crucial to guard against gluttony and cultivate a heart that finds its ultimate satisfaction in God alone (Prov 23:20-21; 1 Pet 4:3-5; Phil 3:19; Prov 25:16; Prov 23:20-21; 1 Cor 6:13).

Grief: An emotional response stemming from the depths of the human soul, precipitated by the experience of loss. This poignant emotion often manifests as intense sorrow, pain, and heartfelt lamentation. While grief is an inescapable aspect of the human condition, the Holy Scriptures offer invaluable wisdom, solace, and hope to those wrestling with the weight of their loss. By turning to biblical narratives and teachings, individuals can navigate through the shadows of mourning and find solace in God's unwavering love and promises (Isa 53:3; Ps 147:3; Rev 21:4; Matt 5:4; Rom 8:18;1 Pet 5:7).

Guilt: Within the biblical framework, guilt accompanies wrongdoing—violating God's righteous standards. When one sins, guilt is the consequence with implications for both one's emotional and spiritual state. This dual representation demonstrates humanity's inherent understanding of and reaction to breaches in divine law. Just as sin manifests through willful transgressions, the sensation of guilt is an inner testimony to one's deviation from God's path. Consequently, recognizing and addressing guilt is pivotal in repentance, redemption, and divine reconciliation (Job 10:7; John 3:17; Ps 32:5; 1 John 1:9; Rom 8:1; James 5:16; Heb 8:12).

Health: Defined as the holistic state in which an individual experiences freedom from physical ailments or injuries, this physical state is also complemented by mental and social well-being. In biblical counseling, proper health is also interwoven with spiritual well-being, where one's body and spirit are aligned with God's purpose and design as outlined in Scripture. This health perspective recognizes the inherent interconnectedness of our physical, mental, emotional, and spiritual facets, all essential for living a life that brings glory and honor to God (3 John 1:2; Prov 17:22; 1 Cor 6:19-20; Jer 17:14; Rom 12:1; Jer 33:6; Matt 11:28).

Impotence/Sexual Dysfunction: In biblical counseling, this refers to an individual's inability or diminished capacity to engage in or enjoy sexual intimacy as intended by God in the marital union. Rooted in various causes—whether physiological, psychological, or spiritual—this challenge underscores the interconnectedness of the human body, mind, and spirit. Addressing such concerns requires a compassionate, holistic approach grounded in understanding humanity's design and purpose as delineated in Scripture, ensuring that the God-ordained gift of marital intimacy is experienced in a manner that glorifies Him (Rom 4:19-25; Ps 113:9; Prov 3:5-6; Eph 6:10; Rom 8:28).

In-Laws: These are the relationships formed not merely by marriage but also by God's sovereign design, intertwining lives for mutual edification, support, and care. The Scriptures frequently underscore the significance of family ties, both by blood and covenant. This connection encompasses not only immediate relations but also extends to broader members of the household, even those not bound by kinship. When rooted in love and understanding, these relationships testify to God's divine plan for community, familial unity, and a picture of God's spiritual family (Gen 29:25-26; Matt 19:4-6; Ruth 1:16-17; Gen 2:24; Eph 4:2-3).

Laziness: A lack of motivation for work or necessary tasks leads to inaction. At its core, laziness can be a spiritual issue, reflecting a heart misaligned from God's purpose for mankind. The Bible consistently portrays work as a task that serves and glorifies God. Thus, laziness is not just a reluctance to engage in physical labor but can be seen as a resistance to fulfilling the God-given mandate to labor and be fruitful. It's vital to differentiate between the genuine need for rest, as God modeled on the seventh day, and the habitual avoidance of responsibility. When counseling, it's essential to discern the heart behind the inaction, guiding individuals to line up with God's purpose and find joy in their labor for His glory (Prov 6:6-8; Prov 20:4; 2 Thess 3:10; Gen 2:15, Prov 24:33-34; Col 3:23).

Loneliness: Derived from the biblical understanding that it is not suitable for man to be alone, loneliness is the sense of isolation and disconnection from others. As sheep are safest under the vigilant watch of their Shepherd, so too are believers safeguarded in the fellowship of the Body of Christ. Straying from this communal fold can leave one vulnerable, akin to a solitary house susceptible to robbery or a lone vessel on turbulent waters, prone to the perils of the adversarial pirate, Satan. In biblical counseling, addressing loneliness requires comforting the afflicted and guiding them toward godly fellowship, reminding them of the strength of collective worship and shared faith (Ps 68:6; Isa 41:10; Ps 27:10; Matt 28:18-20; Prov 17:17; Eccl 4:9-10).

Lust: A sinful desire emanating from the heart, characterized by an intense longing that often leads individuals away from God's righteous path. It is the inner genesis of transgressions, anchoring itself in the heart, the epicenter of moral discernment and spiritual vigor. Lusts are the very entities that captivate our desires, diverting a person's focus from divine purpose and truth. If left unchecked, such overpowering urges can disrupt one's relationship with the Lord and the pursuit of His righteousness (Matt 5:28; Job 31:1; 1 Cor 6:18-20; Eph 2:3-7; Prov 4:23; Prov 5:18-19).

Marriage: Sometimes referred to as "holy matrimony," marriage represents a union God instituted. This sacred bond, designed for one man and one woman, is oriented towards procreation and is underscored by a covenantal promise. It is a lifelong commitment reflecting Christ's unwavering love for the Church. In this relationship, couples are called to love, honor, and cherish one another, mirroring God's steadfast love and faithfulness for them and for others (Eph 5:25; Prov 18:22; 1 Cor 13:4-7; Prov 5:18-20; Mark 10:9).

Heart Issue Definitions

Moodiness: A disposition characterized by abrupt shifts in emotional states, often transitioning swiftly from contentment to anger or sadness. While mood fluctuations are a natural part of the human experience, consistent patterns of moodiness may indicate underlying heart issues that need addressing through godly wisdom, self-examination, and the application of biblical truths. In biblical counseling, the goal is not merely to suppress or regulate emotions but to understand their root cause and align one's heart with the transformative power of God's Word (Ps 42:11; 1 Cor 13:11; 2 Cor 4:7-9; Isa 26:3, Ps 23:1-3).

Overwhelmed/Stress: Stress often arises from our innate tendencies, much like the vulnerabilities of sheep, who are naturally dumb, defenseless, and directionless. In these moments of feeling overwhelmed, Believers must remember to turn their gaze to the ultimate Shepherd. He is not just any shepherd, but one characterized by compassion, unwavering care, and remarkable courage. In facing life's challenges, trusting in this Shepherd provides us solace and direction based on biblical truths (Ps 61:2; 1 Kgs 19:4-8; Matt 11:28-30; 2 Cor 4:8-9; Ps 34:18).

Perfectionism: An incessant pursuit of faultlessness, often rooted in a desire for human approval or a misguided understanding of one's worth. The relentless pursuit of flawlessness can be spiritually crippling, leading one to rely on their own strength rather than God's grace. Just as every day has its night, every soul has its struggles. In pursuing perfection, believers must remember that true completeness is found not in personal efforts but in Christ's redemptive work. When His children surrender their imperfections to Him, they are transformed, not to worldly standards of perfection, but into His likeness, which surpasses all understanding (Matt 5:48; Phil 3:12-14; Mark 10:20-22, 26-27; 2 Cor 12:9; Eph 5:27).

Pornography: Derived from the Greek words *porne* (prostitute) and *graphos* (writing), it has historically referred to writings about prostitutes or fornication. In contemporary contexts, pornography is defined as any material—in the form of pictures, videos, or text—created to arouse the viewer or reader sexually. The Bible, while not explicitly using the term "pornography," speaks unequivocally about lust and immoral sexual behaviors (Prov 31:30; Matt 5:28; 1 Cor 6:18-20; 10:13; Job 31:1).

Procrastination: The act of willfully delaying the doing of something that should be done is the definition of procrastination. For many, it becomes a consistent and habitual response to significant and minor tasks. Though "procrastination" is not explicitly mentioned in the Bible, the Word offers wisdom that speaks against the spirit of delay and complacency. In biblical counseling, procrastination can be seen as a lack of trust in God's provision and strength or resistance to His calling. Overcoming this desire to delay requires seeking God's wisdom, relying on His strength, and regularly reflecting upon our stewardship of the time and resources He has given us (Eccl 11:4, Prov 20:4, Prov 13:4; Eph 5:15-16; Prov 6:10-11; 27:1).

PTSD – Post-Traumatic Stress Disorder: An emotional and mental response stemming from direct or indirect exposure to traumatic events, leading to manifestations such as intense anxiety, intrusive memories, and distressing dreams. While the Bible does not have a definition of PTSD, the Bible doesn't shy away from acknowledging the depths of human suffering. For those wrestling with PTSD, the Bible becomes a source of comfort and restoration, affirming that God understands pain, is present in suffering, and offers hope for healing based on His unfailing love and faithfulness (Ps 23:1-3; 73:16, 26; Isa 26:3; 1 Pet 5:6-8, Ps 147:3; Isa 41:10).

Rebellion: Rebellion is ultimately an act of defiance against God. God's tolerance for rebellion is limited, as it is akin to brazenly challenging Him directly. It is a willful and obstinate resistance to God's sovereign authority. When people rebel, they are not merely rejecting human ordinances but directly opposing the Almighty Himself. For believers seeking to reorient their lives with biblical truths, understanding rebellion's gravity is crucial in returning their hearts to a humble submission under God's loving dominion (1 Sam 15:23; Heb 13:17; Prov 17:11; Titus 3:1-2).

Rejection: An intense feeling of isolation and abandonment often leads to a sense of unworthiness. Many biblical figures felt rejection, and their stories provide valuable insight into how faith can offer comfort and guidance in seasons like this. Rejection is an emotional experience marked by feelings of isolation, abandonment, and a deep-seated sense of unworthiness. Throughout the Bible, numerous individuals faced rejection, from Joseph being sold by his brothers to David being pursued by King Saul, and even Jesus being denied by Peter and crucified by those He came to save. When one feels the sting of rejection, it's crucial to remember that personal worth is not defined by the acceptance of others but by his/her identity in Christ (Ps 71:9; Isa 43:1; Ps 94:14; 55:22; Eph 4:31-32; Rom 14:23).

Relational Idolatry: The act of elevating human relationships to a status above one's relationship with God is a clear expression of idolatry. Embedded in a desire for validation or the fear of being alone, individuals can become ensnared in patterns where they derive their worth and identity from other humans rather than God. Such misplaced priorities can lead to unhealthy dynamics, including excessive reliance on others for emotional support, seeking approval, or basing self-worth on relationship status. (Prov 18:1; Phil 2:3-4; Ex 20:3; Matt 10:37; Phil 3:8).

Sexual Immorality: The term "sexual immorality," derived from the Greek Word *porneia*, predominantly refers to fornication, which is the act of engaging in sexual relations between individuals who are not united in the covenant of marriage. The Bible is clear regarding the sacredness of the marital bond and the sanctity of the sexual union within that bond. To act as though married outside this divine institution is to tread outside the boundaries God has lovingly set for the protection and well-being of His creation. Embracing God's design for sexuality within the confines of marriage fosters a pure relationship that honors both the Creator and the sanctity of human bodies (1 Cor 6:18-20; Rom 13:13-14; 1 Thess 4:3-5; Heb 13:4; Matt 15:19; 5:28).

Sleep/Insomnia: Periodic mind and body rest in altered consciousness produces positive benefits. Sleep, as designed by our Creator, is a divinely ordained period of rest for both the mind and body, reminiscent of God's rest on the seventh day. Insomnia, or the struggle to find this rest, can reflect inner turmoil or spiritual unrest (Mark 6:31; Ps 127:2; Prov 3:24; Eccl 5:12; Ps 127:2; 4:8; 56:3).

Spouse Abuse: Spouse abuse starkly contrasts with the divine design for marital relationships. Spouse abuse, often termed "domestic violence" or "intimate partner violence," manifests as a pattern of behavior intended to rule over a partner. Such behavior contradicts the biblical command for husbands to love their wives "as Christ loves the church" and for wives to respect their husbands. Abuse, be it physical, sexual, economic, or psychological, represents a gross deviation from God's commandment to "love your neighbor as yourself." Believers are called to uphold relationships marked by love, respect, and self-sacrifice, reflecting Christ's love for His church. The act of abusing one's spouse not only harms the victim but also breaks the sacred covenant of marriage (Zeph 2:3 [for the abuser]; Prov 23:15-16 [for the abuser]; Ps 3:1-6 [for the victim]; Ps 34:18 [for the victim]; Eph 5:25-28; Ps 11:5-6; Col 3:19; 1 Peter 3:7).

Suicidal Thoughts: A sense of hopelessness and despair leads individuals to contemplate ending their own lives. Such pain echoes the lives of many biblical figures, like Elijah, who once prayed for his own death, saying, "It is enough! Now, O Lord, take away my life" (1 Kgs 19:4). Jonah, too, wished for death in his distress. In navigating these harrowing feelings, it's crucial to seek refuge in God's promises and the faith community's support, and to remember that every life holds immense value in God's eyes (Isa 61:1-3; Heb 12:1-2; Ps 34:18; Jer 29:11; Matt 11:28).

Time Usage: Believers are to serve God as they fulfill their God-assigned responsibilities, making the best use of their time for the glory of God. Time, a divine gift entrusted to God's people, requires intentional stewardship rooted in a deep understanding of God's purpose. While the world races against the clock, believers are called to serve God even in the most mundane tasks, radiating His heavenly Spirit through their attitudes and actions. Daily responsibilities might limit available moments, but by infusing each second with the intent to honor God, even the briefest periods become sanctified. Managing time is not solely about the quantity but the quality of moments spent in genuine service to the Lord, transforming fleeting instants into eternal investments (James 4:13-15; Prov 23:4; Eph 5:15-16; Ps 90:12; Col 4:5).

Weary: Weariness is a state of physical, emotional, and sometimes spiritual exhaustion. It emerges not just from daily struggles but also from the burdens of life's relentless demands. Weariness, while a product of a fallen nature and world, becomes an invitation to find rest and rejuvenation in God's presence, encapsulating the divine promise of refreshment and renewal for the soul (Matt 11:28-30; Ps 119:44-48; Gal 6:9-10; Isa 40:30-31).

ADULTERY

Adultery signifies the breach of marital fidelity through engaging in sexual relationships outside the marriage covenant. Beyond the spiritual ramifications, committing adultery can yield emotional and relational distress for all parties involved. Within the biblical context, it is a grave sin that disrupts the sacred bond between spouses and fractures one's relationship with God.

> *You shall not commit adultery.*
> **Ex 20:14**

God's command to be faithful in marriage is repeated throughout Scripture. Those who sin through unfaithfulness to their spouse must realize that this unfaithfulness began with unfaithfulness to God. The covenant of marriage is threefold between a man, a woman, and God. To break a covenant with a spouse is a sign of a broken covenant with God.

> *As obedient children, do not be conformed to the former lusts which were yours in your ignorance, but like the Holy One who called you, be holy yourself also in all your behavior; because it is written, "you shall be holy because I am holy."*
> **1 Pet 1:14-16**

Committing adultery showcases that the person has no fear of the Lord and has no regard for God's name. This act is a betrayal of holiness, godliness, and righteousness. Adultery is a breach of a sacred covenant between two people derived from a broken relationship between the sinner and God. When a man becomes a lover of self, the affection of his heart thus becomes disoriented and disordered. Instead of engaging body and soul to love and glorify God, he honors and exalts himself. 1 Peter 1:14-16 commands saints to walk holistically and confronts those who fall short. Peter addresses the brethren as "obedient children," indicating that they no longer live in active rebellion against God as before in their previous ignorant and blinded state. Furthermore, Peter points out to them in verse 15 that the Holy God has called Christians to be holy because He is, and we shall all be like Him. Christians have been regenerated as new creations with a new identity distinct and separated from their old way of living, marked by lusts and open disobedience. A new and higher calling is placed upon us: to be holy in all our behavior (v. 15). For anyone to be able to live a life that is tuned to God's commandment and will, it requires constant dying to self and living unto Christ.

> *He who commits adultery lacks sense;*
> *he who does it destroys himself.*
> **Prov 6:32**

Engaging in adultery displays a lack of wisdom in the offender, because the act ultimately causes destruction. Adultery goes beyond just a simple mistake; it goes against God's intended plan for marriage and the covenant that man and wife entered with Him. The destruction mentioned in this verse has multiple consequences, impacting the sinner's relationship with their spouse and God. This verse serves as a warning against the allure of adultery as there are significant repercussions. Some of those repercussions include a loss of trust from the spouse, more anger/discord in the home, increased likelihood of fighting, and in the worst-case scenario, possible divorce.

Adultery

The one who conceals his sins will not prosper,
but whoever confesses and renounces them will find mercy.
Prov 28:13

Most adultery is done in secrecy without the other spouse's knowledge. When people do this, sin eats away at their hearts. Each encounter's momentary satisfaction is surrounded by thoughts of fear and anxiety, bringing other sins alongside their adultery. Sin will eventually be brought to light, and reputations will be tarnished. However, when people confess their sins, God is faithful to forgive, and the church community should be willing to work with the adulterer toward reconciliation and forgiveness as a beautiful picture of what Christ did on the cross for every sinner.

You have heard that it was said, "You shall not
commit adultery." But I say to you that everyone who
looks at a woman with lustful intent has already
committed adultery with her in his heart.
Matt 5:27-28

Adultery starts with a lustful thought. The Lord knew our hearts and said that if we even consider committing adultery, we have already committed it. The progression of adultery, whether quickly or slowly, starts with a thought, an unmet expectation, or some hole we are trying to fill. This is why we need to set our eyes on God (Isa 26:3) and not let our minds wander. Someone does not wake up one morning saying he/she will commit adultery against his/her spouse. When our character is tested, we will demonstrate the character we have previously shown; we will not demonstrate an extraordinary measure of character we have never shown before. Just as in the book of Daniel, Shadrach, Meshach, and Abednego's obedience to the Lord did not start when they refused to bow down to the King's statue; it started when they chose not to defile themselves by eating and drinking water and vegetables. We need to be demonstrating character that aligns us with Scripture. Living this way means watching our language, guarding our eyes and minds from pornographic images, and being mindful of the music we listen to and any information we absorb from the people or technology around us.

PRACTICAL ADVICE + HOMEWORK

Confess Sin: Love of self lies behind the sin of adultery, and you must recognize that truth as you humbly confess this sin. Knowing that God is faithful to forgive and cleanse your heart following this confession encourages this humble and obedient action. (**Homework:** Stop right now and confess the sin of pride and self-love and its accompanying unfaithfulness to God and your spouse).

Renew Your Mind through Scripture: All proper relationships begin with God. (**Homework:** Read the following biblical texts to understand God's call to faithfulness to Himself and to your spouse: Genesis 2:15-25, Ephesians 5:1-33 and 22-32. Answer these questions from the biblical text you just read: What did you learn about God and His plan for marriage? What did you learn about your responsibility in marriage? Considering these truths, how do your thinking, feelings, and actions need to change?)

Obey God: Be faithful in your marriage. (**Homework:** Spend time with God in His Word each day, attend worship at your church each week, plan and carry out regular date nights, be consistent in expressing love through edifying communication [Eph 4:29] and regular sexual intimacy [1 Cor 7:3-5]).

Honor the Commandments of God: Respect the sanctity of marriage outlined in the Bible. Uphold His commandment that marriage is firmly grounded in God's prohibition against adultery. (**Homework:** Take time each day to reflect on Exodus 20:14 and commit to keeping this commandment close to your heart. Remember that you entered a covenant with God. If you don't know how powerful that is, research it and write down what that means.)

Adultery

Boundaries: Whatever the cause of adultery was (a person, porn etc.), no longer have communication or access to them. The Scripture states, *"And if your right-hand causes you to sin, cut it off and throw it away. For it is better that you lose one of your members than that your whole body go into hell"* (Matt 5:30). (**Homework:** Cut off all communication with this person, delete any websites or social media pages that could be temptations, and establish boundaries where needed. There is software you can put on your phone as well to keep you from re-establishing access.)

Understand the Consequences: You can choose to be obedient to the Word of God or live in disobedience. Every time you live outside God's will, there are serious repercussions. (**Homework:** Take this week to study Proverbs 6:32 and carefully consider the damage adultery can inflict on your life. Journal your reflections to gain wisdom in this matter. If you have children, not only are you hurting your spouse, but your choices are also impacting your kids. If your kids are aware, share why it won't happen again.)

Protect Your Heart and Mind: Adultery is more than just a physical act; Jesus states that even lusting is adulterous. Don't put yourself in challenging situations where you may be tempted to sin. This includes locations where you go and the content which you watch/listen. (**Homework:** Dedicate fifteen minutes every morning to prayer, seeking guidance from God as you reflect on what is found in Matthew 5:28.)

Engagement in Acts of Service towards Your Spouse: There is a saying, "A kind word goes a long way." The same is true for kind acts. It would be even better if they were random acts of kindness that you never mention. These acts could include washing extra laundry while your spouse is away and not telling them you did it. (**Homework:** Look for ways to express your affection and dedication, drawing inspiration from what is found in 1 Corinthians 13. A husband could simply fill his wife's car with gas. A wife might buy tickets to a baseball game when his favorite team comes to town.)

DISCUSSION STARTERS

1. **Sacred Covenant and Faithfulness:** Reflecting on Exodus 20:14 and the threefold covenant of marriage between a man, a woman, and their God, how do you perceive the gravity of adultery as not just unfaithfulness to a spouse but also as a breach with God? Can you identify moments or decisions in your relationship that may have paved the way for unfaithfulness, and how might recognizing these moments guide you toward restoration?

2. **Guarding One's Heart and Mind:** In Matthew 5:27-28, Jesus expounds on adultery, suggesting that even a lustful glance can equate to committing the act in one's heart. How do you understand this teaching in your daily life, especially in the age of technology? What safeguards can be established to ensure your heart and mind align with God's design for marital fidelity?

3. **The Power of Confession and Reconciliation:** Proverbs 28:13 emphasizes the mercy that follows confession and renunciation of sins. How do you see the act of confession —to God and your spouse—playing a role in the healing process after an act of adultery? How might the church community support you in seeking redemption and rebuilding trust in your marriage?

ANGER

An intense emotional response characterized by displeasure and antagonism, typically brought about by a perceived wrong or offense. While the Bible does acknowledge the legitimacy of God's just anger towards sin, it also cautions believers against uncontrolled or prolonged human anger, advising instead for self-restraint and reflection. The Word of God further encourages followers to pursue peace, forgiveness, and understanding in the face of conflict.

> *Be angry and do not sin. Don't let the sun go down*
> *on your anger, and don't give the devil an opportunity.*
> **Eph 4:26-27**

Anger is a powerful emotion that impacts our lives but doesn't have to control us. Paul's passage offers wisdom for those who struggle with anger by acknowledging its presence while pointing out the importance of how we handle it. The verse lets us know that feeling angry is not necessarily wrong. But it does caution us against acting out in anger. This distinction allows us to recognize our emotions are real, but it does not have to dictate our actions. The advice to address and resolve anger before the end of the day suggests a wise approach we should follow. It encourages believers to confront and resolve whatever issues may be causing us to be angry instead of letting them linger and worsen over time.

A Biblical Handbook for Counseling Heart Issues

My dear brothers and sisters, understand this: Everyone should be quick to listen, slow to speak, and slow to anger, for human anger does not accomplish God's righteousness.
James 1:19-20

The emotion of anger, which is sinful when rooted in pride, is used to manipulate others. A person who is in pride "wants what he/she wants when he/she wants it," and he/she will use anger to try and get others to give him/her what he/she wants in exchange for peace in the relationship. This passage from James illustrates the emptiness of these efforts, for God never uses sinful human anger to accomplish His purposes. This text also provides a remedy, for those in Christ can listen and speak carefully as they yield to the control of God's Spirit. In this way, they can respond in Christlike ways. When we allow ourselves to get angry and rage, we allow the devil to have a foothold on us (Eph 4:27). We allow him to manipulate us and keep us in a downward spiral. The devil wants us to overact and get angry because, just like it says in James, when we get angry, we cannot produce righteous anger. Therefore, we must leave judgment and anger up to God. Everyone must stand before God and answer for the sins they have committed, so we need to leave the judgment up to Him.

A gentle answer turns away anger, but a harsh word stirs up wrath. The tongue of the wise makes knowledge attractive, but the mouth of fools blurts out foolishness. The eyes of the Lord are everywhere, observing the wicked and the good.
Prov 15:1-3

Dealing with anger can be a challenge for individuals. This verse guides anyone facing anger, highlighting the importance of using words and acknowledging that God sees it all. The passage teaches us that responding calmly and peacefully anger can defuse tension. It emphasizes the choices we have regarding our reactions, either by responding gently or resorting to harsh words, each with its consequences. Reminding those we counsel that God is aware of everything happening adds a sense of accountability. It encourages self-control, wisdom, and decision making that reflect integrity. Ultimately, this passage offers advice on managing conflicts between people while providing a perspective on following biblical principles. The verses above present a strategy for diffusing anger and setting us up for a life of wisdom and understanding. What we view as essential and primary may not line up with Scripture. Feelings of rage typically stem from a selfishness or pride-filled motive that moves away from what God says is reasonable and necessary. The difficulty is looking past our anger when we are enraged, but Scripture teaches that if we slow down our thoughts and listen, we can handle situations skillfully without causing physical or emotional harm.

> *A person's insight gives him patience, and his virtue*
> *is to overlook an offense. A king's rage is like the roaring*
> *of a lion, but his favor is like dew on the grass.*
> **Prov 19:11-12**

This proverb offers insights for those struggling with anger by highlighting the importance of patience and letting go of offenses. It emphasizes that wisdom and understanding can help us exercise self-restraint and choose not to react to every slight or offense, demonstrating strength through composure. The passage also suggests that uncontrolled anger, like a lion's roar, can have an impact comparable to a king's terrifying wrath. By embracing this truth, individuals can cultivate a mindset that prioritizes forgiveness and self-control over seeking retaliation. These verses remind us that mastering our anger leads to honor and respect in relationships and society. This approach encourages us to respond calmly despite provocation, guiding us to manage anger effectively.

PRACTICAL ADVICE + HOMEWORK

Confess Sin: Pride lies behind the sin of unrighteous anger, and you must recognize that truth as you humbly confess this sin. Knowing that God is faithful to forgive and cleanse your heart following this confession encourages this humble and obedient action. (**Homework:** Stop right now and confess the sin of pride and its accompanying anger to God and to anyone you have wronged in your anger).

Renew Your Mind through Scripture: Understanding anger from God's perspective is critical to the change process. (**Homework:** Read the following biblical text to understand God's call to give up sinful anger: Ephesians 4:22-27 and 31-32. Answer these questions from the biblical text you just read: What did you learn about God's view of anger? What did you learn about what you should do when you are angry? How do your thinking, feelings, and actions need to change considering these truths?)

Obey God: Respond with the fruit of the Spirit rather than fleshly anger. (**Homework:** Spend time with God in His Word each day, attend worship at your church each week, ask others to hold you accountable when you respond in anger, and humbly accept their correction (Matt 18:15).

Timely Resolution: Don't let anger fester. It is like an acid eating away at you from the inside out; seek resolution or find ways to calm yourself before the day ends. This echoes the scriptural admonition in Ephesians 4:26 not to let the sun go down on one's anger, emphasizing prompt reconciliation. (**Homework:** At the end of each day, reflect on any moments of anger and actively release them through prayer or other methods to eliminate pent-up anger. Some possible activities include going to the gym, meditating, going for a walk, undertaking an art project, etc.)

Identify Your Anger: We need to identify places where anger takes over and then set boundaries to help us avoid anger. While setting these boundaries, pray through these areas and ask God to come into these places in your lives. (**Homework:** Reflect and figure out a place in your life where anger takes over. Spend time on your knees, confess to God these areas, and ask Him to come into these places.)

Practice Active Listening: Before reacting in anger, take the time to listen and understand the other person's perspective. (**Homework**: The next time you disagree, count to ten before responding, focusing on understanding the other person's view. If you want to respond immediately via text message or email, write what you want to say in the note section of your phone, wait thirty minutes, and reconsider what you want to send.)

Cut It Out: In moments of anger, stop whatever you are doing and if possible, leave the triggering situation (for instance, stop watching sports, stop playing video games, or stop reading social media or news articles). The problem with hanging around things that trigger your anger is that your anger will not suddenly go away. In terms of watching sports, keep up with alerts on your phone or check the score tomorrow. In terms of playing video games, practice self-control by finding something else to do when you feel angry, like reading, going outside for a short time, or something else that does not involve screens. Regarding social media and news articles, take a break from those for a day and stay away from screens if possible. (**Homework**: Memorize James 1:19-20 and write or type it out whenever you get angry. Doing this will not only help you memorize the passage, but it will train your mind to think of it when you do get angry. Instead of making bad habits out of anger, create helpful habits that reinforce daily biblical principles. You will find that this behavior will bring freedom and help you realize that your emotions do not control you, but you can control your reactions when your emotions swell inside you.)

Choose Words Wisely: Words can escalate or defuse situations; strive for gentleness and clarity in your speech. This reflects the wisdom in Proverbs 15:1, where a gentle answer can turn away wrath. (**Homework**: Journal about recent arguments and how different words might have led to a different outcome. Be intentional about being quick to listen and slow to speak.)

DISCUSSION STARTERS

1. **Differentiating Righteous and Unrighteous Anger:** Ephesians 4:26-27 reminds us that anger in and of itself isn't sinful; it's how we handle the emotion that can be sinful. How can we identify when our anger aligns with God's justice versus when it stems from our own selfish desires or misunderstandings? What biblical accounts or stories highlight the difference between righteous and unrighteous anger?

2. **The Power of Words and Responses:** Proverbs 15:1 and James 1:19-20 provide insights into how our words and reactions can diffuse or escalate situations. How have you seen the power of a gentle response or active listening? Share personal experiences when choosing to respond with kindness or restraint resulted in peace and understanding.

3. **The Role of Patience and Overlooking Offenses:** Proverbs 19:11-12 highlights the virtue of overlooking an offense. In a world that often encourages us to stand up for ourselves and confront every slight, how can we find the balance between defending what's right and choosing to let go for the sake of peace? How does this Proverb relate to Jesus' teachings on forgiveness and turning the other cheek?

ANOREXIA AND
BULIMIA

C hronic disorders where individuals severely restrict their food intake
or engage in binge eating followed by purging. Grounded in an intense
fear of weight gain and accompanied by a distorted perception of one's body,
these conditions often mirror spiritual distress, highlighting deep-seated
emotional pain and a desire for control. The Word of God reminds His people of God's love and affirms that their bodies are not mere physical entities
but temples of the Holy Spirit, crafted with purpose and care.

Do you not know that your body is a temple of the Holy Spirit within you,
whom you have from God, and that you are not your own? For you have
been bought with a price. Therefore, glorify God in your body.
1 Cor 6:19-20

Believers must recognize that they do not belong to themselves. The moment they surrendered to Christ, they gave Him their hearts and their
physical bodies. They now steward His possession. Stewards do not own
their master's property; they manage it, knowing they will give an account
to the owner. The goal is to glorify Him with their whole being. Therefore, bodily abuse through undereating or vomiting is rebellion against
His ownership to exercise control over what no longer belongs to them.

Therefore, I urge you, brethren, by the mercies of God, to present your bodies
a living and holy sacrifice, acceptable to God, which is your spiritual service

of worship. And do not be conformed to this world, but be transformed by the renewing of your mind, so that you may prove what the will of God is, that which is good and acceptable and perfect.
Rom 12:1-2

Presenting our bodies as living and holy sacrifices does not mean harming ourselves via literal sacrifice or depriving ourselves of bodily necessities as if the ascetic lifestyle is superior in holiness. Physical beauty is often no more than a cultural definition. In the Middle Ages, women considered "large" by today's standards in Western culture were considered beautiful. Cultural norms and views are not consistently biblical. When someone struggles with anorexia/bulimia, we must understand that our service of worship includes the care for our bodies and the right way of thinking about our bodies. The Scriptures teach in Romans 12 that we ought to let our minds be transformed to think as Christ thinks, and regarding the physical body and nutrition, we need the transformation of the mind by Christ to combat cultural thinking we may have adopted that competes with Christ's desires for us.

The eating disorder comes from a dysfunctional heart that craves control and obsesses over lies about beauty, worth, and identity. The root issues for eating disorders are a depraved mind that believes lies rather than God's truth, a lack of gratitude toward God for the way the body is made, and an idolatrous heart that worships one's own body rather than God and is tempted to control matters such as the way the body looks in ways that usurp God's sovereignty and authority. A person who struggles with an eating disorder views their body in a way no different than the world and the surrounding culture, which objectifies it, and thus fails to see the sanctity of the physical body God breathes into. The body thus devolves into something that can be casually altered and treated.

I praise you because I am fearfully and wonderfully made; your works are wonderful; I know that full well.
Ps 139:14

Anorexia and Bulemia

Dealing with anorexia and bulimia often involves a challenging journey toward overcoming this devastating, life-dominating sin. The Psalmist provides a passage that is relevant to those struggling with eating disorders, because it stresses the inherent worth and beauty of the individual, mainly who they are in Christ. These issues often arise from a distorted body image and dissatisfaction with his/her appearance. This verse serves as a counter-narrative to worldly pressures, affirming that God makes every person wonderfully and in His image. Image bearers embracing this truth can help someone with anorexia or bulimia see their body not as something to be controlled or despised but as a marvelous work He created. In the healing process, this perspective brings about gratitude for the unique design that God has given them. While reflecting on this verse, individuals are encouraged to shift his/her focus from what the world says instead recognize his/her value in the eyes of God.

> *Cast all your anxiety on him because he cares for you.*
> **1 Pet 5:7**

Many individuals with eating problems experience intense anxiety about weight gain, body image, or a loss of control, and they may turn to restrictive eating or bingeing/purging as ways to manage these fears. Peter offers peace and hope by turning to God and casting these anxieties upon Him. It acknowledges God's genuine care and compassion for each person, emphasizing that they are not alone in their struggle. This biblical guidance can provide comfort and support, enabling a shift away from "just getting by" and towards a reliance on God's love and understanding.

> *Therefore, this is what the LORD of Armies, the God of Israel, says: I am about to punish the king of Babylon and his land just as I punished the king of Assyria. I will return Israel to his grazing land, and he will feed on Carmel and Bashan; he will be satisfied in the hill country of Ephraim and of Gilead. In those days and at that time—this is the LORD's declaration—one*

will search for Israel's iniquity, but there will be none, and for Judah's sins, but they will not be found, for I will forgive those I leave as a remnant.
Jer 50:18-20

The world and its influences will constantly surround us with ideas and images that pressure us to conform to it. However, in the same way God was faithful to forgive and restore Israel, God is faithful to forgive us when we repent and turn to Him in faith and obedience. The world cannot stand against God, and the false ideas and images that plague our minds will be replaced with the blessing and providence of God. His goal is not our suffering aimlessly but rather to foster dependence on His great strength. We must turn from our oppressors and towards the loving and forgiving God.

But the Lord said to Samuel, "Do not look on his appearance or on the height of his stature, because I have rejected him. For the Lord sees not as man sees: man looks on the outward appearance, but the Lord looks on the heart."
1 Sam 16:7

Our bodies are created for the purpose of serving and worshiping God. Anything outside of this does not pertain to our purpose. We often seek approval from ourselves or others when it comes to how we look. We want people to look at us a certain way so that they think a certain way about us. When it comes to eating disorders, there is usually something more. Uncover the root issue first.

PRACTICAL ADVICE + HOMEWORK

Confess Sin: A prideful desire to be in control lies behind the sin of anorexia and bulimia, and you must recognize that truth as you humbly confess this sin. Knowing that God is faithful to forgive and cleanse your heart following this confession encourages this humble and obedient action. (**Homework:** Stop right now and confess the sin of pride and the abusive behavior that it has produced to God. Remember, if you confess the behavior, change will not occur. You must confess the *root* to kill the outward *fruit*).

Renew Your Mind through Scripture: Understanding anorexia and bulimia from God's perspective is critical to the change process. (**Homework**: Read the following biblical text to understand God's call to give up sinful eating habits: Psalm 139:1-18. Answer these questions from the biblical text you just read: What did you learn about God in this text? What did you learn about yourself? How do your thinking, feelings, and actions need to change considering these truths?)

Obey God: Be faithful in your eating. (**Homework**: Spend time with God in His Word each day [Job 23:12], attend worship at your church each week, and ask God to direct your eating, knowing that He has a prescribed portion for you [the daily or necessary food referenced in Job 23:12 means "the portion prescribed for me"]. Humbly confess this sin to other believers and ask them to pray for you and hold you accountable to eat as a faithful steward should [James 5:16]).

Honor Your Body as God's Temple: Acknowledge your body's value and strive to take care of it as a sacred trust from God. (**Homework**: Reflect on 1 Corinthians 6:19-20 daily, writing a journal entry about ways to glorify God with your body.)

Close Your Eyes: Take a break from social media, YouTube, and similar websites and focus on reading through Scripture, preferably a Gospel, when tempted to reach for your phone. Because you are created in the image of God, you should not hold the world's standards as highly as you currently do. The goal of taking a break is not to get away from the world but to retrain your mind to focus on God's standard for your life. Since Jesus is God Himself in physical form, His example of a holy life should be followed by every believer. Closing your eyes to the world and opening them to God's Word will bring "the peace of God, which surpasses all understanding" (Phil 4:7a). (**Homework**: Begin reading through two chapters of *Gentle and Lowly* by Dane Ortlund and be ready to discuss them in the next meeting. The goal is to see what Jesus meant by giving rest to all believers. Since Jesus is gentle and lowly, He is approachable to all people. Unlike the world, Jesus makes it possible for us to live up to God's standards through His grace and teachings in the Bible. Ortlund does a fantastic job in describing these things.)[6]

Define Beauty: Why we do what we do is often based on our beliefs. What we believe is often based on what we have been taught. (**Homework**: Define beauty according to two or three different cultures worldwide. Ask yourself what you agree with or find desirable in those cultures. Then compare it with what you can find in the Bible that defines beauty.)

Embrace Your Unique Design: Work on accepting yourself as fearfully and wonderfully made by God. This helps to cultivate accepting who you are in Christ by highlighting God's intentional creation. (**Homework**: Spend time meditating on Psalm 139:14 this week, creating a list of your unique qualities that reflect God's design. Also, journal how to use your unique qualities to bring God praise, glory, and honor.)

Seek Medical Help and Support: These issues often require medical intervention, support from loved ones, and biblical counseling. (**Homework**: Seek help from a medical doctor specializing in nutrition in addition to visiting your primary care provider if you haven't already, and communicate openly with a supportive community about your struggles.)

DISCUSSION STARTERS

1. **Body as a Temple in Worship:** Reflecting on 1 Corinthians 6:19-20, how does the knowledge that your body is a temple of the Holy Spirit influence how you perceive and treat it? How can you shift

---

6   Dane Ortlund, *Gentle and Lowly: The Heart of Christ for Sinners and Sufferers* (Grand Rapids, MI: Crossway, 2020).

from viewing your body through the lens of worldly standards to seeing it as a vessel meant to glorify God? Given that stewardship is about managing what God has given you, how does this truth impact your daily choices related to nutrition and self-care?

2. **Challenging Worldly Beauty Standards:** Romans 12:1-2 urges us not to be conformed to this world. How do you see the worldly standards of beauty influencing your perceptions and attitudes? How might "the renewing of your mind" transform your understanding of beauty and self-worth? As culture's definition of beauty has shifted, how can you ground your identity in God's unchanging truth rather than fleeting societal views?

3. **God's Intentional Design and Self-Value:** Psalm 139:14 declares that we are fearfully and wonderfully made. How does this psalmist's proclamation resonate with you in moments of struggle with body image? Can you identify the lies that challenge this truth in your life? How might embracing God's unique design for you pave the way for healing and gratitude, countering the worldly pressures that push for a distorted self-image?

ANXIETY / WORRY

A condition of the immaterial heart characterized by unease or apprehension about potential outcomes or the well-being of others. This sentiment can range from a valid unease related to life's demands to intense and consuming fears arising from a skewed viewpoint of life's challenges. While Jesus understood and acknowledged the natural human inclination towards concern for necessities such as sustenance or shelter, He urged His followers to maintain a godly perspective. By prioritizing God's kingdom and righteousness, believers are reminded that other concerns will be addressed in God's providence and perfect timing.

> *Don't worry about anything, but in everything, through prayer*
> *and petition with thanksgiving, present your requests to God.*
> *And the Peace of God, which surpasses all understanding,*
> *will guard your hearts and minds in Christ Jesus.*
> **Phil 4:6-7**

Struggling with anxiety can be an overwhelming experience, and many seek guidance and comfort to overcome it. This passage is particularly relevant for those who struggle with anxiety because it provides a roadmap to peace through prayer and gratitude. It encourages those you counsel to turn their worries into prayers, laying out specific concerns before God and thanking Him for His constant care. This passage states that by adopting an attitude of prayer and supplication, people can find a peace that surpasses all understanding, even amid anxiety-inducing circumstances. This peace is described as a guard for the heart and mind, signifying protection against the turmoil and uneasiness that anxiety can bring. The message is not a dismissal of anxiety but rather a way to process and handle it by relying on faith and connection to God. This passage's emphasis on open communication with God and trust in His provision offers a spiritual mechanism for anxiety. It speaks directly to the restless heart, offering comfort and wisdom to those wrestling with worry, emphasizing that they are not alone in their struggle.

> *Finally, brothers and sisters, whatever is true, whatever is honorable, whatever is just, whatever is pure, whatever is lovely, whatever is commendable—if there is any moral excellence and if there is anything praiseworthy—dwell on these things. Do what you have learned and received andheard from me, and seen in me, and the God of Peace will be with you.*
> **Phil 4:8-9**

This passage encourages individuals to focus their minds on things that are true, noble, right, pure, lovely, admirable, excellent, and praiseworthy. For those struggling with anxiety, this mandate can be a grounding practice that shifts attention away from fears and worries. Anxiety often involves dwelling on potential adverse outcomes or uncertainties; this verse redirects that focus on virtues found in the Word. It's not a superficial avoidance of problems but rather a constructive approach to frame challenges within a perspective of faith and hope. Paul provides a biblical guide for managing anxiety by focusing on biblical truth and what brings God praise, glory, and honor.

Paul emphasizes the importance of practicing biblical truth, offering valuable instruction for those dealing with anxiety. Encouraging individuals to concentrate on what is true, honorable, just, pure, lovely, and commendable shifts attention away from worry and fear. Focusing on these truths can create a mindset that encourages those you counsel to stop thinking anxious thoughts and focus more on God's peace. Anxiety often arises from uncertainty and unrealistic/irrational fears. Emphasize focusing on Christ, which can form a wall against such fears. A blueprint for a life guided by wisdom, virtue, and faith is provided in this passage, which presents a practical and spiritual means of addressing anxiety.

> *Search me, God, and know my heart; test me and know my concerns.*
> *See if there is any offensive way in me; lead me in the everlasting way.*
> **Ps 139:23-24**

This text is most accurately translated from the Hebrew as follows: *"Search me, God, and know my heart; Put me to the test and know my anxious thoughts; And see if there is any hurtful way in me. And lead me in the everlasting way."*

This alternative translation is significant because of what it teaches about anxiety. When God searches and tests individuals, He does so by examining hearts. While people often think of anxiety as an unexplained emotion, this text clarifies that anxiety results from how someone thinks in his or her heart. While outward circumstances can be hurtful, this text explains that inner thoughts are the most hurtful part of any difficulty. Ultimately, anxiety is a self-inflicted wound in which individuals harm themselves with their own anxious thoughts. The Psalmist's prayer to be led in the way everlasting implies that anxiety-producing thoughts lead one away from God, and a humble cry to be led back is part of the necessary remedy for these fears.

> *Trust in the LORD with all your heart, and do not rely on your own under-*
> *standing; in all your ways know him, and he will make your paths straight.*
> *Don't be wise in your own eyes; fear the LORD and turn away from evil. This*
> *will be healing for your body and strengthening for your bones."*
> **Prov 3:5-8**

One of the biggest struggles we have with anxiety is the double-minded nature of overthinking. This passage teaches us that through trusting in God and NOT in our own thoughts or wisdom, reality will unfold as God plans it. The wisdom that comes through depending on God helps turn people away from the evil that dominates their minds and allows healing and strength to fill their bodies. The mind is the gateway to the body, and a mind that trusts God leads to a body that knows rest.

> *Tremble, and do not sin; Meditate in your heart*
> *upon your bed and be still. Selah. Offer the*
> *sacrifices of righteousness, and trust in the Lord.*
> **Ps 4:4-5**

Psalm 4 is a short Psalm of David crying out in distress and anxiety. For those struggling with anxiety and worry, sometimes we feel as if there is nothing we can do to stop the pain, nor anything we can do to prevent the anxiousness from coming upon us. Our bodies will be triggered by stimuli that lead us into a worried state, but God does not hold us accountable for the things out of our control. It is our response *to* anxiousness, like David's, for which God holds us accountable. David says that it is possible to "tremble" yet not sin. When we are trembling with anxiety or worry, we must meditate on how trustworthy and faithful God is in our struggle and be still. Being still is hard, but we must learn to do it as David did.

> *You will keep in perfect peace those whose*
> *minds are steadfast, because they trust in you.*
> **Isa 26:3**

Anxiety is less about gaining control of your life and more about trusting God. Feeling anxious about something is a natural response because we know we cannot control the situation. When we find ourselves here, we need to trust God has us right where He wants us. To trust God, we need to know who He is. When we read the Bible and spend time with Him, we need to do it through the lens of "what does this tell me about God?" not "what does this tell me about me?" If we grow greater in our knowledge of God and better understand who He is, then we can rest in the fact that God has everything in control.

PRACTICAL ADVICE + HOMEWORK

Confess Sin: Distrust of God lies behind the sin of anxiety and worry, and you must recognize that truth as you humbly confess this sin (Jer 17:5-8). Knowing that God is faithful to forgive and cleanse your heart following this confession encourages this humble and obedient action. (**Homework:** Stop right now and confess the sin of your distrust of God. You must confess this root to kill the fruit of fear and worry).

Renew Your Mind through Scripture: Understanding anxiety and worry from God's perspective is critical to change. (**Homework:** Read the following biblical texts to understand God's call to give up fear and worry: Jeremiah 17:5-8; Luke 10:38-42; and Philippians 4:5b-7. Answer these questions from the biblical text you just read: What did you learn about God in this text? What did you learn about yourself? How do your thinking, feelings, and actions need to change considering these truths?)

Obey God: Be faithful in putting off anxiety and worry and putting on prayer with thanksgiving in its place. (**Homework:** Spend time with God in His Word each day, attend worship at your church each week, keep a journal of thanksgiving and offer it back to God in prayer, memorize and mediate on Philippians 4:5b-7, and use this text to direct your responses whenever you start to feel afraid).

Root Cause: When you are anxious about something, there is usually a deeper cause; some triggers might make you feel anxious. (**Homework:** Spend time reflecting and journaling what makes you anxious this week. Then, evaluate if a common theme presents itself. Spend time praying God would come into these parts in your life where you are not fully trusting Him.)

Reading Through the Pain: When anxious thoughts arise, stop what you are doing and read aloud Proverbs 3:5-8. Though this may seem like a hassle, you are making a physical gesture to remind yourself that God is in control, not your circumstances. In moments of anxiety, physically leaving where you are, mentally leaving your mindset, and replacing your anxious thoughts with Scripture also trains your mind to focus on God in these situations. Please do this as often as you feel that anxiety is taking over your mind, no matter how often it happens in a day. (**Homework:** Journal specific times when anxiety starts, write out what thoughts you are having, pray that God would still your heart, and write the time your anxiety ends. This exercise will give evidence to you and your counselor that your anxiety has a start and end time, showing that it does not last forever. This also pairs with reading through Proverbs 3:5-8. As you write down your thoughts, they will be juxtaposed with biblical truth, making you compare them and see if they align with Scripture. *Spoiler alert*: they probably will not.)

Be Still: Psalm 46:10 says, "Be still and know that I am God." As a crying baby needs to be held close and rocked to sleep as it cries and screams, the baby eventually drifts off to sleep peacefully. This image displays you and I amid our worry—the Father must hold us until we drift off into a stillness that comforts us. (**Homework:** When you are anxious, try to stop what you are doing and pray. Write down what upset you or triggered this moment and ask the Lord to help you endure. Journal these thoughts to pray about them when you are not upset.)

Release Burdens: Remember that God invites us to cast our burdens onto Him, trusting in His Love and care for us. Believers are to present their worries to God in prayer, remembering that there is a promise of peace, and that God will guard their hearts and minds. (**Homework:** Write down your primary sources of anxiety on slips of paper, pray, and place them in a "worry jar," symbolizing your act of giving them to God.)

Live in the Present: Resist the urge to agonize over the future; focus on the blessings and tasks of today. This is consistent with Matthew 6:34 about not worrying about tomorrow, instead focusing on gratitude. (**Homework:** Each morning, list three things you're grateful for, and at night, reflect on one moment from the day when you felt peace or joy.)

DISCUSSION STARTERS

1. **The Heart's Cry Amidst Anxiety:** Psalm 139:23-24 encourages us to ask God to search and know our hearts, especially our anxious thoughts. Reflect on a recent time when anxiety weighed heavily on your heart. What were the root thoughts or beliefs that fueled this anxiety? Recognizing that anxiety often arises from our innermost thoughts, how can surrendering these fears to God and seeking His everlasting way bring you peace and redirect your heart toward Him?

2. **The Power of Trust Over Overthinking:** The verses from Proverbs 3:5-8 emphasize the importance of trusting in the Lord rather than relying on our own understanding. How have moments of overthinking or self-reliance caused unrest in your life? By trusting God and His promises, how can you experience healing and strength in your mind and throughout your entire being?

3. **Scripture as the Anchor in Anxious Times:** Philippians 4:8 guides where our minds should dwell, especially during moments of anxiety. Can you recall a recent situation where your focus shifted away from these truths and towards worries or fears? How might intentionally grounding your thoughts in what is true, honorable, and praiseworthy change your response to anxious triggers and better align your perspective with God's promises?

APATHY

Derived from the Greek term *apathēs*, meaning "without passion," this refers to indifference or lack of emotional investment in one's surroundings, relationships, and/or responsibilities. Within biblical counseling, apathy can be perceived as spiritual inaction, where believers neglect God's calling and His divine purpose for their lives.

> *And whatever you do, in word or in deed, do*
> *everything in the name of the Lord Jesus,*
> *giving thanks to God the Father through him.*
> **Col 3:17**

When struggling with apathy, identifying a God-honoring purpose and lining up every aspect of life with that purpose can be a powerful solution. Living with intentionality and commitment, whether in word or action, infuses life with meaning and joy, transcending mere obligation or routine. This approach transforms ordinary responsibilities into opportunities for spiritual growth and expressions of your faith. It calls for a life of enthusiasm and passion, finding God in the day-to-day things. For those feeling disconnected or indifferent, connecting daily actions to something greater gives them significance and value. By engaging fully in life and seeing beyond the superficial, a person can overcome lack of concern and live a fulfilled life seeking to honor God.

But I said, "I have toiled in vain; I have spent My strength for nothing
and vanity; Yet surely the justice due to Me is with the Lord,
and My reward with My God."
Isa 49:4

Isaiah tells us much about the Messiah and His mission. This passage gives insight into the Messiah's feelings regarding the extensive work and pain endured to be the Savior mankind needs. A point came where the Messiah would be tempted to think, "Nothing I do or have done matters, so why even try" (which is apathy)? Is it not true that we tend to want to give up and not care anymore when we see no purpose or vision for anything we seem to be doing or care about? We submit to apathy and this false thinking and spiral out of control. However, the Messiah responds to the temptation of apathy with the right biblical thinking—regardless of whether I see the purpose being fulfilled, I am called to do the right thing by God, to obey! God will reward me, and there is purpose in my work.

And at that time, I will search Jerusalem with lamps
and punish those who settle down comfortably, who
say to themselves: The LORD will do nothing—good or
bad. Their wealth will become plunder and their houses a ruin.
They will build houses but never live in them, plant vineyards
but never drink their wine.
Zeph 1:12-13

God has clearly set what He requires of people, but if we ignore these requirements, pain and suffering will still come and ruin us. Without the foundation of God and His blessings, people will not experience peace and satisfaction in this life. It will be like building a house that is destroyed upon completion. The work was in vain, and the outcome is the same as not building in the first place. We will not know peace and satisfaction unless we do as God commands.

Apathy

Whatever you do, do it from the heart, as something
done for the Lord and not for people, knowing that you
will receive the reward of an inheritance from the Lord.
You serve the Lord Christ.
Col 3:23-24

Apathy can be debilitating, leading to a lack of enthusiasm or interest in everyday undertakings. Embracing a mindset where all actions are seen as a service to God can revive a sense of meaning. When work and daily duties are approached with the attitude of doing them to bring God praise, glory, and honor, they take on renewed significance. This shift in perspective can transform ordinary or repetitive responsibilities into expressions of faith. Building a connection between your day-to-day life and God can help you overcome feelings of indifference and become deeply engaged in acts of service to Him. This way of approaching life encourages a deep, inner motivation and can be a powerful remedy to apathy. Additionally, what is found in this passage can provide a transformative perspective, encouraging believers to work with all their hearts as working for the Lord.

A sensible person sees danger and takes cover, but
the inexperienced keep going and are punished.
Prov 22:3

This verse features the value of looking ahead and taking proactive steps in the face of impending challenges. Apathy often leads to a lack of concern or motivation to act, especially in matters that require prudence and careful planning. Solomon emphasizes recognizing potential dangers and taking decisive action to avoid them. This wisdom encourages taking the initiative, urging individuals to be engaged and aware of their surroundings. It contrasts with apathetic attitudes, where a person may ignore warning signs or fail to take necessary precautions. By following the wisdom of this proverb, one can cultivate a more thoughtful and vigilant approach to life's challenges. Applying this exercise promotes a sense of purpose and determination rather than indifference.

PRACTICAL ADVICE + HOMEWORK

Confess Sin: Pride lies behind the sin of apathy, and you must recognize that truth as you humbly confess this sin. Knowing that God is faithful to forgive and cleanse your heart following this confession, provides encouragement for this humble and obedient action. (**Homework**: Stop right now and confess the sin of apathy and the pride it is rooted in. Remember, the prideful root must be extinguished through confession so that the apathetic emotional fruit can be extinguished.)

Renew Your Mind through Scripture: Understanding apathy from God's perspective is a critical part of the change process. (**Homework**: Read the following biblical text to understand God's call to give up apathy: Revelation 3:14-20. Answer these questions from the biblical text you just read: What did you learn about God's view of apathy? What did you learn about what you should do when you are apathetic? How do your thinking, feelings, and actions need to change in light of these truths?)

Obey God: Yield to God's Spirit rather than giving into apathy. (**Homework**: Spend time with God in His Word each day, attend worship at your church each week, and make a list of your responsibilities and schedule each one, carrying them out for the glory of God [Matt 5:16]).

Evaluate Your Spiritual Temperature: Recognize the dangers of being lukewarm in your faith and commitments. This is similar to the warning in Revelation 3:16 against being lukewarm, encouraging consideration of any spiritual stagnation. Don't be lukewarm. (**Homework**: Reflect on areas where you feel most apathetic and identify one spiritual practice that might ignite more passion or purpose in that area.)

Evaluate Your Work: Why exactly are you apathetic? Is it because you are lazy or because you have worked extremely hard and do not see the purpose of the labor you are engaging in? Sometimes, apathy is the result of our laziness; sometimes, it is a result of our discouragement. (**Homework**:

Evaluate what you are doing today considering God's calling on your life, such as a spouse, parent, employee, etc. Prioritize what you know matters to God, asking God to remind you that your reward is with Him.)

Cultivate Zeal and Enthusiasm: Embrace your duties and commitments with enthusiasm, remembering that every effort can be a service to the Lord. This has its basis in Colossians 3:23, emphasizing that whatever we do, we should do it heartily, as for the Lord, thus transforming everyday routines into spiritual service. (**Homework:** Choose one job or commitment this week and approach it with renewed enthusiasm, as if doing it for God directly.)

Persevere in Doing Good: Even when you don't feel like it, push through the feelings of apathy and continue to do good, trusting that the fruits of your labor will appear in time. Doing this resonates with what is found in Galatians 6:9, where persistence in good works is encouraged even when enthusiasm declines. (**Homework:** Commit to a new act of kindness or service for the next week, regardless of how you feel each day.)

Pray at All Times: When you feel unmotivated to do anything, pray that God will give you the desire to get up and do what needs to be done. This is what dependence looks like. Prayer is not a magical incantation that will immediately give us what we desire, but it helps us go to the feet of Christ and give our hearts to Him. Apathy can be challenging if you do not want to overcome it, so let God know! Sometimes, we can be motivated to do the wrong things, so dependence allows God to show us what we need and what we need to do. (**Homework:** For the next meeting, write five things you like and why. In times of apathy, finding positive things in life can be challenging, so starting off with things that interest you can build a foundation of positivity. With this list in hand, point to the things that motivate you. If any items on the list are sinful, address them first and point to biblical truth appropriately.)

DISCUSSION STARTERS

1. **Intentional Living in Christ's Name:** Reflecting on Colossians 3:17, consider the areas where apathy has taken root in your life. How might seeing every action, big or small, as an act of worship and dedication to the Lord transform your approach to daily tasks? How can incorporating gratitude into your daily routine help combat feelings of indifference and infuse purpose into even the most mundane activities?

2. **Finding Purpose Amidst Disheartenment:** In Isaiah 49:4, the prophet expressed discouragement, feeling as if his efforts might have been in vain. Yet, he found solace in the Lord's promises. Have there been times in your life when you felt your efforts were fruitless or lacked meaning? How can anchoring your worth and purpose in God's perspective, rather than the immediate outcomes, renew your passion and drive?

3. **Apathy Versus Spiritual Zeal:** Zephaniah 1:12-13 warns against complacency and the dangers of taking God's presence and blessings for granted. Reflect on moments when you've felt distant or disinterested in your spiritual journey. How might aligning your daily actions and thoughts with God's purpose rekindle a spiritual zeal, ensuring your efforts aren't in vain?

BITTERNESS

Grounded in Hebrews 12:15, bitterness can be described as a long-lasting animosity that festers within an individual's heart. This emotion can often stem from an unresolved conflict or offense, leading to persistent anger, resentment, and even thoughts of revenge. Such a disposition affects one's relationship with others and can impede one's relationship with God. It is imperative to address bitterness through the lens of Scripture, emphasizing the need for genuine forgiveness, as modeled by Christ, to restore the soul and foster spiritual growth.

> *Let all bitterness, anger and wrath, shouting and slander*
> *be removed from you, along with all malice.*
> **Eph 4:31**

Struggling with bitterness can impact personal relationships and your spiritual well-being. Ephesians 4:31 speaks directly to this struggle, calling for removing all bitterness, rage, anger, harsh words, and slander. The passage urges individuals to replace these non-God-honoring emotions with kindness, compassion, and forgiveness. Doing so sets a standard for personal conduct that promotes healing and reconciliation. This can benefit those wrestling with bitterness, providing a clear path to transforming their relationships and personal character. Following this biblical advice will lead to personal growth and more fulfilling interactions with others. It serves as a remedy for those who find themselves trapped in cycles of bitterness and resentment.

What, then, are we to say about these things? If God is for us, who is against us? He did not even spare his own Son but gave him up for us all. How will he not also with him grant us everything? Who can bring an accusation against God's elect? God is the one who justifies. Who is the one who condemns? Christ Jesus is the one who died, but even more, has been raised; he also is at the right hand of God and intercedes for us.
Rom 8:31-34

When believers are unforgiving and bitter towards their fellow believers, the truths from Romans 8 need to transform their thinking. Every child of God should recognize that God is for them; they are justified and no longer under condemnation. While these truths cause rejoicing, victims of wrongdoing must also recognize that they are equally true for their fellow believers who have wronged them. Every child of God has the same benefit: a God who is for them, justification, freedom from condemnation, and a Savior who uses what He knows about them to intercede for them. The only unknown factor is the human response. Will those harmed continue to condemn their oppressors based on what they know, or will they be like Jesus Christ and use what they know to be intercessors?

He has laid siege against me, encircling me with bitterness and hardship... Because of the LORD's faithful love, we do not perish, for his mercies never end.
Lam 3:5, 22

Bitterness is the extended anger over an injustice or wrongdoing that never finds forgiveness, resulting in hostility towards another. However, sometimes people find themselves in situations where they say their bitterness results from God's work. Jeremiah writes that, in his flesh, he sees that the immense suffering in his life is a result of the calling God gave him as a prophet. Bitterness has overtaken him at times because he holds God responsible. People sometimes move from holding the offender responsible for the injustice to holding God responsible. It seems that God does not care or act to right the wrong or end the suffering, and thus they become bitter with God. Jeremiah gives the antidote in verse 22 with the reminder to trust in His lovingkindness (*hesed* in Hebrew), knowing that God will not be unjust; instead, He will be faithful to us amid injustice. We can always trust in Him.

> *For I see you are poisoned by bitterness and bound by wickedness.*
> **Acts 8:23**

Bitterness can often seep into a person's soul, affecting their behavior and relationships. Acts 8:23 describes a situation where bitterness was likened to being trapped in sin, warning about its destructive nature. This passage provides insight into the impact that bitterness can have on a person's spiritual condition. It is a vivid reminder that unresolved bitterness can lead to deeper spiritual problems and separate us from God. By recognizing and addressing bitterness, individuals can pursue healing and spiritual growth, positioning themselves more closely with the teachings and examples found in the Bible. The passage should cause reflection and encourage those struggling with bitterness to seek reconciliation and restoration with others (Acts 8:24). It emphasizes the importance of not allowing bitterness to fester, as doing so can have spiritual consequences.

> *Make sure that no one falls short of the grace of*
> *God and that no root of bitterness springs up,*
> *causing trouble and defiling many.*
> **Heb 12:15**

Bitterness can worsen within a person, leading to spiritual, physical, and emotional troubles. Paul cautions against allowing a "root of bitterness" to grow and cause trouble, thereby defiling many. The imagery in this passage emphasizes how bitterness can spread and affect the individual and those around them. By recognizing the destructive nature of bitterness and heeding the warning contained in this verse, individuals are encouraged to pursue peace and holiness. They are prompted to actively guard their hearts and relationships, ensuring that resentment doesn't take root. Meditating upon this passage should eventually lead the bitter person to have compassion, forgiveness, and restoration. It serves as a stark reminder that unchecked bitterness can have far-reaching consequences and provides a call to action to counteract its spread.

PRACTICAL ADVICE + HOMEWORK

Confess Sin: A prideful and judgmental spirit lies behind the sin of bitterness and unforgiveness, and you must recognize that truth as you humbly confess this sin. Knowing that God is faithful to forgive and cleanse your heart following this confession provides encouragement for this humble and obedient action (1 John 1:9). (**Homework:** Stop right now and confess the sin of your prideful and judgmental spirit towards others who have sinned against you. You must confess this root to kill the fruit of bitterness and unforgiveness).

Renew Your Mind through Scripture: Understanding bitterness and unforgiveness from God's perspective is critical to the change process. (**Homework:** Read the following biblical texts to understand God's call to give up bitterness and unforgiveness: Leviticus 19:17-18; Matthew 18:21-35; Romans 12:14-21. Answer these questions from the biblical text you just read: What did you learn about God in this text? What did you learn about yourself? How do your thinking, feelings, and actions need to change considering these truths?)

Obey God: Be faithful in putting off bitterness and unforgiveness through confession. (**Homework:** Spend time with God in His Word each day. Attend worship at your church each week. Use the pattern laid out in Luke 6:27-28 to relate to your oppressors by choosing to love them, do good to them, return blessing for cursing, and faithfully pray for them).

Bitterness

Recognize and Address Bitterness: Self-awareness is the first step. Understanding and admitting where bitterness may have taken root in your heart encourages introspection and acknowledgment of the issue, aligning with Hebrews 12:15, which warns against the root of bitterness. (**Homework:** Journal about a recent or past event that may have planted seeds of bitterness and express your feelings in writing.)

Are You Mad at God?: As you investigate the cause of your bitterness, ask yourself if you need to ask the Lord for forgiveness if you have held Him responsible for wrongdoing in your life. (**Homework:** Pray to the Lord that He would reveal to you if you have held bitterness towards Him in a lack of trust of His faithfulness. Confess this as sin before Him and learn to walk in that trusting of His faithfulness even if you cannot see it.)

Seek Forgiveness and Offer It: Remember the grace and forgiveness God extends to us and strive to extend it to others. This is grounded in what Jesus taught in Matthew 6:14-15, emphasizing the importance of forgiving others as God has forgiven us. (**Homework:** Identify at least one person you need to forgive and take a step towards reconciliation, whether initiating a conversation or writing a letter. If this is not possible due to the individual(s) not being open to reconciliation, lay everything at the feet of Christ.)

Cultivate a Heart of Gratitude: Changing your perspective from dwelling on the things that cause you pain to appreciating the things that bring you joy has the power to turn bitterness into gratitude. This aligns with the message conveyed in 1 Thessalonians 5:18, which encourages us to maintain a spirit of thankfulness for our circumstances, redirecting our attention from our wounds to the blessings we receive. (**Homework:** Each day for a week, list three things you're grateful for, mainly focusing on areas where you've felt resentment.)

Pray for Healing: Take the time to bring your bitterness to God. Offer it up to Christ, seeking healing and wisdom. This practice invites individuals to entrust their burdens to God, just as Philippians 4:6-7 advises us to pray about everything, including our feelings of bitterness. (**Homework:** Dedicate ten minutes each day for a week to pray specifically about your feelings of bitterness and ask for God's perspective.)

DISCUSSION STARTERS

1. **Overcoming Bitterness with Kindness and Compassion:** Reflecting on Ephesians 4:31, where we're instructed to remove all bitterness and embrace kindness and forgiveness, how do you see bitterness manifesting in your interactions with others? How might a conscious effort to replace bitterness with kindness and compassion impact your personal well-being and your relationships with others?

2. **God's Justification Amidst Our Bitterness:** Romans 8:31-34 reminds us of God's unwavering support and Christ's intercession. When feelings of bitterness arise, especially towards fellow believers, how can internalizing these truths about God's love and justification help release those feelings? How does understanding God's stance towards us influence our perspective toward those who may have wronged us?

3. **Transformative Grace Amidst Bitterness:** The warning in Hebrews 12:15 about the "root of bitterness" highlights its deep-seated and pervasive nature. Can you recognize situations or experiences that might have sown seeds of bitterness within you? In what ways can immersing yourself in God's grace and love prevent this bitterness from taking deeper root and spreading to others?

CHILDREN

Beyond the practicalities of day-to-day routines, a biblical vision for parenting encompasses a reflective responsibility entrusted by God. It signifies the intentional guardianship parents undertake, not just for their children's physical well-being but also for their spiritual growth. Anchored in God's Word, this perspective views children not merely as offspring but as eternal souls given by God into the care of parents. Parenting becomes a holy task, where guidance, discipline, and love cultivate a child's heart in preparation for a relationship with the Creator. This immense responsibility underscores the significance of parents' role in shepherding their child into the path of righteousness for His name's sake.

Children, obey your parents in the Lord, because
this is right. Honor your father and mother, which is
the first commandment with a promise, so that it may go
well with you and that you may have a long life in the land.
Eph 6:1-3

God's commands for children in Christian families are clear and include obedience to their parents out of hearts that honor them. This means children have a duty to listen and then conform to their parents' instructions. The attitudes and actions come from hearts that honor and respect those God has placed over them as His authorities. Children who resist God's authority exercised through godly parents must be reminded of these truths and called to repentance for their rebellion against God and their parents.

> *Start a youth out on his way; even when*
> *he grows old, he will not depart from it.*
> **Prov 22:6**

Rearing children is a demanding undertaking requiring wisdom and understanding. The idea found in Proverbs 22:6 emphasizes the role of guidance and educating your child from a young age. It speaks to the notion that instilling solid biblical principles and ethical values in a child's early years will set them on a path they will likely follow. Parents and guardians are encouraged to actively participate in their children's moral development, setting an example and providing direction. This concept offers reassurance that the lessons taught early on have a lasting impact. It's a principle that resonates across different cultures and has been cited in various contexts related to child-rearing. Thus, the verse becomes a fundamental resource for those seeking to raise children with integrity, faith, and strong character.

> *Fathers, don't stir up anger in your children but bring*
> *them up in the training and instruction of the Lord.*
> **Eph 6:4**

Ephesians 6:4 directs parents, particularly fathers, about how they should treat their children. It highlights the importance of nurturing and instruction rather than provoking and causing resentment. The values in this passage underscore the role of parents in teaching their children about faith and righteousness. Following this counsel makes parents likelier to have a loving and respectful relationship with their children, making spiritual and moral education more effective. The teachings found here have enduring relevance and can be applied to various aspects of parenting, helping to create a harmonious and biblically grounded family environment. Ultimately, this passage serves as a reminder of the parental responsibility to raise children with compassion and understanding, aligning values based on the Word of God.

> ***Discipline your child, and it will bring you***
> ***peace of mind and give you delight.***
> **Prov 29:17**

This verse highlights the importance of consistent discipline in a child's upbringing. It suggests that proper wisdom and correction lead to a more harmonious home environment. By instilling boundaries and biblical values, parents raise children whose goal should be obedience to God's Word. This should bring the parents peace of mind, knowing their child lives in a God-honoring way. This proverb encapsulates how a disciplined upbringing brings long-term rewards, both in the child's behavior and in the joy they bring to their parents. Essentially, structured and loving discipline today paves the way for a brighter, more peaceful tomorrow.

> ***You shall love the Lord your God with all your heart and***
> ***with all your soul and with all your might. These words,***
> ***which I am commanding you today, shall be on your heart.***
> ***You shall teach them diligently to your sons, and shall talk***
> ***of them when you sit in your house, and when you walk by***
> ***the way, and when you lie down, and when you rise up.***
> **Deut 6:5-7**

Moses spoke these words (known as the *Shema*) to the people of Israel as they prepared to enter the Promised Land after spending forty years in the wilderness. To cultivate a nation of holy people and families, it was imperative for parents to: First, love God inwardly and through the actions of their lives. This was not meant to be just behavioral repetition, but an intimate understanding of God and His heart. Second, parents were to teach their children who God was and His ways of living so that they could also fulfill God's holy purposes in their lives. Parents were to be diligent, intentionally putting forth effort, to use every applicable moment and event to point their children to the Lord, His ways, and His will.

PRACTICAL ADVICE + HOMEWORK

Confess Sin: A prideful and independent spirit lies behind the sin of rebellion against your parents, and you must humbly confess this sin. Knowing that God is faithful to forgive and cleanse your heart following this confession encourages this humble and obedient action. (**Homework:** Stop right now and confess the sin of your prideful rebellion against your parents to God and to them. Do so humbly, recognizing that submission and obedience to God are reflected in your submission and obedience to your parents).

Renew Your Mind through Scripture: Understanding rebellion from God's perspective is critical to change. (**Homework:** Read the following biblical texts to understand God's call to give up rebellion: Deuteronomy 1:26-33. Answer these questions from the biblical text you just read: What did you learn about God in this text? What did you learn about yourself? How does rebellion express itself in speech, thoughts about God, and shifting blame for personal sin? How do your thoughts, feelings, and actions need to change considering these truths?)

Obey God: Make Him first in your heart and life. (**Homework:** Spend time with God in His Word each day, attend worship at your church each week, and submit to God's authority exercised through your parents as you obediently carry out their commands).

Commitment to Lifelong Teaching: Make sure that the teachings of the Bible influence your family's daily routines. By doing so, you can ensure that your child's spiritual growth is a part of their upbringing. This aligns with the commandment in Deuteronomy 6:6-7 to educate children about God's commandments and make faith a regular aspect of their lives.

Children

(**Homework:** Set aside dedicated time each day for a family devotion or Bible reading.)

Foster a Nurturing Environment: Maintaining loving communication, understanding, and patience regarding discipline is crucial. When considering how to offer correction, it is crucial to root an act of discipline in biblical truth and wisdom. This approach aligns with Ephesians 6:4, which encourages discipline rooted in love and understanding rather than provoking negativity. (**Homework:** When addressing behavioral issues, briefly discuss the situation and its consequences with your child.)

Maintain Open Communication: Open the lines of communication, allowing your child to freely express feelings, doubts, or questions about faith and life, as this helps build trust and understanding, supported by the encouragement in James 1:19 to be quick to listen. (**Homework:** Have a weekly "heart-to-heart" chat where each family member shares something they're grateful for and struggling with. It is time for children to have an opportunity to share without fear of judgment. *Example:* If your son doesn't come to you to share that he's doing drugs and you find out on your own—significant punishment. If your son tells you on his own—the punishment won't be as severe.)

Lead by Example: Embody the teachings of the Bible in your own actions so your child can have a tangible model to emulate. This reflects the Christ-like example in 1 Corinthians 11:1, providing children with tangible models of faith in action. (**Homework:** Reflect on your efforts over the past week and identify one way to better embody a Christ-like attitude daily. Remember, your kids are watching you; they are always watching. So be a man/woman with a heart and desire to obey everything in the Bible, not just the easy parts.)

Engage in a Local Church Family Ministry: The local church is designed to be a center of "equipping the saints for the work of service" (Eph 4:12), and discipling children in the Lord's will and ways that fall under that purpose. What better place to learn to be a disciple-making parent than alongside like-minded parents? (**Homework:** Reach out to your pastor or the pastor on staff at your church that directly oversees family ministry and/or children and student ministries based on the age of your children. If you do not have a church, or if your pastor cannot help, contact a friend you trust who can help you find a pastor or church that can provide assistance.)

DISCUSSION STARTERS

1. **Understanding Biblical Obedience:** Ephesians 6:1-3 speaks of the importance of children obeying and honoring their parents. How do you understand the term "honor" in your relationship with your parents? How can reflecting on God's design for familial relationships help you better fulfill this commandment and experience the promised blessings?

2. **The Foundations of Childhood:** Proverbs 22:6 emphasizes the role of early guidance in a child's life. Can you recall biblical principles or teachings that were instilled in you from a young age? How have these principles influenced your choices and path as you've grown older? Furthermore, how can parents today utilize this wisdom to set their children on a godly path?

3. **Parental Compassion and Discipline:** In Ephesians 6:4 and Proverbs 29:17, we are shown two contrasting yet complementary aspects of parenting—nurturing without provoking resentment and the importance of discipline. How have you experienced these principles in your upbringing, and how do they influence your views on parenting now? How can striking a balance between love and discipline result in a God-honoring upbringing?

CHILDHOOD SEXUAL ABUSE

In the light of Scripture, which underscores the sanctity and dignity of every individual, sexual abuse is a grievous sin and violation. It is a traumatic experience where a child is used for the sexual gratification of an adult or older child. Such abuse can disrupt a person's understanding of his/her God-given value and sense of self-worth, leading to challenges in trust, intimacy, and emotional and relational well-being.

> *He heals the brokenhearted and binds up their wounds.*
> **Ps 147:3**

Survivors of childhood sexual abuse often struggle with feelings of brokenness, betrayal, and deep pain, both emotionally and sometimes physically. This verse acknowledges the reality of a broken heart. It presents God as a Healer willing and able to mend what has been shattered. It is a declaration of God's healing ability and a tender and compassionate promise to hurting people. For survivors, the imagery of God binding up their wounds can be a powerful metaphor for restoration, offering hope and assurance that healing is possible. By focusing on this Scripture, survivors may find comfort and encouragement to seek God's healing presence in their journey toward recovery and wholeness. This verse can be a cornerstone in building faith and trust in a loving God who sees, understands, and actively seeks to heal the scars left by such a devastating experience.

> *Wash yourselves, make yourselves clean; Remove*
> *the evil of your deeds from My sight. Cease to do evil,*
> *learn to do good; Seek justice, reprove the ruthless,*
> *defend the orphan, plead for the widow.*
> **Isa 1:16-17**

Childhood sexual abuse happens, and the church must teach people how to respond to such a heinous violation of an innocent child. Many victims fall into a trap in which they believe *they* are responsible, that they must stay quiet, and that they will cause problems or ruin people's lives (especially their abuser) if *they* speak up and seek justice. However, Isaiah writes that the Lord demands that the church defend children and seek justice. This is what living a clean life looks like. We must encourage the abused, or those struggling with knowing abuse has happened, to know that God's will is the reproof of the evil doer. While mercy and forgiveness can be exhibited, accountability is helpful for both the abuser and the victim. It is never the victim's fault for the decisions the abuser made when they chose to abuse.

> *The Lord is my rock, my fortress, and my deliverer,*
> *my God, my rock where I seek refuge.*
> **Ps 18:2**

This verse speaks to the fundamental need for safety, protection, and stability, which is often shattered in the experience of abuse. For survivors, the imagery of God as a rock and fortress can provide a sense of security, emphasizing His unchanging nature and His role as a protective refuge. The person experiencing the feeling of vulnerability that often accompanies the memories of abuse might find solace in the concept of God as a deliverer. It may inspire survivors to rebuild trust and lean on God's strength. Moreover, the verse's theme resonates with the journey of healing, where seeking refuge in God becomes essential to recovery. In biblical counseling for childhood sexual abuse, this verse can act as an anchor, offering an enduring sense of God's care and protection that supports the complex process of healing and restoration.

You Yourself have recorded my wanderings.
Put my tears in Your bottle. Are they not in Your book?
Ps 56:8

Dealing with the emotional aftermath of childhood sexual abuse often involves wrestling with grief, shame, and a sense of being unseen. This verse assures the survivors that their pain, tears, and every moment of suffering are seen and acknowledged by God. It's a powerful expression of validation for someone who might feel their pain has been ignored or minimized. The imagery of God collecting tears in a bottle underscores the value and significance He places on every tear shed. For those struggling with the long-term effects of childhood sexual abuse, this verse can be a foundational truth, emphasizing that they are seen, valued, and cared for by God. It offers comfort and a sense of being understood, knowing their Heavenly Father does not overlook their deepest hurts.

We know that all things work together for the good of those who love God,
who are called according to his purpose. For those he foreknew he also
predestined to be conformed to the image of his Son, so that he would be the
firstborn among many brothers and sisters.
Rom 8:28-29

Children who have experienced sexual abuse struggle to reconcile their experiences with the revealed nature of God as loving, good, kind, and powerful. Renewing their minds with His truth is essential for their restoration to Him. While their experiences have not been good, God can redeem their souls and their experiences with His goodness. Ultimately, He plans to use their pain for their good as He molds them into the image of His Son through it.

PRACTICAL ADVICE + HOMEWORK

Confess Sin: A heart that refuses to trust God may develop in you as a sexual abuse survivor, and if so, you must humbly confess this sin. Knowing that God is faithful to forgive and cleanse your heart following this confession encourages this humble and obedient action. (**Homework:** Stop right now and confess the sin of your distrust of God to Him).

Renew Your Mind through Scripture: Understanding trust and distrust from God's perspective is critical to change. (**Homework:** Read the following biblical texts to understand God's call to trust Him: Proverbs 3:5-6; Jeremiah 17:5-8; Psalm 26:3-4. Answer these questions from the biblical texts you just read: What did you learn about God in this text? What did you learn about yourself? How do your thoughts, feelings, and actions need to change considering these truths?)

Obey God: Commit to trusting Him no matter what He allows to happen in your life (Job 13:15). (**Homework:** Spend time with God in His Word each day, attend worship at your church each week, memorize Proverbs 3:5-6, and ask God to help you live in obedience to these truths).

Seek Healing with God: Embrace God as the healer of your broken heart, trusting His love and compassion. Ultimately, we want a complete reliance on God's loving nature, exemplified in Psalm 147:3, where He heals the brokenhearted. (**Homework:** Reflect daily on Psalm 147:3, journaling about your feelings and how you can seek God's healing.)

Find Refuge in God: Psalm 18:2 depicts God as a fortress and rock. Look to Him as your fortress and rock, understanding that He offers safety and protection in His care. (**Homework:** Meditate on Psalm 18:2 this week, visualizing yourself in the refuge of God's love and care.)

Acknowledge Your Pain with God: Allow yourself to be honest with God about your pain. Knowing that He sees and values your tears helps facilitate an open and honest relationship with Him, reflecting the sentiment of Psalm 56:8 that He values our tears and understands our pain. (**Homework:** Spend your mornings in prayer with Psalm 56:8, expressing your pain to God and asking for His comfort.)

Seek Community and Accountability: You can't go through life as a "Lone Ranger." God created us for community and time spent with those who can point us back to biblical truth. Getting lost in our thinking is easy, so community and accountability are essential. Spend time with people who will remind you that your thoughts and actions must bring God praise, glory, and honor. (**Homework:** Spend time this week identifying who your community will be and individuals who can disciple you. Be open and honest about everything you are going through with trusted Christian friends/leaders.)

Seek Legal and Pastoral Support: God's will is for everyone to be at peace and for reconciliation to result. However, abuse can be exasperated by covering up the situation and not holding the abuser accountable. (**Homework:** If you or someone you know has been involved in child sexual abuse, reach out to a trusted pastor or friend who can get you in touch with the proper authorities that will assist in accountability in a Christlike manner.)

DISCUSSION STARTERS

1. **Experiencing God's Healing:** Psalm 147:3 proclaims the loving nature of God as He heals the brokenhearted and mends their wounds. How can you open your heart to allow the Lord's healing

touch to work within you, especially when confronting the pain of past sexual abuse? In your moments of despair, how can you lean into this truth to find restoration and renewal in Him?

2. **Seeking Justice with Righteous Intention:** In Isaiah 1:16-17, God commands us to seek justice, stand up against evil, and defend the vulnerable. Given the trauma you or others may have faced, how do you interpret this call to act justly and defend the oppressed? How can the church, alongside abuse survivors, foster an environment where evil is reproved and righteousness prevails?

3. **Finding Strength and Refuge in the Lord:** As you ponder on Psalm 18:2, which portrays God as a rock, fortress, and deliverer, how does this imagery resonate with your experiences and journey toward healing from abuse? How can embracing the notion of God as your steadfast protector and refuge empower you to rebuild trust, find solace, and lean into His unwavering strength in moments of vulnerability?

COMMUNICATION

A God-ordained mechanism by which one soul's inner reflections and intents are faithfully conveyed through speech to another, ensuring clarity and mutual understanding. Drawing upon the Word, effective communication seeks to transmit information and foster connection, edification, and unity in alignment with God's design for relationships.

A gentle answer turns away anger,
but a harsh word stirs up wrath.
Prov 15:1

It is crucial to approach interactions with wisdom and gentleness. Proverbs 15:1 provides wise advice about the power of a soft answer to turn away wrath instead of harsh words that can stir up anger. This principle encourages individuals to consider their tone and choice of words when communicating with others. It reminds us that thoughtful and measured responses can defuse tension and create positive dialogue. The truths found in this proverb can be applied in various contexts, including personal relationships, business settings, and even online communication. We cultivate a more respectful and understanding atmosphere by embracing the wisdom of offering gentle answers instead of reacting harshly. The widespread applicability of this proverb makes it a fundamental tool for communication skills and nurturing healthier relationships.

A Biblical Handbook for Counseling Heart Issues

My dear brothers and sisters, understand this:
Everyone should be quick to listen, slow to speak, and slow to anger.
James 1:19

Effective communication is essential from personal relationships to professional settings. The principle found in James 1:19 emphasizes the importance of being quick to listen, slow to speak, and slow to anger. This truth promotes a thoughtful and caring approach to conversation, where one actively listens and thinks before responding. By encouraging patience and careful consideration in communication, misunderstandings can be minimized, and mutual respect can be built. This wisdom is universally applicable and transcends cultural and social differences. By following this advice, individuals can improve more meaningful and constructive dialogues. Ultimately, the insight offered in this passage advocates for a more harmonious and compassionate approach to interacting with others.

No foul language should come from your mouth,
but only what is good for building up someone in need,
so that it gives grace to those who hear.
Eph 4:29

This verse provides wisdom on how words should uplift others rather than tear them down. This counsel emphasizes speaking about what is reasonable and necessary for building others up according to their needs. This approach to communication promotes consideration, understanding, and mutual respect. Adhering to this Bible verse can create an environment where trust and compassion flourish. It's not just about avoiding harmful speech, but focusing on words that offer grace to those who hear. Applying this principle can transform everyday interactions, making them more meaningful and impactful.

Like apples of gold in settings of silver is
a word spoken in right circumstances.
Prov 25:11

When communicating, just because a thought is true, right, or needed doesn't mean it should always be spoken when it comes to mind. *How* we communicate with our words and actions is just as important as what we communicate with our words and actions. The table centerpiece of gold and silver would be a beautiful and valuable fixture that all at the table could mutually appreciate as they share a meal, and such unity can be obtained through communication that is edifying, God-honoring, and delivered at the right time and in the right way.

PRACTICAL ADVICE + HOMEWORK

Confess Sin: If you use hurtful speech to harm others and build yourself up, you must humbly confess this sin to God and to those you have wounded. Knowing that God is faithful to forgive and cleanse your heart following this confession encourages this humble and obedient action. (**Homework:** Stop right now and confess the sin of hurtful speech and the prideful heart from which it flows to God and to others and ask for their forgiveness).

Renew Your Mind through Scripture: Understanding sinful speech from God's perspective is critical to change. (**Homework:** Read the following biblical texts to understand God's call to speak in ways that honor Him: Galatians 5:13-15; James 3:1-12; and 1 Peter 3:8-12. Answer these questions from the biblical texts you just read: What did you learn about God in this text? What did you learn about yourself? How do your thoughts, feelings, and actions need to change considering these truths?)

Obey God: Commit to speaking in ways that honor and reflect Him to your hearers. (**Homework:** Spend time with God in His Word each day, attend worship at your church each week, memorize Ephesians 4:29-30, and put these truths into practice each day).

Prioritize Listening: Effective communication starts with genuine listening. Understand what someone is trying to say before seeking to be understood. This echoes James 1:19, emphasizing the importance of being quick to listen and slow to speak. (**Homework:** Practice active listening in your next conversation, focusing entirely on the speaker, without formulating your response until they're finished.)

Speak with Kindness: Choose your words carefully to promote peace and understanding. This reflects Proverbs 15:1, urging kind words to prevent strife and promote peace. (**Homework:** For the next week, intentionally pause before responding to any discussion, especially in potentially heated moments.)

Build Others Up: 1 Thessalonians 5:11 instructs Christians to encourage one another, recognizing the power of words. (**Homework:** Every day for the next week, compliment or affirm at least one person in your life.)

Avoid Negative Speech: The Bible warns against gossip and slander in Proverbs 6:16-19 and Ephesians 4:29. (**Homework:** Make a conscious effort to avoid negative talk for a day, then reflect on how it made you feel.)

Avoid Poor Circumstances when Communicating: Sometimes we want to communicate to our spouse, friends, boss, or children something weighing on our hearts, yet it is not heard or received well due to the circumstances. For example, when it comes to communicating in this way with your spouse, avoid initiating deep or confrontational conversations late at night right before bedtime with a spouse. Wait until the morning and then schedule a time to discuss such topics. When it comes to communicating a serious matter with your pastor, avoid offering criticism or complaining to him right before his Sunday sermon so as not to discourage him. (**Homework:** Do NOT avoid hard conversations; make sure to have them under the most reasonable circumstances.)

DISCUSSION STARTERS

1. **The Power of Gentle Words**: Reflecting on Proverbs 15:1, have you recently encountered situations where a soft response could've made a difference? How can consistently applying this principle transform your relationships, especially during tension or disagreement?

2. **Actively Listening in Conversations:** James 1:19 stresses the importance of listening quickly and slowly speaking. Can you recall when failing to listen led to misunderstandings or hurt feelings? How might embracing this biblical principle more intentionally shape your interactions and foster genuine understanding?

3. **Elevating Speech to Build Up:** Ephesians 4:29 calls believers to use speech that edifies and imparts grace. Can you recognize moments when your words didn't reflect this biblical directive? How can focusing on this passage challenge and change your daily communication habits, ensuring your words uplift rather than harm?

CONFLICT

Interpersonal conflict is fundamentally anchored in the sinfulness of human nature. In the book of James, God articulates that the core of disputes and contentions arises from unchecked passions and yearnings within man. Delving deeper, the wisdom of Proverbs identifies individuals who propagate discord as being dominated by emotions and attitudes such as anger, greediness, and animosity. It is paramount in biblical counseling to address these sinful dispositions with the transformative power of God's Word, guiding individuals toward understanding reconciliation and a heart aligned with God's will.

If your brother sins against you, go tell him his fault, between you and him alone. If he listens to you, you have won your brother. But if he won't listen, take one or two others with you, so that by the testimony of two or three witnesses every fact may be established.
Matt 18:15-16

Conflict is inevitable unless you are a hermit living alone in a cave. Still, it doesn't have to lead to division or resentment. In Matthew 18:15-16, Jesus offers a design for grievances between individuals to be addressed within a church both directly and privately. Instead of gossiping or retaliating, this biblical paradigm promotes a loving confrontation for reconciliation. If the issue isn't resolved, the next step involves bringing one or two others to help mediate. This approach emphasizes the value of the relationship over the issue at hand, seeking to heal rather than harm. By following this principle, parties involved in a conflict can find a path toward a resolution that respects the dignity and worth of everyone involved. The wisdom of this passage offers a way to navigate conflict that promotes understanding, compassion, and unity.

> *What is the source of wars and fights among you? Don't they come from your passions that wage war within you? You desire and do not have. You murder and covet and cannot obtain. You fight and wage war. You do not have because you do not ask. You ask and don't receive because you ask with wrong motives, so that you may spend it on your pleasures.*
> **James 4:1-3**

When believers have conflict, they do so because of competing and conflicting desires. These desires motivate each party to war and fight for what they want while seeing their adversary as an obstacle to fulfilling those desires. Attempts to remove the other person acting as an obstacle result in conflict. A heart that desires the glory of God, no matter the situation, is spared these kinds of conflicts.

> *If possible, as far as it depends on you, live at peace with everyone.*
> **Rom 12:18**

In dealing with conflict, finding common ground and harmony can be challenging. Romans 12:18 advises individuals to strive for peace with others, as much as it depends on them. This biblical truth underscores the importance of personal responsibility in maintaining peace, even if it means compromising or setting aside individual differences. It encourages a proactive approach to resolving disagreements by seeking understanding and mutual respect rather than escalating tension. Furthermore, the verse doesn't guarantee that peace can always be achieved, but emphasizes doing one's part in pursuing it. This wisdom offers a balanced approach to conflict management, recognizing that while striving for peace is ideal, it may not always be fully attainable. The principle serves as a reminder that effort and intention in resolving conflicts are vital, even if the desired outcome is not guaranteed.

> ***A hot-tempered person stirs up conflict,***
> ***but one slow to anger calms strife.***
> **Prov 15:18**

Managing conflict requires wisdom, patience, and understanding. Proverbs 15:18 highlights the contrast between stirring up conflict and calming a dispute. A hot-tempered person can exacerbate a situation, whereas someone slow to anger can defuse tension. This principle encourages taking a step back and evaluating a situation calmly rather than reacting impulsively. It teaches that control over one's emotions can lead to resolution rather than escalation. By following this wisdom, people can approach conflicts more peacefully and thoughtfully. Ultimately, this wisdom can help improve relationships and be applied in various areas of life, from personal relationships at home to the workplace.

> ***Above all, keep fervent in your love for one***
> ***another, because love covers a multitude of sins.***
> **1 Pet 4:8**

Conflicts are always a result of the Fall, but sometimes a perceived conflict is not worth escalating to confrontation. Christians must be zealous in pursuing loving interactions rather than always looking for a fight. God never turns a blind eye toward sin; at the same time, God does not always address every tiny sin we commit at the exact moment we commit it. Christians should evaluate whether the offense in question needs to be confronted or whether it can be covered by grace at the moment and conflict avoided.

PRACTICAL ADVICE + HOMEWORK

Confess Sin: A heart that seeks the fulfillment of personal desires lies behind sinful conflict. You must recognize that truth as you humbly confess this sin. Knowing that God is faithful to forgive and cleanse your heart following this confession encourages this humble and obedient action (1 John 1:9). (**Homework:** Stop right now and confess the sinful pursuit of your personal desires to God and to your brother or sister in Christ who you have wounded through this selfish pursuit).

Renew Your Mind through Scripture: Restoring relationships is possible following conflict when you take God's truth to heart. (**Homework:** Read the following biblical text to understand how God wishes you to address conflict: Matthew 5:43-48 and Luke 6:27-28. Answer these questions from the biblical text you just read: What did you learn about God in this text? What did you learn about your responsibility when you are mistreated? How do your thinking, feelings, and actions need to change considering these truths?)

Obey God: Seek to glorify Him amid conflict. (**Homework:** Spend time with God in His Word each day, attend worship at your church each week, accept God's assignment from Luke 6:27-28 to respond to others with whom you have conflict by choosing to love, speak blessing, do good, and pray for them.

Initiate Conversations in Private: Address conflicts head-on by communicating privately with the individual involved. The promotion of understanding is reflected in Matthew 18:15, which instructs believers to resolve grievances personally in this way. (**Homework:** Think of a recent minor disagreement. Reflect on how approaching the person personally might have influenced the outcome, even if it's just a hypothetical scenario.)

Seek Peace Actively: Make every effort to maintain peace, understanding that you can only control your actions and responses. Re-read Hebrews

12:14 and Romans 12:18, passages that encourage the effort to live peaceably with others, acknowledging that our control is limited to our actions and responses. (**Homework:** In disagreements this week, focus on finding common ground and solutions rather than assigning blame.)

Practice Patience: Responding with patience can de-escalate situations and promote understanding. Proverbs 15:18 highlights how a patient and gentle answer turns away wrath. (**Homework:** The next time you're faced with a conflict, take several deep breaths before responding, allowing yourself time to consider the most constructive reply.)

Avoid Retaliation: Rather than seeking vengeance or holding grudges, try understanding the other person's perspective. This action is in line with Romans 12:19, which cautions against taking vengeance into our own hands and instead promoting empathy and peace instead. (**Homework:** Reflect on a past conflict where you might have sought to "get even" and think about a more peace-promoting response.)

Avoid Escalating Conflict, if Possible: God says to "do justice, to love kindness" (Micah 6:8). We should never cower away from the conflict that needs to be fought. Still, we should always see if kindness and mercy can be given rather than escalating a matter to a potential fight. (**Homework:** Spend time evaluating whether the offense that has been committed or the perceived offense is a sin against God. Seek wisdom from a neutral party that is familiar with Scripture. If the offense needs confrontation for growth, confront. If the offense can be covered by grace, forgive the offending party and move on, avoiding conflict.)

DISCUSSION STARTERS

1. **Addressing Grievances Biblically:** Reflecting on Matthew 18:15-16, how do you currently handle grievances against someone? What steps can you take to adopt the biblical approach to rec-

onciliation mentioned in these verses? How might this direct, private conversation foster a deeper sense of understanding and intimacy in your relationships?

2. **Navigating Heart Desires in Conflict:** With James 4:1-3 in mind, have you identified the underlying desires or passions that may cause conflict in your life? How can recognizing and surrendering these desires to God's will lead to harmonious relationships and prevent unnecessary disagreements?

3. **Personal Responsibility in Conflict Resolution:** Romans 12:18 encourages us to do our part in striving for peace. How do you currently take responsibility for peace in your relationships? How can this principle reshape your perspective on conflict, emphasizing mutual understanding and compromise?

CONTROL

Biblically understood as the capacity given by God to humans to influence and guide behaviors, choices, and the progression of situations. It reflects humanity's God-given dominion over creation while emphasizing the need for self-restraint and discipline. In interpersonal interactions, control is supposed to be an exercise of love, guidance, and stewardship, always aligned with God's will and directives, rather than a mere imposition of one's desires or dominance over others.

So, you too consider yourselves dead to sin and alive to God in Christ Jesus. Therefore, do not let sin reign in your mortal body, so that you obey its desires. And do not offer any parts of it to sin as weapons for unrighteousness. But as those who are alive from the dead, offer yourselves to God, and all the parts of yourselves to God as weapons for righteousness.
Rom 6:11-13

Believers must submit their hearts to God to think and act rightly. The outcome of a life is the result of who is in control. Yielding to self and its desires leads to a life of sin. Yielding to God and His control leads to a life that is useful to Him as He builds His kingdom.

A person's heart plans his way,
but the Lord determines his steps.
Prov 16:9

Individuals often seek control to gain assurance and direction in their lives. Proverbs 16:9 acknowledges our tendency to plan and orchestrate every aspect of life. Still, it reminds readers that ultimate control resides with God. This proverb underscores the importance of setting intentions and making plans but leaving room for flexibility and recognizing that there may be a broader plan at work. By accepting that control is not entirely in one's hands, a person can find peace and trust in the process rather than becoming overwhelmed by the need to control every detail. Embracing this perspective encourages a balance between personal responsibility and surrendering to the flow of life. It fosters humility and trust and offers a practical and philosophical approach to the complexities of control.

> *The LORD will fight for you while you keep silent.*
> **Ex 14:14**

After leaving Egypt, the Hebrews found themselves cornered at the Sea, with an impending Egyptian attack that would surely kill them. They had fought for control, nagging Moses, blaming him for their troubles, and even complaining about God's deliverance. For the next forty years, they would do the same, constantly trying to take their destinies and well-being into their own hands. Moses stood before the people to remind them that sometimes God brings His people to a place in their lives where His miraculous power is the ONLY way for their rescue. Today, believers' command in the moment is to stay silent, to not move, to not speak, to just stand by and watch. Doing so is hard for those struggling with control, but when things seem out of their control or they seek to manipulate outcomes (especially manipulation through ungodly means), they must stop and wait on God.

> *I know, Lord, that a person's way of life is not his own;*
> *no one who walks determines his own steps.*
> **Jer 10:23**

Control

Control over life's circumstances is an ability that many people strive to possess, but such a pursuit can often lead to stress and frustration. Jeremiah 10:23 shows that we cannot direct our own steps (see also Ps 37:23-24). This understanding helps us recognize the limitations of human control and the wisdom in seeking wisdom from God. By relinquishing the illusion of total control, one can find peace in trusting a greater plan at work. This does not mean abandoning responsibility, but aligning actions and decisions with faith and wisdom. Embracing this perspective can lead to a more balanced and fulfilled life, where control is exercised with humility and discernment.

> *Do not fear, for I am with you; do not be afraid,*
> *for I am your God. I will strengthen you; I will help you;*
> *I will hold on to you with my righteous right hand.*
> **Isa 41:10**

The desire for control in life's situations is often rooted in fear and uncertainty. Isaiah 41:10, although not directly about control, speaks to the fears that often drive us to seek control, offering reassurance that God is with us and will strengthen us. The need to control every detail diminishes by relying on God, as faith and trust take precedence. This passage can inspire individuals to release their grip on control, recognizing that they are supported and upheld by their Father in Heaven. It encourages leaning into God rather than succumbing to fear. This shift in perspective from self-reliance to reliance on Him helps foster a sense of peace, even when circumstances are unpredictable. Ultimately, it's a reminder that we don't have to bear the burden of control alone; we have the support of God.

PRACTICAL ADVICE + HOMEWORK

Confess Sin: Love of self lies behind the sinful desire to be in control. You must recognize that truth as you humbly confess this sin. Knowing that God is faithful to forgive and cleanse your heart following this confession provides encouragement for this humble and obedient action.

(**Homework:** Stop right now and confess the sin of selfishness and its accompanying sinful controlling behavior to God).

Renew Your Mind through Scripture: Submission to God and His control is essential for righteous living. (**Homework:** Read the following biblical text to understand God's call to submit to Him: Mark 14:32-36. Answer these questions from the biblical text you just read: What did you learn about God? What did you learn about submission through Jesus' responses to His Father? How do your thinking, feelings, and actions need to change considering these truths?)

Obey God: Yield to Him daily. (**Homework:** Spend time with God in His Word each day, attend worship at your church each week, and commit to God to think, feel, and act according to His directives in Scripture rather than to your fleshly thoughts and desires. Memorize Romans 6:11-13).

Acknowledge Limited Control: We should remember that even though we can make plans, God ultimately guides our journey. (**Homework:** Reflect on a past situation where your plans didn't unfold as expected and identify how God might have been at work.)

Entrust Your Plans to God: Instead of stressing over the need for control, entrust your anxieties and plans to God through prayer and focus on casting all anxieties on God, because He cares for us. (**Homework:** Write down three things you're trying to control right now and commit to praying over them daily for a week.)

Avoid Over-Analyzing: Overthinking can exacerbate the desire for control, because we can't always foresee or control outcomes (**Homework:** When faced with a decision this week, give yourself time to think, decide, and then let it go, trusting that God is in control.)

Seek God's Wisdom: Regularly seek God's direction and wisdom. Recognizing His sovereign control over everything mirrors James 1:5, reassuring believers to ask God for wisdom in all situations. (**Homework:** Start each morning with a prayer, asking God to guide your daily decisions.)

Stop Trying So Hard: If God enabled us to do "everything" for ourselves, then why do we need Him? If God enabled us to "fix" or "control" every detail in our lives and others, why do we need Him? (**Homework:** What area of your life do you get upset if you lose control over? Have a mature friend/pastor walk with you through deciding if this is something you should actively be involved in, or if you need to let someone else, especially God, take the reins starting today as you back off.

Discussion Starters

1. **The Illusion of Control:** Romans 6:11-13 teaches believers the importance of yielding themselves to God rather than sin. Can you reflect on moments where you felt you had control but realized it was an illusion? How can surrendering to God's control, rather than our own desires, lead to a fruitful and fulfilling life?

2. **Acknowledging God's Sovereignty:** Proverbs 16:9 and Jeremiah 10:23 emphasize God's ultimate control over our lives and plans. How have you grappled with the balance between planning for your future and submitting to God's sovereignty? How can embracing the truth that God determines our steps bring peace and clarity to your path?

3. **Waiting on God's Timing:** Reflecting on Exodus 14:14, when have you felt backed into a corner with seemingly no way out? How did you respond in that situation? How might surrendering and waiting on God's intervention in those moments transform your understanding of control and reliance on Him?

CRITICAL SPIRIT

A disposition characterized by persistent, harsh judgments towards others, often magnifying their shortcomings while overlooking their virtues. Rooted in a lack of grace and mercy, this mindset can strain relationships, cause disunity within the body of Christ, and foster inner unrest. The address of a critical spirit requires a heart examination, repentance, and seeking God's transformative love to cultivate a spirit of humility and grace.

It came about after the LORD had spoken these words to Job,
that the LORD said to Eliphaz the Temanite, "My wrath is kindled
against you and against your two friends, because you have not spoken
of Me what is right as my servant Job has.
Job 42:7, NASB 95

Sometimes we tend to be overly critical, judgmental, and downright mean towards others for one reason: We hold bad theology and application of theology. Job's friends delivered long speeches to Job trying to make sense of his troubles, and they were off target with most of it. God chastised these three men because they did not speak rightly of the Lord regarding His work in Job's life and Job's responses to the Lord. Sometimes, we are critical because we think we know exactly what God is doing and what others should be doing, when in reality, we have no idea! Our perceptions are not always reality, and a good friend will seek to understand the situation in its entirety, seek the Lord's will and ways via Scriptures, and only then, in humility, offer a judgment on a situation. To do any less risks the danger of being critical in spirit.

> *Therefore, every one of you who judges is without excuse. For when you judge another, you condemn yourself, since you, the judge, do the same things. Now we know that God's judgment on those who do such things is based on the truth. Do you think—anyone of you who judges those who do such things yet do the same—that you will escape God's judgment?*
> **Romans 2:1-3**

Believers must recognize that God is the rightful judge in this context. He is the One who has the right to discern sin in men's hearts, pass judgment on those hearts, and condemn them accordingly (Jer 17:9-10). Christians are not to usurp His role. Doing so demonstrates a lack of understanding about our own sinful natures. Trusting injustice to God does not negate the obligation to confront sin within a church (Matt 18:15), but it does remind Christians that they have no right to condemn others unjustly and without cause.

Paul also warns against the hypocrisy of judging others when we are guilty of the same faults. This passage illuminates the double standard often present in a critical spirit, where one may harshly judge others' flaws while ignoring or excusing their own. It emphasizes that God's judgment is based on truth, and we are all accountable to Him. Reflecting on this passage, a person struggling with a critical spirit can gain insight into their behavior's inconsistency with biblical values, and its potential spiritual danger. This passage serves as a reminder to approach others with humility, compassion, and self-awareness, understanding that God alone is the just judge, and we all need His grace. It can be a significant step in recognizing and overcoming a critical attitude.

> *Do not judge, so that you won't be judged. For you will be judged by the same standard with which you judge others, and you will be measured by the same measure you use.*
> **Matt 7:1-2**

Critical Spirit

A critical spirit often stems from a habit of judging others. Matthew 7:1 serves as a potent warning for someone struggling with a critical spirit. This verse directs us to refrain from judging others, recognizing that the measure we use will be returned to us. For an individual prone to criticism and judgment, this scripture challenges them to examine their behaviors and attitudes, emphasizing that they are not beyond judgment. It encourages a perspective shift from focusing on the faults of others to self-reflection and personal growth. The verse promotes empathy and compassion, urging an understanding of others' struggles rather than a rush to condemnation. By heeding this teaching, an individual can replace a critical spirit with a more gracious and Christ-like approach, fostering improved relationships and personal contentment. The clarity and wisdom encapsulated here can be a transformative guide for someone seeking to overcome a critical and judgmental attitude.

> **Above all, maintain constant love for one another,**
> **since love covers a multitude of sins.**
> **1 Pet 4:8**

This verse emphasizes the preeminence of love, urging a constant forgiving attitude toward others. For someone struggling with a tendency to harshly judge or focus on the faults of others, this Scripture serves as a reminder that love should be at the core of our interactions. Love not only nurtures positive relationships but also has the power to "cover" offenses, fostering forgiveness and understanding. By reflecting on this verse, an individual can be encouraged to replace judgment with compassion, extending grace and mercy as God does for us. Focusing on what Peter shared can act as a transformative guide, steering one's heart away from criticism and towards a loving and forgiving perspective that mirrors Christ's love for us.

PRACTICAL ADVICE + HOMEWORK

Confess Sin: Pride lies behind the sinful desire to judge, condemn, and punish others with a critical spirit. You must recognize that truth as you humbly confess this sin. Knowing that God is faithful to forgive and cleanse your heart following this confession encourages this humble and obedient action. (**Homework:** Stop right now and confess the sin of pride, a critical spirit, and unjust judgment of others to God.)

Renew Your Mind through Scripture: God's Word instructs us to speak truth in love rather than to unjustly criticize others. (**Homework:** Read the following biblical texts to understand God's call to leave judgment to Him: Jeremiah 17:9-10 and Romans 12:19-21. Answer these questions from the biblical text you just read: What did you learn about God? What did you learn about yourself? Considering these truths, how do your thinking, feelings, and actions need to change?)

Obey God: Yield to God as Judge. (**Homework:** Spend time with God in His Word each day, attend worship at your church each week, and renew your mind by memorizing Jeremiah 17:9-10 and Romans 12:18-21.)

Avoid Judging Others: Recognize that judgment is reserved for God and that striving to view others with compassion is rooted in Jesus' teaching in Matthew 7:1, which emphasizes the importance of extending grace rather than judgment. (**Homework:** Reflect daily on Matthew 7:1, considering ways to extend grace rather than judgment.)

Seek Truth with Humility: No believer is always right, nor are his/her perceptions and/or impressions consistently accurate. In fact, wisdom dictates that believers should assume the possibility that they could be wrong or misinformed. (**Homework:** Ask yourself if your thoughts towards another are based on reality and verifiable fact. If not, seek to understand the situation better and filter all conclusions or speculations through Scripture and prayer.)

Cultivate Love: Practice loving others unconditionally, recognizing that love fosters forgiveness, which calls attention to 1 Peter 4:8 and the healing power of unconditional love. This fundamental Christian quality counters critical attitudes. (**Homework:** Meditate on 1 Peter 4:8 this week, identifying practical ways to show love to those around you.)

Focus on Godly Thoughts: Training your mind to dwell on what is honorable and commendable will encourage a positive mindset, replacing criticism with appreciation. (**Homework:** Spend ten minutes each morning reflecting on Philippians 4:8, listing things you appreciate in others.)

DISCUSSION STARTERS

1. **Understanding God's Judgments and Our Roles:** Considering Romans 2:1-3, which illustrates God's rightful position as judge and our tendency to wrongly assume this role, how have you witnessed the dangers of assuming God's role of judgment in your own life or in the lives of those around you? In pondering the depth of God's wisdom and knowledge in discerning the heart, how can this understanding affect your attitude and interactions with others, particularly when tempted to judge?

2. **The Balance of Confrontation and Compassion:** Considering that Matthew 18:15 instructs us to confront sin within the church, yet numerous verses (*e.g.*, Matt 7:1 and 1 Pet 4:8) teach us about the danger of a critical spirit and the importance of love, how can you practically maintain this balance in your interactions? How might you prepare your heart to approach others with grace, truth, and love, ensuring that any correction is biblically based and motivated by genuine concern?

3. **The Root of a Critical Spirit:** Reflecting upon the premise that pride is the root behind a desire to judge others unjustly, as seen

in the advice provided, in what ways have you identified pride influencing your interactions and perceptions? How can internalizing scriptures like Jeremiah 17:9-10 and Romans 12:19-21 reshape your understanding and prompt a heart of humility?

DECEPTION

An act whereby individuals mislead or misrepresent the truth, often driven by their own desires, fear, or pride. The Bible unequivocally denounces such dishonesty, urging believers to embody truthfulness in their thoughts, words, and actions. Sincerity and transparency should be paramount in Christian relationships and interactions, reflecting Christ's character.

Lying lips are detestable to the Lord,
but faithful people are his delight.
Prov 12:22

Deception can lead to broken trust and strained relationships, making it a concerning habit for anyone. Proverbs 12:22 underlines the value of honesty, stating that lying is detestable to the Lord. At the same time, those who are truthful are His delight. This simple wisdom reminds us that integrity is vital in human interactions. We align ourselves with admirable and, most importantly, biblically significant values by embracing honesty and avoiding deception. Living a life of truth helps to build trust and respect among peers and reflects a commitment to moral excellence. For someone struggling with deception, understanding and internalizing this biblical truth can be a decisive step toward personal transformation and integrity.

Therefore, putting away lying, speak the truth, each one
to his neighbor, because we are members of one another.
Eph 4:25

One of the consequences of deception is that it can erode trust and damage relationships with others. Paul urges individuals to put away falsehood and speak the truth with one another, as they are all part of the same community. By embracing honesty, a person can further trust, authenticity, and integrity in his/her interactions. This advice transcends simple truth-telling and promotes a mindset where honesty is valued as a fundamental virtue. It can be a guiding principle for someone struggling with deception, offering a clear and moral directive. Following this wisdom enhances personal growth and strengthens connections with others, allowing for more genuine and fulfilling relationships. Thus, it serves as a vital reminder for anyone seeking to overcome the temptation to deceive.

Then I replied to him, "There is nothing to these rumors you
are spreading; you are inventing them in your own mind."
For they were all trying to intimidate us, saying, "They will drop
their hands from the work, and it will never be finished."
But now, my God, strengthen my hands.
Neh 6:8-9

Perception is not reality, primarily when that perception is based on bold lies. Nehemiah was facing men willing to create bold lies against him to deceive the King of Persia, in order to have Nehemiah punished. It is unlikely that these men truly believed that Nehemiah was practicing evil. They viewed the Jews negatively and with such hatred that they were willing to deceive others. Nehemiah faced deception with a response of ignoring these false charges and continuing His work, praying for strength from God.

Do not lie to one another, since you have
put off the old self with its practices.
Col 3:9

"Do not lie to one another," pinpoints the direct prohibition against deception. This warning is set within the larger context of taking off the old sinful nature and embracing a new self. The verse underscores its incompatibility with biblical living by highlighting deception as part of the old nature. The emphasis on "to one another" suggests the importance of truthfulness in fostering trust and unity within the body of Christ. Lying is portrayed as contrary to the process of spiritual renewal and growth. Truth becomes an integral part of spiritual maturity and sanctification. Colossians 3:9 is a powerful reminder that honesty is central to Christ-centered life.

PRACTICAL ADVICE + HOMEWORK

Confess Sin: Deception in a child of the God who cannot lie (Num 23:19 and Titus 1:2) keeps that believer from accurately imaging Him. You must recognize that truth as you humbly confess this sin. Knowing that God is faithful to forgive and cleanse your heart following this confession encourages this humble and obedient action. (**Homework:** Stop right now and confess the sin of deception to God and to any others who have heard those lies.)

Renew Your Mind through Scripture: God's Word instructs us to speak truth rather than lies. (**Homework:** Read the following biblical texts to understand God's call to speak truth even as He does: Leviticus 19:11; Psalm 15:1-3; Mark 7:20-23; and 1 Timothy 1:9-11. Answer these questions from the biblical text you just read: What did you learn about God? What did you learn about yourself? How do your thinking, feelings, and actions need to change considering these truths?)

Obey God: Always speak the truth in love. (**Homework:** Spend time with God in His Word each day, attend worship at your church each week, list those to whom you have lied, contact them, and humbly ask their forgiveness.)

Value Truthfulness: Understanding that God treasures honesty is foundational for trust in relationships, and echoes the biblical analogy of a city without walls being defenseless. (**Homework:** Reflect on recent situations where you might have stretched the truth or avoided complete honesty. Commit to apologizing and rectifying those situations.)

Stand Against Deception: Do not let lies told against you deter you from being obedient to the Lord. Conversely, if you struggle with the temptation of deceiving others because you allow yourself to be deceived, then you must repent. (**Homework:** If you find yourself as a victim of deception, try to fact-gather as much as possible so that you can make informed decisions. Repent of any untruths you've believed.)

Acknowledge the Weight of Deception: Recognize the harm deception can cause to yourself and others. (**Homework:** Write a list of the potential negative consequences that can arise from telling even a "small" lie.)

Practice Open Communication: Prioritize open and honest communication, even when the truth is complicated. (**Homework:** Choose a day this week to be especially conscious of your words, ensuring they are truthful and transparent in every conversation.)

Seek Personal Transformation: Strive for personal growth by shedding old habits of deception and embracing a new self, one grounded in truth. (**Homework:** Spend time in prayer each morning this week, asking God to reveal areas where you might be prone to deception and to strengthen your truthfulness.)

DISCUSSION STARTERS

1. **Valuing God's Perspective on Truth:** Proverbs 12:22 emphasizes the Lord's disdain for lying lips and His delight in those who are

faithful. How do you see this priority of truth mirrored in your daily interactions? How can keeping this divine perspective in mind motivate you to pursue honesty even when it feels challenging?

2. **Integrity in Community:** Ephesians 4:25 instructs us to discard lying, underlining the interconnectedness we all share. How have you witnessed the ripple effects of deception or honesty within your community or relationships? In what ways can embracing God's directive to speak the truth impact not just individual lives but the entire community?

3. **Facing False Accusations with Resilience:** Nehemiah 6:8-9 showcases Nehemiah's strength in the face of deceitful accusations, turning to God for reinforcement. Have you ever encountered a situation where others have falsely accused or misrepresented you? How did you respond, and how can Nehemiah's example of reliance on God guide you in similar circumstances in the future?

DECISION MAKING

A multifaceted process grounded in discernment and informed by Scripture. It encompasses the formation of judgments grounded in biblical wisdom and understanding. This process often necessitates demonstrating resoluteness and determination in one's choices, aligning actions with the will and teachings of God. In circumstances of conflict or ambiguity, decision-making can signify a resolution guided by prayer, Scripture, and godly counsel, leading to a choice that upholds righteousness and justice.

> *Trust in the Lord with all your heart, and do not*
> *rely on your own understanding; in all your ways*
> *know him, and he will make your paths straight.*
> **Prov 3:5-6**

Decision-making can be stressful, especially when faced with uncertainty or a lack of clear direction. This passage emphasizes the necessity of wholehearted reliance on God rather than mere human intellect or instincts. It advocates acknowledging God in all our ways, suggesting that every decision, big or small, should be made in alignment with God's will. The promise is clear in return: "He will make your paths straight," indicating God's wisdom and direction. This scripture underscores the idea that our perspectives are limited, but God's vantage point is all-encompassing. Therefore, entrusting our decisions to Him ensures we're on the best possible path. Proverbs 3:5-6 offers a blueprint for decision-making rooted in faith, humility, and dependence on the Lord.

> *Now therefore, I pray You, if I have found favor in*
> *Your sight, let me know Your ways that I may know*
> *You, so that I may find favor in Your sight.*
> **Ex 33:13a, NASB 95**

Moses understood discipleship and learning because he was an educated man. God displayed favor upon Moses, and through that favor, Moses was able to lead God's people out of Egypt. Moses made a request that if he continued to lead the people, God would need to show him His ways. Moses knew that if God showed him how He operated throughout history, then he would know something about the person of God. Once Moses learned about the person of God, based on how He operated in history among His creation, he was able to find favor (be pleasing) in God's sight.

We get to know someone by learning their story, observing their life, and interacting with them. When making decisions, if we have read God's story (the Bible), and we have sought to understand the God of the Bible, then the Holy Spirit within us will bring to remembrance all that we have read and heard to teach us what decisions we are to make in life.

> *Now if any of you lacks wisdom, he should*
> *ask God—who gives to all generously and*
> *ungrudgingly—and it will be given to him.*
> **James 1:5**

Making decisions, especially significant ones, can be daunting, often leaving people feeling uncertain and stressed. By asking for God's wisdom, one acknowledges the limitations of human understanding and opens to guidance that transcends mere logic or emotion. This approach to decision-making can instill a sense of peace and clarity, knowing that the wisdom sought is pure and unerring. It reinforces the idea that one cannot face tough decisions alone but can rely on God for direction. It's a perspective that applies to major life decisions and daily choices, aligning one's actions with a broader, spiritual purpose.

> *Don't worry about anything, but in everything, through prayer*
> *and petition with thanksgiving, present your requests to God*
> **Phil 4:6**

This verse commands believers to pray to God about our concerns and decisions. It implies that all Christians should turn to God for wisdom instead of succumbing to worry or overthinking. By emphasizing "every situation," the verse acknowledges the relevance of God's counsel in all decision-making processes, big or small. The inclusion of "with thanksgiving" suggests an attitude of gratitude and trust in God's sovereignty. It affirms that believers can find clarity and direction by maintaining a close relationship with God. Paul is illuminating the path of faithful decision-making rooted in prayer and trust in God's wisdom.

PRACTICAL ADVICE + HOMEWORK

Confess Sin: A tendency to trust self instead of God when making decisions requires confessing this sin. Knowing that God is faithful to forgive and cleanse your heart following this confession encourages this humble and obedient action. (**Homework:** Stop right now and confess any sin of trusting self instead of God).

Renew Your Mind through Scripture: God's Word instructs us to trust Him no matter our circumstances. (**Homework:** Read the following biblical texts to understand God's command to trust Him: Psalm 37:3-5, Psalm 62:5-8, and Proverbs 3:5-6. Answer these questions from the biblical text you just read: What did you learn about God? What did you learn about yourself? How do your thinking, feelings, and actions need to change considering these truths?)

A Biblical Handbook for Counseling Heart Issues

Obey God: Trust Him no matter what He allows. (**Homework:** Spend time with God in His Word each day, attend worship at your church each week, pray about your decisions daily, at every moment they come to mind, and whenever you are tempted to worry about them).

Seek God's Wisdom: Always prioritize seeking God's guidance in your decisions, trusting He knows what's best for you, and seek Him out through prayer. (**Homework:** List three upcoming choices you're facing. Spend a few minutes in prayer about each, asking for God's direction.)

Avoid Anxiety: Instead of worrying about decisions, bring them before God in prayer, seeking His peace; present worries to God in prayer, seeking His peace in decision-making. (**Homework:** Set aside time to pray about any decisions causing anxiety this week, handing your worries to God.)

Consult Scripture: The Bible is a bastion of wisdom and truth; make it a habit to consult it regularly. Be wise and interact daily with God's Word, affirming the Bible's role as a guide in life's choices (Ps 119:105). (**Homework:** Spend ten minutes daily reading Scripture, noting any verses that provide insight or wisdom into your decisions.)

Seek Counsel: Getting perspectives from trusted individuals grounded in their walk with God is wise. You can show your trust in the Lord by trusting in the wisdom found in the Word and seeking counsel with godly friends or mentors for well-rounded perspectives. (**Homework:** Talk to a trusted friend or mentor about a significant decision you're facing, seeking their godly advice and perspective.)

What would God have Done: Like "Consulting Scripture" as homework, seek the Scriptures to find any narratives where biblical figures were dealing with the same circumstances as you, or issues that share similar principles. (**Homework:** Find two-three passages with the help of a trusted Bible teacher that deal with your issue, and journal how God handled the situation, how the people involved responded, and what obedience God desired.)

DISCUSSION STARTERS

1. **Complete Reliance on the Lord:** Given the instruction of Proverbs 3:5-6 to "Trust in the Lord with all your heart," how do you currently perceive your reliance on God versus your own understanding in daily decision-making? How might recognizing God's ultimate wisdom and guidance reshape how you approach decisions, big or small?

2. **Understanding God's Ways:** Moses sought to know God's ways to better please Him, as evidenced in Exodus 33:13. How does this desire resonate with your personal walk with God? How can familiarizing yourself with God's past actions in Scripture shape your confidence and direction in present-day decisions?

3. **Seeking Biblical Wisdom in Decisions:** James 1:5 emphasizes that God grants wisdom to those who ask. Reflecting on your life, can you pinpoint times you sought God's wisdom? How did it impact the outcome, and how can you more consistently seek His wisdom in all decisions moving forward?

DEPRESSION

This issue results in an emotional state marked by despondency, discouragement, and sorrow. This condition often aligns with feelings of personal powerlessness and a diminished zest for life. Scriptural narratives depict several individuals who demonstrated signs of depression stemming from varied circumstances. As believers turn to the Scriptures, they find solace and guidance in navigating this complex emotional terrain, recognizing that God's presence and promises offer hope that counters their despair.

The righteous cry out, and the Lord hears, and
rescues them from all their troubles. The Lord is
near the brokenhearted; he saves those crushed in Spirit.
Ps 34:17-18

For someone struggling with depression, seeking comfort and understanding is often a crucial part of the healing process. Psalm 34:17-18 speaks of the closeness of God to the brokenhearted and His attentiveness to their cry. It reassures that even in despair, one is never alone; a compassionate presence is ready to hear and respond. This passage can be a source of hope because it emphasizes that our Father in Heaven acknowledges the feelings of sadness and isolation. It encourages reaching out in prayer or reflection, working on a connection that might alleviate some pain. By focusing on this spiritual dimension, an individual may find a supportive framework that helps overcome depression.

Why, my soul, are you so dejected? Why are you
in such turmoil? Put your hope in God, for I will
still praise him, my Savior, and my God.
Ps 42:11

Dealing with depression often involves a journey toward hope and heal-ing, which can be complex. Psalm 42:11 speaks to the soul, urging individ-uals to put their hope in God despite feelings of despair and turmoil. This message encourages us to look beyond our current circumstances and to find solace in God. The verse's poignant question, "Why, my soul, are you so dejected?" reflects an internal dialogue that many facing depression might recognize. One can find a pathway out of despair by focusing on faith and hope in God, knowing He loves us. It's a reminder that emo-tions are transient, and healing and peace are attainable through Him. The verse's message is not a quick fix but a perspective shift, providing comfort and encouragement for those in need.

Come to me, all of you who are weary and burdened, and I will give you rest.
Matt 11:28

Battling depression can be an exhausting and overwhelming experience, often leading to feelings of hopelessness and despair. In Matthew 11:28, the invitation to come to Jesus for rest and relief is a powerful reminder of the compassion and understanding available for those weary and bur-dened. This passage offers a sense of hope, accentuating that help is avail-able for those who seek it. By turning to Christ, individuals struggling with depression may find a source of comfort and strength beyond their own capabilities. This concept resonates deeply with many who feel over-whelmed by their struggles and seek solace and healing. Amid depres-sion, this invitation to find rest in a caring and understanding presence can be a beacon of hope, guiding the way toward peace.

So, I say, "My strength has perished, and so has my
hope from the Lord ... The Lord is my portion,"

says my soul, "Therefore I have hope in Him."
Lam 3:18, 24, NASB 95

When Jeremiah recorded these words, he was struggling with the nation of Judah and their unwillingness to submit to God's will. The Babylonians were coming to defeat them, and his people thought he was a spy and treated him harshly. He saw no hope before him, and his spirit was crushed. However, as he then writes, he was reminded that there is always hope in the Lord. Christians must understand that events and circumstances in a fallen world will happen, and they will test our resolve to trust God is sovereign and has a plan for us. Being proactive amid despair in bringing our thoughts captive to Christ is imperative to combating depression. Even if you do not feel, see, or even struggle to believe it, get up today and live as if our hope in Christ is real.

PRACTICAL ADVICE + HOMEWORK

Confess Sin: At the heart of genuine depression (not righteous sorrow and grief over loss) lies a distrust of God. (**Homework:** If this is true in your situation, stop right now and confess the sin of failing to trust God.)

Renew Your Mind through Scripture: God's Word reminds us that He is trustworthy. (**Homework:** Read the following biblical text to understand God's call to trust Him no matter our circumstances: Jeremiah 17:5-8. Answer these questions from the biblical text you just read: What did you learn about God? What did you learn about trust? How do your thinking, feelings, and actions need to change considering these truths?)

Obey God: Focus on the truth about God and His character. (**Homework:** Spend time with God in His Word each day, attend worship at your church each week, list responsibilities you are failing to fulfill, and complete one more each week.)

Seek God in Your Despair and Pray: I don't know about you, but the ability and freedom to pray powerfully helps me. When my prayer life is on order, there is a peace that passes all understanding. Realizing that my heavenly Father, who created the universe, takes time to listen and answer all my prayers brings peace. Yes, he answers all prayers. We must accept that "no" is an answer. (**Homework:** Spend some quiet time reflecting on God's Word and Pray Without Ceasing daily.)

Engage in Act(s) of Service: The author of this manual testifies that he encourages those with whom he works to get out of their heads, to quit wallowing in self-pity, and to help others. During his second month of sobriety, he was told to volunteer at the free state-run detox, Charlie Street in Southern California. He recalls seeing a man with no legs mopping the floor. It was the man's assigned chore in order to attend the detox. The depressed and disabled man's dedication to this day serves as a daily example to the author of how those who deal with depression can find determination to turn their focus from themselves, outward. (**Homework:** Spend some time helping at a homeless shelter or detox center. This activity can assist you in making sure you are not isolating yourself in a desperate attempt at self-care.)

Move from Depressive Disengagement to Personal Engagement: Sometimes, amid our despair, we quit and give up on what we know to be God's will. These things could be simple everyday actions like praying with your kids, fixing lunch for the family, or serving in a ministry opportunity. (**Homework:** Make a list of easy tasks that you can complete, that is, a list of things that matter and have purpose no matter how small, and pray for strength to begin them. Then, complete the tasks one by one.)

Don't Believe the Lies: When battling depression, our minds have a tendency to suggest negative messages to ourselves such as we are unworthy or that no one likes us. The sooner we recognize those unbiblical thoughts, the sooner we can combat them with biblical truth. When we understand our identity as children of God, we realize being created in HIS image makes us infinitely more valuable than we might we feel. (**Homework:** Address each of the negative and unbiblical thoughts. If you need someone to help you distinguish between true and false, find a biblical counselor, pastor, or trusted friend with whom you can talk.)

Have FUN! Go Outside or Exercise: Sometimes depression can run us into the ground. We may feel very tired and fatigued. One of the ways the author has found to be helpful is doing things he loves. For example, when feeling down and out, he calls his sister and asks her if he can spend time with her children. When he sees them running around, laughing, and giving him hugs gives him a feeling a joy and happiness. (**Homework:** Find a hobby/activity that you can do that will bring God praise, glory, and honor.)

DISCUSSION STARTERS

1. **Dependence on God in Despair:** Given the promise in Psalm 34:17-18 that God hears the righteous and is close to the broken-hearted, how can you integrate this truth into your daily life? How might a deeper reliance on God's nearness provide solace in your moments of deep sadness or despair?

2. **Internal Dialogue with the Soul:** In Psalm 42:11, the psalmist speaks directly to his own soul during deep anguish. Can you relate to this internal dialogue? How can meditating on God's unwavering character shift your focus from despair to hope, even in the darkest moments?

3. **Addressing Unbiblical Thoughts:** What unbiblical thoughts or lies have you noticed taking root in your mind? How can you counteract these with the truths of who you are in Christ and your hope in Him?

DISCIPLINED LIVING

Disciplined living is the intentional and faithful stewardship of God-given resources, particularly time and money. Drawing inspiration from Scripture, believers recognize that true godliness stems from a life ordered by spiritual discipline. Central to this spiritual formation are the disciplines of time and money, which when managed in alignment with God's will, pave the way to a life that reflects the character of Christ. Just as Jesus exemplified a life of purpose and sacrifice, disciplined living challenges believers to utilize their resources purposefully, ultimately bringing praise, glory, and honor to the Lord. It also requires control over our impulses, emotions, and desires.

> *A person who does not control his temper*
> *is like a city whose wall is broken down.*
> **Prov 25:28**

Proverbs 25:28 compares a person without self-control to a city with broken walls. This metaphor illustrates the vulnerability and chaos that lack of discipline can bring into a person's life. In the same way that city walls provide protection and structure, self-discipline establishes boundaries and order in our daily lives. Exercising self-control builds resilience against temptations and distractions that might lead us astray. This wisdom from Proverbs offers valuable insight into the importance of disciplined living and how discipline creates a foundation for success, well-being, and personal integrity. We should evaluate and strengthen our boundaries to live a fulfilling and controlled life.

> *The plans of the diligent certainly lead to profit,*
> *but anyone who is reckless certainly becomes poor*
> **Prov 21:5, NASB 95**

The author notes that diligent plans lead to profit, while hasty and poorly thought-out plans lead to poverty. This proverb immediately deals with the growth or gain of wealth, while also implies the discipline needed to do so. Solomon recognizes that hasty plans, often just thrown together without counsel or intentionality, describe foolish people. The wise man will think through every detail, and his plans and efforts will be as valuable as gold. Diligence is the constant and attentive effort towards something, and for Christians, living a disciplined life defined by constant and attentive efforts towards holiness will "lead surely to advantage." In contrast, a reckless life will "surely lead to poverty" in your walk with the Lord.

> *Don't you know that the runners in a stadium all race,*
> *but only one receives the prize? Run in such a way to win the prize.*
> *Now everyone who competes exercises self-control in everything.*
> *They do it to receive a perishable crown, but we an imperishable crown.*
> *So, I do not run like one who runs aimlessly or box like one beating the air.*
> *Instead, I discipline my body and bring it under strict control,*
> *so that after preaching to others, I myself will not be disqualified.*
> **1 Cor 9:24-27**

Paul uses the metaphor of an athlete training for a race to illustrate spiritual discipline. Living a disciplined life requires focus, determination, and the willingness to put in consistent effort toward one's goals. He emphasizes the importance of self-control and striving towards a goal with a clear purpose. Approach life with the same determination and commitment an athlete would apply to their training. Just as athletes use restraint and follow a strict regimen to win a race, we are urged to live disciplined lives for an eternal reward. Disciplined living applies to various areas of life, including personal growth, career advancement, and spiritual development. It serves as a reminder that success in any field requires dedication, purposeful action, and a willingness to stay the course.

For God has not given us a spirit of fear,
but one of power, love, and sound judgment.
2 Tim 1:7

The phrase "sound judgment" in Greek can be translated "self-control" or "self-discipline." This verse emphasizes that the source of our discipline comes from God Himself, equipping us to live purposefully. The contrast of fear with power, love, and self-discipline highlights that disciplined living combats the paralysis that fear can bring. A spirit of self-discipline is essential for believers to resist temptations, stay committed to God's will, and navigate life's challenges. This verse indicates that discipline is not just about rigid control but is rooted in love for God and others. This Scripture reassures us that with the help of God we possess the inner strength to live disciplined lives even in the face of adversity, calling us to lean on God-given resilience and maintain a disciplined life that honors Him.

PRACTICAL ADVICE + HOMEWORK

Confess Sin: The heart of an undisciplined believer is self-serving, aimless, and lazy. These aspects of the old man or flesh must be put off through confession if the man or woman of God is to be helpful in the Master's service. (**Homework:** If this is true in your situation, stop right now and confess the sin of selfish, aimless, and lazy living.)

Renew Your Mind through Scripture: God's Word reminds us that we are workers in His kingdom. (**Homework:** Read the following biblical texts to understand God's call to work diligently in His service: Galatians 5:22-23, Titus 2:11-14, and Hebrews 12:1-11. Answer these questions from the biblical text you just read: What did you learn about God? What did you learn about discipline? How do your thinking, feelings, and actions need to change considering these truths?)

Obey God: Live a disciplined life. (**Homework:** Spend time with God in His Word each day, attend worship at your church each week, ask God to order your days, and seek wisdom about practical steps to grow in disciplined living from those disciplined and orderly.)

Value Self-Control: Recognize that discipline protects and empowers you much like walls protect a city, offering safety from external assaults. (**Homework:** Reflect on a recent situation where a lack of discipline led to an undesirable outcome. Plan steps to handle similar situations with greater self-control in the future.)

Pursue Spiritual Excellence: Approach your spiritual journey with the same dedication and training that athletes apply to their sport. Draw parallels between spiritual growth and athletic training that inspire commitment and diligence. (**Homework:** Identify one spiritual discipline, such as prayer or Bible reading, and commit to practicing it daily for the next week.)

Use Your God-Given Spirit: Embrace the spirit of power, love, and self-control God has given you to live a disciplined life as instructed in 2 Timothy 1:7, invoking the divine gifts of power, love, and self-control. (**Homework:** Memorize 2 Timothy 1:7. When faced with challenges this week, recite the verse as a reminder of your God-given spirit.)

Avoid Aimlessness: Set clear spiritual goals to guide your disciplined efforts echoing the biblical principle of having a clear vision and purpose. (**Homework:** Write down three specific, measurable goals you want to achieve next month and outline steps to accomplish them.)

Pursue Stewardship Excellence: Money touches every aspect of your life and every relationship, and living a disciplined and excellence-driven life regarding how you handle money will impact every aspect of your life and relationships. (**Homework:** Create a budget based on every expense you had for the last thirty days. Have a trusted Christian who excels in stewardship either assist you in building or reviewing your budget and what adjustments need to be made for this coming month.)

DISCUSSION STARTERS

1. **The Protection of Self-Control:** Proverbs 25:28 describes the consequences of the lack of self-control by likening it to a city with broken walls. How do you see this imagery playing out in your personal life when discipline is lacking? Reflecting on this proverb, how can implementing self-control in areas where you have struggled be a protective barrier against temptations or distractions?

2. **The Athlete's Pursuit of Excellence:** In 1 Corinthians 9:24-27, Paul compares the discipline required for athletic training and spiritual growth. Have you ever pursued something with such dedication and purpose, like an athlete training for their sport? How can this metaphor inspire you to bring that determination and discipline into your spiritual journey, ensuring you are not running aimlessly but with God-given purpose?

3. **God's Gift of Discipline**: 2 Timothy 1:7 emphasizes that God gifts us with a spirit of power, love, and self-discipline. Can you recall moments when you have leaned into this divine endowment, particularly during times of fear or adversity? How does knowing that God has equipped you with the strength for disciplined living motivate you to confront and overcome challenges, ensuring your actions and choices honor Him?

DISORGANIZATION

The lack of structure or order in one's life can diminish an individual's capacity to fulfill God's purpose and commands. Godly discipline enables believers to function by godly principles rather than transient desires. Believers establish dominion over fleshly appetites by consciously rejecting impulsive behaviors, ensuring that actions line up with God's will. This deliberate choice, grounded in self-control and the Fruit of the Spirit, allows truth, virtue, and integrity to govern thoughts and actions bring them closer to the image of Christ and equip them for every good work.

But everything is to be done decently and in order.
1 Cor 14:40

This verse underscores the significance of orderliness in the context of worship and prophecy and suggests a broader principle about the importance of structure and organization in all aspects of life. Disorganization can lead to confusion, inefficiency, and missed opportunities much like chaotic worship disrupts spiritual unity. Applying this teaching to daily living encourages us to cultivate habits of organization. This organized approach benefits personal growth and ensures a harmonious community or environment; it provides a scriptural basis for the value of organization in every area of our lives.

For God is not a God of confusion but of
peace, as in all the churches of the saints.
1 Cor 14:33, NASB 95

Paul speaks to the Corinthian church about many issues. One of these issues relates to the confusion and disorder within their church due to theological and practical errors due to both ignorance and intentionality. God is described as a "God of peace," not confusion. Chaos ensues when order is not established, boundaries not kept, and instruction is not heeded. Often, if we are not diligent in keeping our lives "in order" or organized, we are overwhelmed with what seems to be chaos and despair. By conducting their lives according to God's order, the Corinthian church could experience peace rather than chaos. In the same way, if people begin to get aspects of their lives organized and tasks mapped out that must be completed, peace starts to break through what was once thought to be chaos and confusion.

The plans of the diligent certainly lead to profit,
but anyone who is reckless certainly becomes poor.
Prov 21:5

Disorganization can often lead to confusion, inefficiency, and stress in various aspects of life. Proverbs 21:5 emphasizes the importance of careful planning and diligent work contrasting it with the haste that often accompanies disorganization. Applying this wisdom means recognizing the value of thoughtful preparation and the steadiness required to achieve goals. By taking the time to organize thoughts or spaces, one can create a more conducive environment for success. This principle applies to physical surroundings, time management, and goal setting. Understanding that diligent planning leads to profit while haste leads to poverty can be a motivating factor to overcoming disorganization. Applying this proverb to one's life encourages a more organized and disciplined approach to life's challenges fostering success and personal growth.

Disorganization

I went by the field of a slacker and by the vineyard of one lacking sense. Thistles had come up everywhere, weeds covered the ground, and the stone wall was ruined. I saw, and took it to heart; I looked, and received instruction: a little sleep, a little slumber, a little folding of the arms to rest, and your poverty will come like a robber, and your need, like a bandit.
Prov 24:30-34

Solomon provides a vivid depiction of a vineyard belonging to a person lacking judgment and diligence. It is overrun with thorns, covered with weeds, and its wall is broken down. This imagery is a cautionary tale about the consequences of neglect and disorganization. Disorganization will lead to chaos, decay, and lost opportunities much like the unattended vineyard. The passage explicitly highlights the dangers of complacency and procrastination which are common culprits of disorganization. This proverb conveys that even once-fruitful endeavors can quickly deteriorate without regular attention and maintenance. The passage teaches that order, diligence, and proactive care are essential for success. When ignored, the disarray symbolized by the neglected vineyard can impact productivity and prosperity.

PRACTICAL ADVICE + HOMEWORK

Confess Sin: Haphazard and disorderly living fails to reflect a God who is a God of order (1 Cor 14:33). These aspects of the old man or flesh must be put off through confession if the man or woman of God is to accurately reflect his or her Maker. (**Homework:** If this is true in your situation, stop right now and confess the sin of disorderly living.)

Renew Your Mind through Scripture: God's Word reminds us to image His character to a watching world. (**Homework:** Read the following biblical texts to understand God's call to image Him with our lives: Genesis 1:26-27 and Ephesians 4:17-24. Answer these questions from the biblical text you just read: What did you learn about God? What did you learn about discipline? How do your thinking, feelings, and actions need to change considering these truths?)

Obey God: Live an orderly life. (**Homework:** Spend time with God in His Word each day, attend worship at your church each week, ask God to order your days, and seek wisdom about practical steps to grow in disciplined living from people in your life who are disciplined and orderly.)

Prioritize Order: Recognize that being organized goes beyond simply tidying up areas. It also highlights the significance of maintaining a structured life. This showcases the value of order in our surroundings and in managing our lives in a God-honoring way. (**Homework:** Identify one area of your life that is most disorganized. Whether it is your workspace, schedule, or finances, set aside time this week to bring order to it.)

Plan Ahead: The idea that careful planning can result in abundance while impulsive decisions can lead to consequences is reminiscent of the wisdom in Proverbs. It teaches us that through planning and hard work, we can achieve prosperity, but making hasty decisions may lead to failure. (**Homework:** For upcoming events, plan each step to ensure you are prepared and organized.)

Observe & Learn: Solomon discovered through his observation of a field that it is crucial to evaluate the impact of disorganization in your life. This reflection on the consequences of chaos can ultimately foster development and growth. (**Homework:** Reflect on a past event where disorganization led to stress or failure. Write down lessons learned and practical steps to prevent a recurrence.)

Avoid Procrastination: Tackling life promptly rather than postponing it can prevent the accumulation of disorder. This is supported by the biblical call to be diligent and responsible. (**Homework:** Make a "To-Do" list for the week. Prioritize your list and commit to completing each item without delay.)

Seek Expertise: One rule for effective growth is to find a trusted Christian who is "winning" in areas where you want to win and then do what they do. (**Homework:** If you have identified an area of your life that seems to be disorganized, but you do not know where to start or what to do next; search for a seminar, class, group, or an expert in that area of discipleship to ask for their one-on-one help.)

DISCUSSION STARTERS

1. **Orderliness Reflecting Our Creator:** Reflecting on 1 Corinthians 14:40, which emphasizes doing everything decently and in order, how do you see the effects of disorganization affecting your spiritual growth and daily life? How might a disciplined approach to your tasks, grounded in scripture, transform your relationship with God and those around you?

2. **The Consequences of Disorganization:** In Proverbs 21:5, the contrast between the diligent and the reckless highlights the outcomes of careful planning versus impulsive actions. How do you think the diligent planning principle applies to personal organization? How might an organized life contribute to your overall well-being and alignment with God's desires?

3. **Learning from Neglect:** Proverbs 24:30-34 offers a vivid image of a neglected field, demonstrating the consequences of lack of attention and care. Can you identify areas in your life that might resemble this neglected field? How do you feel God calls you to tend to these areas, and what steps might you take to restore order and productivity?

DISCOURAGED/ DOWNCAST

A state in which one experiences a diminishment of confidence or enthusiasm. This issue is often rooted in various life challenges or unmet expectations. In such moments, believers are reminded to hope in God, to seek His face, and to recognize that the ultimate encouragement and strength does come not from circumstances but from the sovereign Lord's unchanging nature and promises.

> *Haven't I commanded you: be strong and courageous?*
> *Do not be afraid or discouraged,*
> *for the Lord your God is with you wherever you go.*
> **Josh 1:9**

At the beginning of a daunting challenge, God commands Joshua to be strong and courageous and not be terrified or discouraged. This directive speaks directly to the heart of anyone facing daunting challenges. It is an excellent reminder that God is with us wherever we go, providing a biblical source of encouragement and strength. Discouragement often stems from fear of the unknown or the magnitude of what is ahead. Referencing this passage reminds us that with His presence, there is no reason to succumb to such feelings. The verse emphasizes the importance of faith and trust in God, especially in moments of doubt. Joshua reminds believers that God is ever-present. With God's support, discouragement can be replaced with courage and purpose. Believers can draw strength in challenging times and approach situations with renewed confidence.

> *When I think of you as I lie on my bed, I meditate*
> *on you during the night watches because you are my*
> *helper; I will rejoice in the shadow of your wings. I*
> *follow close to you; your right hand holds on to me*
> **Ps 63:6-8, NASB 95**

When we are discouraged and have lost confidence in people or circumstances, we must remember the Lord. Remembering and meditating on the Lord is not some abstract theoretical practice, but a real-life action necessary to combat discouragement. The psalmist focuses on memories of God being a "helper" to him in the past. God constantly told his people to "remember the Lord your God" in the Old Testament, and in Hebrews 11, the writer tells us that we can remember many saints of old to strengthen our faith in Him. Interestingly, a strengthened faith is the antidote for discouragement and lack of confidence. Hebrews 11:1 tells us that faith is the assurance and conviction of things unseen and hoped for. When discouraged, remember that the same God who has done so much for others AND you in the past is the same God who is still with you. You can trust Him.

> *The righteous cry out, and the Lord hears, and*
> *rescues them from all their troubles. The Lord is*
> *near the brokenhearted; he saves those crushed in spirit*
> **Ps 34:17-18**

The psalmist emphasizes the closeness of the Lord to those with broken hearts and crushed spirits. These verses offers solace to those feeling discouraged. They reassure believers that God hears and responds when they cry out in pain and distress. The reference to a "broken heart" resonates deeply with anyone experiencing disappointment or discouragement. The Scripture's promise of deliverance from trouble is a beacon of hope in dark times. David conveys the comforting notion that God values vulnerability and genuine emotion, drawing near to those in their lowest moments. In times of distress, this biblical promise reinforces the Christian faith and offers a tangible source of encouragement. These two verses underscore that God's care and support are unwavering, even when one faces deep discouragement.

We are afflicted in every way but not crushed;
we are perplexed but not in despair;
we are persecuted but not abandoned;
we are struck down but not destroyed.
2 Cor 4:8-9

These verses speak directly to facing trials, setbacks, and discouragement, asserting believers may be hard-pressed but not destroyed. Paul's acknowledgement of challenges resonates with anyone feeling overwhelmed or defeated. By distinguishing between being "perplexed" and "in despair," the scripture emphasizes that though we might not always understand our trials, we are never without hope. The contrast between "persecuted" and "abandoned" reiterates God's constant presence even in our darkest hours. Such powerful imagery of being "struck down, but not destroyed" reinforces resilience and God's protection. These verses testify to the inner strength believers possess through their faith in Christ. 2 Corinthians 4:8-9 offers an uplifting message of perseverance, resilience, and God's assurance amidst discouragement and adversity.

PRACTICAL ADVICE + HOMEWORK

Confess Sin: The heart of a discouraged or downcast believer is characterized by misplaced hope. These aspects of the old man or flesh must be put off through confession to be helpful in your Master's service. (**Homework:** If this is true in your situation, stop right now and confess the sin of misplaced hope).

A Biblical Handbook for Counseling Heart Issues

Renew Your Mind through Scripture: God's Word reminds us that we are to hope in Him alone. (**Homework:** Read the following biblical texts to understand God as the sole reason for our hope: Psalm 62:5-8; Jeremiah 17:7-8; and Romans 5:1-5. Answer these questions from the biblical text you just read: What did you learn about God? What did you learn about discipline? How do your thinking, feelings, and actions need to change considering these truths?)

Obey God: Fix your hope on God alone. (**Homework:** Spend time with God in His Word each day. Attend worship at your church each week. Any time you are tempted to be discouraged, place your hope in a God who is in control rather than in the circumstances as you see them).

Remember God's Presence: Recognize that even in discouraging moments, God is with you and offering you strength and courage. This belief agrees with the biblical promise in Joshua 1:9, which assures God's constant companionship even in disheartening times. (**Homework:** Take a quiet moment each day this week to reflect on Joshua 1:9, reminding yourself of God's unwavering presence. It can be hard to remember God's goodness while being discouraged, but you must intentionally focus on Him to get through hard times.)

Cry Out to God: The ability and freedom to pray powerfully helps believers. Peace that surpasses all understanding comes to them when their prayer lives are in order. Realizing that the heavenly Father, who created the universe, takes time to listen and answer all their prayers bring peace. Yes, he answers *all* prayers. We just must accept that "no" and "not yet" are acceptable answers. (**Homework:** Spend some quiet time reflecting on God's Word and pray without ceasing daily.)

Identify God's Help in Your Life: Identifying the exact moments and circumstances in which God has helped you and others can be an uplifting effort as it pulls you out of doubt and despair. It refocuses your mind to dwell on the goodness of God. (**Homework:** Identify specific times and circumstances in your life that God has rescued you out of or provided for you. Ask another believer to do this with you if you are young. Thank God for those past encouragements and ask Him for the strength to keep one's mind uplifted towards Him.)

Reflect on Resilience: Even when facing challenges, remember that with God's help, you can endure and overcome. It involves meditating on 2 Corinthians 4:8-9 and reminding oneself of God's enabling power to endure and overcome adversity. (**Homework:** Meditate on 2 Corinthians 4:8-9 and journal about an experience where you felt discouraged but persevered with God's help.)

Seek Inspiration from Scripture: Surrounding yourself with uplifting Scriptures, music, or testimonies can combat discouragement and promote a nourishing spiritual environment. This fosters encouragement and strength through biblical insights, songs, and testimonies. (**Homework:** Compile a list of songs, verses, or stories that uplift you and turn to them whenever you feel discouraged. Such a list might include Psalm 142, the song *Amazing Grace*, and remembering how far you have come despite the trials and tribulations you have experienced.)

DISCUSSION STARTERS

1. **Drawing Courage from God's Presence:** Reflecting on Joshua 1:9, which emphasizes God's unwavering presence during challenges, how have you experienced God's guidance during your moments of discouragement? In times when you felt downcast or overwhelmed, how has the assurance of God been with you provided comfort or changed your perspective?

2. **Finding Peace Amidst Chaos:** In 1 Corinthians 14:33, we learn that God is not a God of confusion but of peace. How has the

chaos or confusion in your life contributed to feelings of discouragement? How can turning to God's Word and promises help you find peace and clarity during such times?

3. **Endurance Through Adversity:** Given Paul's words in 2 Corinthians 4:8-9, which describe the resilience of believers. Can you recall a time when you felt pressed but not crushed or perplexed but not in despair? How did your faith play a role in overcoming that adversity? How can reflecting on God's enduring love and strength empower you in moments of discouragement?

DRUNKENNESS

A state of diminished cognitive and physical faculties induced by the excessive intake of alcoholic substances. Throughout the Word, drunkenness is denounced as a detrimental behavior incompatible with a life of righteousness and spiritual maturity. The Bible often underscores the virtues of sobriety, alertness, and self-mastery. It places these traits in sharp contrast with the traits of overindulgence in alcohol. A biblical portrait of a person overcome by alcohol is a metaphorical depiction of the despair those who oppose God's will and authority face.

And don't get drunk with wine, which leads
to reckless living, but be filled by the Spirit.
Eph 5:18

Paul directly addresses the issue of drunkenness by instructing believers not to get drunk on wine which leads to debauchery. This verse encourages believers to be filled with the Holy Spirit instead of seeking escape from life's trials or celebrating in intoxication. The juxtaposition between drunkenness and spiritual fulfillment underscores that genuine joy and purpose are found in a relationship with God not in temporary pleasures. Warning against debauchery, the scripture highlights the negative behaviors and consequences of excessive drinking. The Scripture positions sobriety not as a mere avoidance of alcohol but as a proactive pursuit of spiritual growth. Paul's guidance serves as a moral compass, urging

Christians to prioritize their spiritual well-being over worldly indulgence. Through this verse, the Bible promotes a life of self-control, spiritual depth, and meaningful engagement with God over fleeting pleasures like drunkenness.

> *Give beer to the one who is dying and wine to one*
> *whose life is bitter. Let him drink so that he can*
> *forget his poverty and remember his trouble no more*
> **Prov 31:6-7**

Drunkenness is a state in which many who are struggling find themselves. Solomon tells us that those who are perishing (or perceive that they are perishing), those who are bitter in life, those who are in poverty, and those who are just "troubled" tend to find drinking as the antidote for their pain. The idolatry of drunkenness is apparent in this passage for many reasons: 1) Those who are saved never perish, and to live is Christ and to die is gain; 2) Bitterness results from anger and unforgiveness towards man or God that has not been adequately resolved; 3) Poverty is something that overcomes the faithful and the evil at times, but God supplies all our needs; and 4) Trouble is guaranteed in this life, but how we respond to it teaches us to trust the Lord. The person described here has turned to a substance that could lead to "forgetting" the things of the Lord and to lose sight of God's provision and goodness.

> *Wine is a mocker; beer is a brawler;*
> *whoever goes astray because of them is not wise.*
> **Prov 20:1**

This passage straightforwardly warns about the dangers of wine and strong drink by asserting that whoever is led astray by them lacks wisdom. The proverb identifies alcohol as a mocker and strong drink as a brawler by highlighting their deceptive and combative impacts. The verse implies that while alcohol might seem appealing, it often leads to negative and unpredictable behaviors. Stating that those who are deceived by alcohol lack understanding, the Scripture emphasizes the importance of discernment and wise choices. The Bible consistently promotes wisdom and knowledge as virtues and drunkenness as contradictory to a life of bringing God praise, glory, and honor. This proverb serves as a foundational reminder about the deceptive allure of alcohol and its potential to divert individuals from righteous living. It encourages believers to prioritize sobriety and to seek wisdom in all areas of life including their consumption choices.

> *No thieves, greedy people, drunkards, verbally*
> *abusive people, or swindlers will inherit God's kingdom.*
> **1 Cor 6:10**

Paul lists drunkards among those who will not inherit the Kingdom of God. This categorization underscores the spiritual consequences of consistent drunkenness. This Scripture places drunkenness alongside other morally severe failings, which highlights its gravity in the Christian life. Paul urges believers to recognize the spiritual implications of their physical actions. Paul emphasizes the eternal significance of one's earthly behaviors. Drunkenness is something to be left behind and has no place in God's Kingdom. This verse serves as a potent reminder for believers to prioritize sobriety as an integral part of righteous living.

PRACTICAL ADVICE + HOMEWORK

Confess Sin: The heart of a drunkard is an idol-worshiping one. Both unbelievers and believers must turn away from this idol and turn to God. (**Homework:** If this is true in your situation, stop right now and confess the sin of idolatry which has led to your drunkenness. If you are an unbeliever, commit your life to Christ and trust Him to save you—both body and soul.)

Renew Your Mind through Scripture: God's Word reminds us that we are to find comfort in Him alone. (**Homework:** Read the following biblical texts to understand God as our true Source of comfort: John 14:16-18; 2 Corinthians 1:3-7; and 2 Thessalonians 2:16-17. Answer these questions from the biblical text you just read: What did you learn about God? What did you learn about discipline? How do your thinking, feelings, and actions need to change considering these truths?)

Obey God: Turn to Him for comfort. (**Homework:** Spend time with God in His Word each day, attend worship at your church each week, ask fellow believers to hold you accountable to turn to God rather than to alcohol, and avoid places where you will be tempted.)

Seek the Spirit: Instead of seeking escape or solace in alcohol, find joy, comfort, and purpose in the Holy Spirit. This confirms the Bible's command to be filled with the Holy Spirit rather than with wine (Eph 5:18) and emphasize a daily connection with God's comforting presence. (**Homework:** Spend ten minutes daily in quiet reflection or prayer, asking God to fill you with His Spirit.)

Recognize the Deception: While alcohol might offer relief or fun, it can deceive and lead to unwise choices. Reflect on Proverbs 20:1—a reminder that wine's allure can lead to folly and harm. (**Homework:** Reflect on Proverbs 20:1 and write down any negative consequences you have witnessed or experienced due to drunkenness.)

Contemplate Eternal Consequences: Consider the long-term spiritual consequences of continual drunkenness. 1 Corinthians 6:10 highlights the serious spiritual implications of persistent drunkenness. (**Homework:** Meditate on 1 Corinthians 6:10 and journal about what it means for your spiritual journey and eternal destination.)

Remember the Lord's Goodness: Whatever you try to forget in life, understand that the Lord sees it all. Philippians 3:13-14 tells us to forget what is behind by pressing on to what is ahead in Christ! We do not forget by drunkenness but by willful obedience to walk in His ways. (**Homework:**

Get your mind off the things you seek to forget by focusing on how you can serve the Lord right now and do that. Whether it be an act of service or simply refusing to give in to sin, decide and carry it out. Remember that the Lord is with you even during your struggle.)

Replace with Positive Habits: Cultivate healthy habits that offer genuine relaxation and relief without the side effects of alcohol. The hardest part of sobriety is learning how to live life without the mind-alerting substances. (**Homework:** Find an alternative activity. Consider exercise, reading, or a new hobby for the times when tempted to drink or do drugs. In the author's first year of sobriety, all he did was go to work, church, Bible study, gym, martial arts, and hang out with people who supported his decision to get sober.)

DISCUSSION STARTERS

1. **Confronting the Idol of Alcohol:** Given the biblical passages that equate drunkenness with idolatry, how do you identify and address the temptation of alcohol in your life? How can recognizing and confessing this idolatry lead you to a deeper relationship with God and away from the temporary and deceptive comfort of alcohol?

2. **Spiritual Implications of Habitual Drinking:** Reflecting on 1 Corinthians 6:10, which underscores the gravity of consistent drunkenness, how does understanding the eternal consequences impact your perspective on alcohol consumption? How might meditating on our choices' eternal rewards and ramifications realign your priorities and choices?

3. **Seeking True Comfort:** The Scriptures emphasize turning to God for genuine comfort rather than seeking solace in substances like alcohol. How have you experienced or witnessed the fleeting com-

fort of alcohol in contrast to the lasting peace found in Christ? In your moments of distress, pain, or celebration, how can you cultivate a habit of seeking the Holy Spirit's filling as described in Ephesians 5:18?

DYSFUNCTIONAL FAMILY

This issue denotes a disordered family pattern that is characterized by consistent abnormal behaviors and conflicts, frequently resulting in deep emotional scars with damaging consequences. While the wounds from such an environment can be troubling, the Bible provides hope and direction. Restoration and reconciliation can be attained through biblical wisdom, understanding, genuine forgiveness, and deliberate behavioral shifts. The Bible underscores the significance of a family's unity and offers inspired counsel for repairing familial bonds.

> *Honor your father and mother so that you may have a*
> *long life in the land that the Lord your God is giving you.*
> **Ex 20:12**

First, this passage is a commandment to honor parents providing a foundational principle that transcends the complex emotions and behaviors that often arise in challenging family relationships. Framing honor and respect towards parents as a divine command and sets a higher standard for behavior which can guide family interactions. This does not diminish the pain or complexity of dysfunction but instead offers a pathway toward healing and reconciliation. Following this commandment may open doors to understanding and forgiveness which aligns family members' attitudes with God's will. In doing so, it promotes a respect-driven approach that recognizes the inherent value in family relationships. Lastly, the promise of long life in the land underscores the importance of this command, linking it to blessings and well-being, thereby giving hope and perspective to those striving to overcome family dysfunction.

> *A gentle answer turns away anger,*
> *but a harsh word stirs up wrath.*
> **Prov 15:1**

Communication in a dysfunctional family is often fraught with anger and conflict. In families with ongoing tension, misunderstandings, or unresolved conflicts; communication can often escalate into anger and resentment. This verse guides individuals to use gentle words to de-escalate potential conflicts and promote a more peaceful environment. By following this biblical wisdom, family members can learn to communicate more effectively and choose words that foster understanding rather than further strife. Additionally, this approach can create a foundation for healing and reconciliation within the family by encouraging positive change. Embracing the principle of gentle communication, as presented in Proverbs 15:1, not only aligns with Christian values but also offers a practical and compassionate approach to addressing the complex challenges that often characterize dysfunctional family relationships. The guidance provided in this verse is both timeless and universal offering a pathway toward peace and restoration.

> *...Bearing with one another and forgiving one*
> *another if anyone has a grievance against another.*
> *Just as the Lord has forgiven you, so you are also to forgive.*
> **Col 3:13**

In families where tensions, misunderstandings, and grievances often accumulate; this verse serves as a reminder and guide to the Christian duty to forgive. Bearing one another's faults and choosing forgiveness can lead to healing and reconciliation within a family structure. By aligning family members' attitudes and actions with the example of Christ's forgiveness, one cultivates a culture of grace and mercy. This verse acknowledges the reality of grievances and offers a divine solution that transcends human limitations. It challenges individuals to rise above petty conflicts and resentment. It nurtures a renewed family connection based on love and understanding. In the context of a dysfunctional family, Colossians 3:13 is not just a recommendation but a transformative principle that can shift the entire family dynamic toward healing and unity.

> *Children, obey your parents in the Lord, for this is right.*
> *Honor your father and mother (which is the first commandment with a*
> *promise), so that it may be well with you, and that you may live long on the*
> *earth. Fathers, do not provoke your children to anger, but bring them*
> *up in the discipline and instruction of the Lord.*
> **Eph 6:1-4**

Dysfunctional family dynamics are often instigated by sins compounded by repetition from several family members. This unhealthy pattern, coupled with a lack of biblical discipleship, can teach the family there is another way of living and interacting which can promote peace in the home. Understanding the God-ordained relationship that Paul describes between parents and children in the home (as well as between spouses in Eph 5:22-33) is a first step to functionality. Children should obey their authorities, and parents should not provoke children to anger. Disobedience by either party leads to dysfunction in the home. Instead, instruction (learning) and discipline (practicing what is learned) in the Lord are key to growth.

PRACTICAL ADVICE + HOMEWORK

Confess Sin: Sinful division can be addressed through confession of sin to God and to each other. (**Homework:** If this is true in your situation, stop right now and confess the sins you have committed against God and each other to God and each other.)

A Biblical Handbook for Counseling Heart Issues

Renew Your Mind through Scripture: God's Word teaches us that unity within the family and the church is His plan. (**Homework:** Read the following biblical texts to understand God's plan for the family: Colossians 3:18-21; Ephesians 5:1-33; and Ephesians 6:1-4. Answer these questions from the biblical text you just read: What did you learn about God? What did you learn about discipline? How do your thinking, feelings, and actions need to change considering these truths?)

Obey God: Fulfill your responsibility within your family as Scripture instructs. (**Homework:** Spend time with God in His Word each day, attend worship at your church each week, study Colossians 3:18-21; Ephesians 5:1-33; and Ephesians 6:1-4 as a family and hold each other accountable to fulfill God-given responsibilities within the family.)

Honor Your Family: Regardless of difficulties, striving to show respect and honor towards family members is rooted in the Fifth Commandment, found in Exodus 20:12, which emphasizes respect and dignity within familial relationships. (**Homework:** Reflect on Exodus 20:12 daily and consider ways to express honor within your family.)

Choose Gentle Words: Work on communicating with love and gentleness. Avoiding anger and harshness encourages loving communication. Guided by the wisdom of Proverbs 15:1, foster a peaceful environment. (**Homework:** Meditate on Proverbs 15:1 this week practice gentle responses in your family interactions.)

Pursue Forgiveness: Recognize the power of forgiveness and strive to forgive as Christ forgave you. Colossians 3:13, which promotes the healing power of forgiveness, strive to mirror Christ's love and forgiveness. (**Homework:** Spend ten minutes each evening reflecting on Colossians 3:13 and pray for the strength to forgive.)

Seek God and Pray as a Family: Peace that surpasses all understanding comes when our prayer life is in order. Realizing that our heavenly Father, who created the universe, takes time to listen and answer all our prayers brings peace. Yes, He answers *all* prayers. We just have to accept that "no" and "not yet" are answers. (**Homework:** Spend some quiet time reflecting on God's Word and pray without ceasing.)

Be a Light, Even When Others Are Not: Regardless of whether a family member is a rebel against the Lord's ways or not, you are responsible for your actions towards God and others. (**Homework:** Seek to find ways that you are contributing to the dysfunction and repent of those ways. Seek forgiveness and move forward by walking in holiness. The family may never become functional, but through the faithful witness of your life and efforts, he or she very well could.)

DISCUSSION STARTERS

1. **Restoration Amidst Family Fractures:** Genesis 50:20 showcases Joseph's heart when he states, "You intended to harm me, but God intended it for good to accomplish what is now being done, the saving of many lives." This verse teaches us that God can redeem and restore even amid deep familial betrayal. How have you seen God's providence play out in challenging family dynamics? How can embracing God's sovereign hand help foster forgiveness and reconciliation even when past wounds run deep?

2. **The Role of Love and Patience:** 1 Corinthians 13:4-7 beautifully depicts love, emphasizing its patient and kind nature. Given the challenges within a dysfunctional family, how might applying this description of love transform the way you engage with family members? How can internalizing this divine understanding of love guide you toward more harmonious family interactions?

3. **Understanding Generational Patterns:** Exodus 34:7 mentions that the fathers' sins can affect the children up to the third and

fourth generations. While we are not bound by our family's past, it's essential to recognize patterns and behaviors that might have been passed down. Have you identified any generational patterns in your family? How can bringing these patterns into the light, with the help of God's wisdom, lead to breaking cycles and establishing healthier family dynamics?

ENVY

This sinful heart issue is one that Christians are explicitly warned against, as it mirrors the very transgressions of the devil. His envy precipitated his fall from grace. Similarly, this envy led to humanity's estrangement from God. Envy starkly contrasts the biblical mandate to love even those who oppose Believers. When one succumbs to envy, he or she has not only emulated the devil's sin but also has rejected the call to love others unconditionally—even when others have more.

A tranquil heart is life to the body,
but jealousy is rottenness to the bones.
Prov 14:30

Envy is a tricky emotion that can consume us if we are not careful. This verse provides a striking visual to understand its effects and emphasizes the significance of a heart at peace. When we have a peaceful and contented heart, it brings life and vitality to our entire being. Conversely, envy, described as "rottenness to the bones," is not just an emotional or spiritual concern and implies a physical and overall well-being detriment. Just as rot spreads and compromises the integrity of an object, envy can consume and weaken from the inside out. In his wisdom, Solomon nudged us to prioritize internal peace over external comparisons. Biblical counseling serves as a stark reminder to focus on nurturing inner peace and contentment and steer clear of the debilitating effects of envy.

> *Not that I speak from want, for I have learned*
> *to be content in whatever circumstances I am.*
> **Phil 4:11**

Paul tells the Philippians that contentment is a learned skill necessary for believers. Contentment is being at peace with what God has ordained for you to have and experience in life. Envy is the opposite. It is where one is distraught over not having what they think they ought to have. A root heart issue with envy is believing that God has withheld what you ought to have from you and that the desires for your wants are unjustly being neglected. God is sovereign, and you are not. As Job would say, you are to accept the good and the bad from the Lord. You must constantly ensure that our hearts are not envious and believe that God gives us all we need.

> *For where there is envy and selfish ambition,*
> *there is disorder and every evil practice.*
> **James 3:16**

James effectively diagnoses the human heart and the ramifications of letting envy take root. This scripture explains that envy is not a mere individual internal struggle but has ramifications that reverberate through communities. The direct correlation James makes between envy and "disorder and every evil practice" underscores the domino effect of envy. It does not stop at one sin but leads to multifaceted moral breakdowns. In the larger context, James frequently addresses the potency of the tongue and suggests that the expressions of envy can further instigate and amplify harm. This is not merely a surface-level analysis but a truth about the human condition: unchecked emotions and desires, like envy, can become the seedbed for discord and wickedness. Fortunately, James does not leave us without hope. He subtly points toward the antidotes of self-awareness, self-restraint, spiritual growth, and divine wisdom. By leaning into God's Word and seeking His wisdom, believers can cultivate a heart resistant to envy and rooted in righteousness.

Envy

Let us not become conceited, provoking
one another, envying one another.
Gal 5:26

This verse is part of Paul's exhortation about living in the Spirit to the Galatians. Paul identifies envy as hindering spiritual growth and community well-being by urging them not to become conceited or envious. The warning against envy in this context highlights its divisive nature and its potential for tearing apart the unity of the Christian community. In the chapter, Paul contrasts the deeds of the flesh with the fruit of the Spirit and emphasizes that envy belongs to the former category. His instruction reinforces the importance of maintaining humility and mutual respect among believers. Ultimately, the verse underscores the necessity of spiritual transformation and renewal to overcome destructive behaviors like envy.

Do not let your heart envy sinners, but
always be zealous for the fear of the LORD
Prov 23:17

The wisdom of Solomon in Proverbs sheds light on the proper disposition of a believer's heart. Instead of envying those who might seem to prosper despite their sinful ways, believers are encouraged to be fervent in their reverence for God. This verse offers a beautiful juxtaposition as it stresses the transient nature of worldly success against the eternal value of honoring God. It suggests that even if the path of righteousness feels challenging, it is infinitely more valuable than the fleeting pleasures of sin.

PRACTICAL ADVICE + HOMEWORK

Confess Sin: Jealousy and envy are the outward expressions of a discontent heart that compares itself to others. If you are struggling with these sins, you must put off comparing God's plan for your life with His plan for the lives of others. These sins can be addressed through confession to

God. (**Homework:** If this is true in your situation, stop now and confess the jealousy and envy within your heart to God and anyone you have mistreated because of it.)

Renew Your Mind through Scripture: God's Word exhorts us to put off jealousy and envy. (**Homework:** Read the following biblical texts to understand how to deal with these sinful heart attitudes: 1 Corinthians 3:1-3; Galatians 5:16-23; and 1 Peter 2:1-3. Answer these questions from the biblical text you just read: What did you learn about God? What did you learn about envy and jealousy? How do your thoughts, feelings, and actions need to change in light of these truths?)

Obey God: Put off envy and jealousy and seek contentment in your relationship with Christ. (**Homework:** Spend time with God in His Word each day, attend worship at your church each week, and memorize Galatians 5:19-23 to help you think and act upon truth.)

Reflect on Consequences: James 3:16 underscores the disruptive nature of envy in relationships. Consider how envy and jealousy would lead to chaos and adverse outcomes in your circumstances. (**Homework:** Meditate on James 3:16 and journal about the time envy disrupted harmony in your life or relationships.)

Work Harder or Lay it Down: If we do not have what we want it could be because we have not asked God or we have been lazy. Perhaps we want something we do not have, and God knows it would be detrimental. (**Homework:** With the help of a trusted spiritual leader, ask the Lord to reveal the desires of our heart towards what we envy to determine if any of the following is true: Is the desire sinful? Can the desire be obtained through more effective work? Have you asked God to reveal if He even wants you to have that thing.)

Seek Spiritual Growth: Immersing oneself in spiritual disciplines can help shift focus from worldly desires to eternal priorities. This shift shows the importance of immersing oneself in spiritual disciplines and the call to set one's mind on things above rather than earthly things (Col 3:2). This action shifts focus from worldly desires to eternal values. (**Homework:** Dedicate time to read Scripture or a devotional that reinforces the values of contentment and love for neighbors.)

Shift Perspective to Service: Instead of focusing on what we do not have or what others possess, shift the perspective to service. Serving others allows us to put our blessings into perspective and fosters gratitude. When we serve, we see the needs of others and the places they lack, which allows us to appreciate our blessings and reduce room for envy. Jesus himself said, "For even the Son of Man did not come to be served, but to serve ... ." (Mark 10:45). (**Homework:** Volunteer at a local charity, church, or community event once a month. Each time you do, reflect on your life's blessings and the joy of giving to others. Remember that in giving, we often receive more in return in terms of joy and contentment.)

Replace Envy with Prayer: Instead of letting envy take root, use it as a signal to pray. Whenever you feel envious, it is a call to pray to God—not only for yourself but also for the one you're envying. By praying for blessings, understanding, and contentment for both parties; you are actively involving God in transforming a potentially negative emotion into a positive action. (**Homework:** Whenever envy strikes, pause and pray. Pray for yourself to find contentment and understanding and pray for blessings and grace for the individual you envied. Document these moments in a journal, and over time, notice how your perspective on envy and those you once envied changes.)

DISCUSSION STARTERS

1. **The Cost of Coveting:** Given the vivid description in Proverbs 14:30, where jealousy is likened to "rottenness to the bones," how has envy manifested physically or emotionally in your life? How

might embracing the tranquility that God offers lead to a fuller, more abundant life free from the consuming fire of envy?

2. **Learning Contentment in Comparison Culture:** Philippians 4:11 emphasizes Paul's learned contentment, regardless of his circumstances. In today's society, where comparison is a mere click away, how do you navigate the challenge of remaining content with your life's blessings? What steps can you take to focus more on God's provision and less on worldly possessions or status?

3. **Seeds of Discontent and Community Disruption:** James 3:16 highlights the communal ramifications of individual envy. Reflect on a time when envy affected your internal peace and your external relationships. How can recognizing and addressing the ripple effects of envy lead to more harmonious relationships within your community and the larger Body of Christ?

FEAR

In the intricate tapestry of human emotions, fear stands out as a complex response to perceived threats, encompassing feelings of anxiety, dread, and a momentary loss of courage. Both tangible dangers and intangible concerns can trigger this emotion. In the biblical context, the term "fear of God" has a dual significance. On one hand, it refers to a sense of awe, reverence, and respect, acknowledging God's sovereignty and majesty. This reverence is foundational to a right relationship with the Creator and is a guiding principle for righteous living. On the other hand, it can also describe the overwhelming dread and trepidation experienced when confronted with God's manifest presence or the judicious execution of His divine wrath.

> *Do not fear, for I am with you; do not be afraid,*
> *for I am your God. I will strengthen you; I will help*
> *you; I will hold on to you with my righteous right hand.*
> **Isa 41:10**

This verse offers reassurance directly to those consumed by fear. First, it highlights God's unwavering presence in our lives, as He assures us, "I am with you." He is not a distant deity but a close, personal God involved in the intricacies of our lives. Second, God's words, "I am your God," reiterate His covenant relationship with His people. He is not just any god; He is our God, committed to our well-being. Third, this verse promises not just passive support but active intervention. God does not simply witness our struggles. He strengthens, helps, and upholds us through them. The "righteous right hand" imagery conveys God's might and righteousness. That God possesses these two qualities ensures that His acts are mighty and just. With such promises, believers are reminded that surrendering to fear is unnecessary because they are safeguarded by the most High, whose love and power are both unmatched and unceasing.

> *The wicked flee when no one is pursuing,*
> *but the righteous are bold as a lion.*
> **Prov 28:1**

What do you fear? If the Lord is for you, who can be against you? Often, we are fearful because we think we have done something wrong and are about to be punished. When the boss calls us into his office; when a parent or spouse says they need to talk with us; or when your actions have brought society's disapproval to your doorsteps are moments that we begin to fear consequences. Solomon tells us that the wicked flee when they "think" they are being pursued or when they imagine danger is at hand. In contrast, the godly man does not care what is nipping at his heels. Because like the lion who fears no one, the godly man knows he only answers to One, and if that One is pleased with Him there is no reason to be fearful no matter what happens.

> *For God has not given us a spirit of fear,*
> *but one of power, love, and sound judgment.*
> **2 Tim 1:7**

The passage affirms that fear is external to God's intentions for us, pushing us to identify and reject such false narratives. Instead of being ensnared by dread, we are reminded that God equips us with robust resources: power, love, and a sound mind. Power emboldens us and helps us face and triumph over adversities. Love is the antidote to fear fostering selfless acts and genuine connections with others. A sound mind ensures we do not fall prey to confusion but remain anchored in divine wisdom. By meditating on this Scripture, counselees can redirect their focus, recognizing that they are not isolated in their struggles but backed by God's unwavering strength. Through the lens of this verse, the Spirit empowers individuals to live with conviction, purpose, and unwavering faith.

Even when I go through the darkest valley, I fear no danger,
for you are with me; your rod and your staff—they comfort me.
Ps 23:4

David acknowledges the inevitability of facing dark, challenging times in life, yet he emphasizes having a fearless attitude—not because of the believer's strength but because of God's unwavering presence. The mention of God's "rod and staff" symbolizes His protection and guidance, assuring believers they are not alone or defenseless. This Scripture underscores the comfort and confidence one can derive from a relationship with God. It provides a trust model illustrating that with God's presence, fear is displaced. Psalm 23:4 is a reminder to rely on God during fear and uncertainty.

The Lord is my light and my salvation; whom shall
I fear? The Lord is the stronghold of my life;
of whom shall I be afraid?
Ps 27:1

David's unwavering trust in the Lord becomes a blueprint for believers today to confront their fears. When someone experiences fear, it often emerges from feelings of uncertainty, darkness, or being threatened by something or someone. Recognizing God as the "light" brings clarity and guidance in these uncertain moments and illuminates the path forward. Likewise, seeing Him as our "salvation" assures us that there is always deliverance regardless of our struggles. David's words remind us that our fears, no matter how significant, are small compared to God's vast might and love. Therefore, by anchoring our hearts in the truth of Psalm 27:1, we can boldly face life's challenges fully aware that God is our unwavering stronghold. In biblical counseling, this Psalm can be pivotal in reframing one's perspective from fear to faith by grounding one's emotions and reactions in the steadfast promises of God.

> *Therefore, don't worry about tomorrow because tomorrow*
> *will worry about itself. Each day has enough trouble of its own .*
> **Matt 6:34**

Jesus, in His Sermon on the Mount, addressed the common human tendency to worry about the future. For individuals struggling with anxiety and fear, faith can be an anchor. One can find peace and relief by focusing on today and trusting that God has our tomorrows in hand. The Bible repeatedly teaches about the trustworthiness of God and His care for His creation. By internalizing this truth from Matthew, believers can learn to combat the paralyzing effects of fear and anxiety. It underscores the principle of living in the present and not being held captive by future uncertainties. Essentially, this teaching redirects one's focus from the unknowns of tomorrow to the faithfulness of God today. It is an invitation to a life of faith living one day at a time and relying on God's consistent provision and care.

PRACTICAL ADVICE + HOMEWORK

Confess Sin: If you are fearful, you must confess this sin. At the heart of this sinful emotion is a prideful desire to have life as you wish it to be and an unwillingness to trust God and His plan for your life (Jer 17:7-8). The fear of not having what you desire produces emotional misery. (**Homework:** If this is true in your case, stop right now and confess this sin to God.)

Renew Your Mind through Scripture: God commands us to fear not (Isa 43:1-5). (**Homework:** Read the following biblical texts to understand God's perspective on fear: Isaiah 43:1-5; Psalm 118: 1-6; Luke 12:4-7 and Romans 8:15-25. Answer these questions from the biblical texts you just read: What did you learn about God? What did you learn about yourself? How do your thinking, feelings and actions need to change considering these truths?)

Obey God: Put off fear and put on faith. (**Homework:** Spend time with God in His Word each day, attend worship at your church each week, ask God to help you learn to walk by faith instead of by sight, memorize Hebrews 12:1-2 to help you remember and meditate on truth when you are tempted to be fearful.)

Acknowledge God's Presence: Recognize that God promises to be with you; offering strength and support in fearful moments instills confidence in God's constant support, a foundational biblical truth. (**Homework:** Memorize Isaiah 41:10, repeating it to yourself during moments of anxiety or fear.)

Embrace Your God-given Spirit: Understand that God grants you a spirit of power, love, and self-discipline not a spirit of fear. This forces the individual to lean on God's empowerment, enhancing personal resilience against fear. (**Homework:** Reflect on 2 Timothy 1:7 and identify one fear to confront this week using the power and love God grants you.)

Seek Comfort in God's Protection: Remember God's protective and comforting nature even in daunting situations. Meditation brings about trust in God's protective nature and comfort. (**Homework:** Spend time meditating on Psalm 23 and journal about how its truths can apply to your current fear.)

Who Issues the Consequences We Fear: If we are in immediate danger or harm, it is normal to experience fear. However, we must be bold like a lion if we experience something fearful out of obedience to God. Even if we are experiencing something fearful out of disobedience, the Lord is merciful. We can trust that He will only do that which is edifying to our lives and His glory. (**Homework:** Are you suffering at the hands of man for your obedience? Your disobedience? Your sins or your righteous living? Journal your answers to these questions and ask the Lord to give you the strength to be bold like David when he asked for the Lord's discipline and mercy. Read 1 Chronicles 21:13.)

Face Your Fears: Confronting fears head-on can often diminish their hold on you. It embodies a practical application of faith and recognizes that confronting fears with God's support can alleviate their power. (**Homework:** Write down a specific fear, then take one small step this week to confront or address it while trusting in God's support.)

DISCUSSION STARTERS

1. **Finding Strength in God's Assurance:** Considering Isaiah 41:10 which emphasizes God's unwavering presence and support, how have you experienced or felt God's strengthening hand during times of fear? How might a deeper trust in His promise to uphold you with His righteous hand help diminish the fears you are currently facing?

2. **The Battle Between Fear and Faith:** Reflecting on Proverbs 28:1 which contrasts the wicked man's actions with the boldness of the righteous, how do you navigate the balance between faith and fear in your life? How can an increased reliance on God's promises and a deeper understanding of His character embolden you to face your fears with lion-like courage?

3. **Embracing God's Gifted Spirit:** Given 2 Timothy 1:7 which assures believers that God has granted them a spirit of power, love, and sound judgment; how have you felt empowered to confront your fears? How can leaning into this spirit God has bestowed upon you guide you toward love-driven actions and sound decisions amidst fearful situations?

FINANCES

As delineated in Scripture, financial stewardship encompasses more than the mere accumulation of wealth. It is a threefold principle that balances enjoyment, investment, and generosity. There is joy in the blessings God provides, yet a heart inclined towards generosity reflects the nature of a giving God. An unwillingness to give can lead to spiritual deprivation akin to a monkey trapped by its own greed and unwilling to release its hold on food to free his hand.

> *The rich rule over the poor, and*
> *the borrower is a slave to the lender.*
> **Prov 22:7**

Solomon, who some argue was the wealthiest man of all time, highlights the power dynamics inherent in wealth and debt. It points out the vulnerability that comes with being in debt comparing it to a form of bondage. This Scripture serves as a cautionary note on the dangers of borrowing and the importance of financial prudence. By understanding this, individuals can better navigate their financial decisions to avoid undue obligations. It promotes the value of financial independence and the freedom that comes with it. Proverbs 22:7 is a foundational verse emphasizing the significance of wise financial stewardship.

"No one can serve two masters since either he will hate
one and love the other, or he will be devoted to one and
despise the other. You cannot serve both God and money."
Matt 6:24

Jesus highlights the inherent tension between material and spiritual loyalties. It asserts that individuals should not prioritize worldly wealth. This Scripture is a caution against allowing financial pursuits to eclipse one's spiritual commitments. It is clear: one's allegiance cannot be split between the temporal and the eternal. When someone is overwhelmed by financial concerns or ambitions, this verse nudges him or her to reassess their heart's orientation. Is he/she seeking wealth for self-glory or stewarding resources in a way that glorifies God? This Scripture is not about denouncing money but ensuring it does not become an idol in one's life. As counselors, guiding individuals to this realization allows them to make financial decisions rooted in biblical values and helps ensure their aim is to honor God rather than just amass wealth.

For the love of money is a root of all kinds of evil,
and by craving it, some have wandered away from the
faith and pierced themselves with many griefs.
1 Tim 6:10

Paul distinguishes between money and the overwhelming love or craving for it. He suggests that wealth can be a snare when placed above God. When someone's heart is fixed on financial gain, he/she may drift from their foundational beliefs and open doors to many troubles. This Scripture is not painting money as inherently wrong but rather is stating that the deep-seated love of it is evil. In counseling, one can use this verse to help individuals discern their motivations and desires concerning finances. It is an invitation to keep one's priorities straight by ensuring that the pursuit of money does not come at the cost of one's spiritual well-being. For believers, this is a reminder to trust God with their finances and acknowledge Him as the provider with wisdom in financial decisions. The core takeaway? Keep God at the center and allow money to serve, not rule, one's life.

... You wicked, lazy slave, you knew that I reap where I did not sow and gather where I scattered no seed. Then you ought to have put my money in the bank, and on my arrival, I would have received my money back with interest.
Matt 25:26-27

The parable of the talents (Matt 25:14-30) is a financial example of managers who steward the owner's money/resources well and who do poorly. The success was not just that two men doubled the master's money but that the two who doubled managed the money in a manner consistent with the owner's wishes and desires. The owner entrusted each manager with the amount that the owner believed they could manage. The manager in this specific verse was viewed as wicked because he failed to do what the owner knew he was capable of, nor did he delegate his responsibility to another (or, the bank). Instead, he wasted the opportunity. Christians are managers of God's money. He is the owner and entrusts us to care for our family and others in need and to give to missional projects like the Church out of our resources. Managing our resources directly affects our day-to-day lives and blessings from the Lord.

Dishonest money dwindles away, but whoever gathers money little by little makes it grow.
Prov 13:11

This wisdom from Solomon serves as a beacon for those tempted by shortcuts in acquiring wealth. Rather than seeking instant gratification, Solomon emphasizes the importance of slow and steady accumulation, which often leads to more sustainable and lasting prosperity. Furthermore, the verse warns of the fleeting nature of dishonest money which might seem appealing at first but is bound to evaporate quickly. It is about how much money one gathers and the character and integrity behind that accumulation. In times of financial strain, seeking quick fixes is natural, but the

Bible reminds us to remain steadfast and upright. A righteous path often leads to more lasting rewards even though it is sometimes longer. This Scripture challenges believers to take the honest, diligent route in a world of get-rich-quick schemes and shortcuts. It is a call to perseverance by urging us to trust in the principles laid out in the Word of God especially regarding our financial well-being.

> *The plans of the diligent lead surely to abundance,*
> *but everyone who is hasty comes only to poverty*
> **Prov 21:5**

This proverb sheds light on God's wisdom regarding financial steward-ship. Solomon's words remind us that being diligent—consistent and thoughtful in our actions—leads to financial blessings. In contrast, rush-ing into decisions without proper insight or prayerful consideration can quickly deplete our resources. The Word here encourages believers to take their financial commitments to the Lord in prayer by seeking His guidance. Just as Joseph was a prudent manager in Egypt, this verse urges us to be wise managers of what God entrusts us. A key takeaway for those undergoing biblical counseling would be to ground their financial deci-sions on biblical principles by maintain patience and relying on God's di-rection. In a world filled with enticing shortcuts and quick schemes, lean-ing into God's word provides a stable foundation. This scripture serves as a warning and a promise of God's provision for those who are faithful and diligent.

PRACTICAL ADVICE + HOMEWORK

Confess Sin: If you worship money, you must confess this sin to God. At the heart of this sinful behavior is a prideful desire to please and comfort yourself with money and the things it can buy. You must recognize that if God has given you more resources than you need, it is not for your in-creased consumption but to share with those who have need (Eph 4:28).

(**Homework:** If this is true in your case, stop right now and confess this sin to God.)

Renew Your Mind through Scripture: God commands us to use our resources to help those who have needs (Eph 4:28). (**Homework:** Read the following biblical texts to understand how God expects us to use our financial resources: Matthew 6:19-21; Ephesians 4:22-28; and 1 Timothy 6:17-19. Answer these questions from the biblical texts you read: What did you learn about God? What did you learn about yourself? How do your thinking, feelings, and actions need to change considering these truths?)

Obey God: Follow his precepts on possessions and use the resources He has entrusted to you in ways that glorify Him. (**Homework:** Spend time with God in His Word each day, attend worship at your church each week, and generously give to those who have needs but do it in secret, so God is put on display and glorified rather than you.)

Avoid Debt: Understand the importance of living within your means to avoid the pitfalls of debt. There is wisdom in living within means, and reviewing and planning debt payments applies this knowledge directly. (**Homework:** Review your current debts, if any, and create a plan or strategy to start paying them down.)

Evaluate Priorities: Reflect on whether your pursuit of wealth overshadows your relationship with God. (**Homework:** Spend fifteen minutes meditating on Matthew 6:2 and journal about your relationship with money and God.)

Guard Your Heart: An unhealthy focus on or love for money can lead to numerous problems and makes the counselee understand the importance of valuing non-material blessings, which is an idea central to the biblical teaching on contentment. (**Homework:** List three non-material blessings you are grateful for and thereby shifting focus from financial wealth.)

Budget Wisely: Prioritizing, creating, and sticking to a budget to ensure responsible financial stewardship is essential because responsible stewardship of financial resources is consistent with the Word of God. (**Homework:** If you have not already, start a simple budget this week and monitor your income and expenses.)

Married or Single, You Can Prosper: If you are married, your accountability partner is your spouse. If you are single, you need an accountability partner already winning at financial stewardship (not a friend in just a bad financial situation as you are). Either way, you must commit to having someone have full access to your financial expenses, behaviors, and plans who can hold you accountable. (**Homework:** Sit down with your spouse or a close friend, repent of any apparent financial sins, and commit to walking alongside each other to grow in perspective and skillsets needed to be faithful stewards.)

DISCUSSION STARTERS

1. **Stewardship and Bondage:** Reflecting on Proverbs 22:7 which highlights the dynamic between the rich and the poor and the consequences of debt, how do you perceive your current financial obligations? How has debt, if any, impacted your freedom and decision-making? How can adopting a biblical perspective on stewardship and avoiding unnecessary debts bring about a sense of liberation in your life?

2. **Serving God or Money:** Considering Jesus' words in Matthew 6:24, where He emphasizes the impossibility of serving God and money, how do you evaluate your current relationship with wealth? Do you ever feel torn between material pursuits and spiritual commitments? How can focusing more on God's kingdom and less on worldly wealth align your priorities and bring true contentment?

3. **The True Value of Money:** Drawing from 1 Timothy 6:10 which speaks to the dangers of loving money, have you experienced any moments where pursuing wealth has overshadowed other essential aspects of your life? How can a shift from focusing on monetary gains to valuing spiritual blessings and relationships change your perspective on wealth and its true purpose?

GLUTTONY

An overindulgence that extends beyond food and is synonymous with a heart that is unsatisfied with God's provisions and seeks to consume all excess on self. The Scriptures link gluttony with sinful behaviors including stubbornness, rebellion, disobedience, drunkenness, and wastefulness. The Hebrew term, often translated as "glutton," can also encompass the characteristics of a wastrel, profligate, or one given to riotous and excessive living. Jesus' accusation of being "a glutton and a drunkard" was rooted in this broader understanding and implied a life led without restraint or respect for divine boundaries. Beyond its spiritual implications, the vice of gluttony has tangible consequences. Gluttony dulls the spirit, brings about lethargy, fosters laziness, and leads to poverty. As believers, it is crucial to guard against gluttony and cultivate a heart that finds its ultimate satisfaction in God alone.

> *Don't associate with those who drink too much*
> *wine or with those who gorge themselves on meat.*
> *For the drunkard and the glutton will become poor,*
> *and grogginess will clothe them in rags.*
> **Prov 23:20-21**

This Scripture offers caution against the dangers of gluttony. By juxtaposing overindulgence in food with excessive drinking, the passage equates gluttony with the severe implications of drunkenness. The Bible frequently emphasizes balance and moderation. The pitfalls of excess consumption are highlighted through warnings of poverty and grogginess. Beyond material implications, an underlying message about spiritual and emotional consequences is tied to unchecked indulgence. Ultimately, these verses serve as a timely reminder for believers to exercise wisdom and self-control in all aspects of life.

For the time already past is sufficient for you to have carried out the desire of the Gentiles, having pursued a course of sensuality, lusts, drunkenness, carousing, drinking parties and abominable idolatries. In all this, they are surprised that you do not run with them into the same excesses of dissipation, and they malign you; but they will give account to Him who is ready to judge the living and the dead.
1 Pet 4:3-5

The "excesses of dissipation" or excessive seeking of pleasure is described as the lost person or "Gentile." Peter indicates that such would be sinful. Gluttony, while mainly thought of as related to excess food, is at the heart the excess seeking of pleasure through something tangible that is sinful due to its excess. We must be ready to give an account to God based on how we live our lives. Whether it be excessive food, engaging in excessive "fun," or anything that we perceive to make us feel better—when the "excessive" becomes harmful physically and/or spiritually, we must recognize gluttony for what it is: sinful.

Their end is destruction; their God is their stomach; their glory is in their shame; and they are focused on earthly things
Phil 3:19

Paul's letter to the church of Philippi provides a perspective on the dangers of making our fleshly desires the ultimate priority in life. The reference to individuals whose "god is their stomach" illustrates the consequences of succumbing to physical desires like overeating at the expense of spiritual well-being. It is a potent reminder that being driven by our physical appetites can lead us astray from our true spiritual path. We risk missing out on the deeper spiritual truths and rewards by focusing solely on earthly desires. This caution against gluttony extends beyond mere consumption. It is about prioritizing the temporary over the eternal. Paul calls readers to examine their priorities and consider if they are elevating fleeting pleasures over lasting spiritual pursuits.

> *If you find honey, eat only what you need;*
> *otherwise, you'll get sick from it and vomit.*
> **Prov 25:16**

In the book of Proverbs, wisdom often comes in the form of witty advice. It is as relevant today as when it was written. The mention of honey, a valuable and delightful treat in ancient times, is a metaphor for life's pleasures. Just as too much honey can lead to physical discomfort, indulging excessively in any pleasure can have negative consequences. This proverb underscores the virtue of moderation by warning against the dangers of excess in all things. The essence is to enjoy life's pleasures without being consumed by them. By advocating for self-control and balance, the wisdom literature speaks directly to the heart of gluttony. It is a timeless reminder that while enjoying life's sweetness is fine, one should always do so in moderation.

> *Do not be with those who are given to wine,*
> *or with those who gorge themselves on meat;*
> *For the heavy drinker and the glutton will come*
> *to poverty, and drowsiness will clothe one with rags.*
> **Prov 23:20-21**

This verse from Proverbs clearly warns against the dangers of excessive indulgence. Solomon advises against association with those who over-consume anything. The verse highlights gluttony's physical and economic consequences, stating that it will lead to poverty and lethargy. It implies that excessive consumption, whether it is of alcohol or food, can lead to ruin both materially and spiritually. It is not just about the direct effects of overindulgence but the ripple effects it can cause in one's life. The wisdom imparted here encourages self-discipline and prudence. Believers are reminded to live with balance and moderation by avoiding the pitfalls of unrestrained consumption.

> *Food is for the stomach and the stomach for food, but*
> *God will do away with both of them. Yet the body is not for immorality,*
> *but for the Lord, and the Lord is for the body.*
> **1 Cor 6:13**

In his letter to the Corinthians, Paul highlights the fleeting nature of our physical desires and bodies. While he acknowledges that food is essential for the body, he emphasizes that both are temporary. By stating this, Paul reminds believers that they should not be enslaved or controlled by their physical appetites. According to Paul, our bodies' true purpose is to serve the Lord. This implies a higher, spiritual purpose beyond mere physical desires or needs. The verse challenges Christians to prioritize spiritual growth and service to God above indulging in fleeting pleasures. It is a call to align our actions and desires with God's will by emphasizing self-control and spiritual purpose over momentary physical gratification.

PRACTICAL ADVICE + HOMEWORK

Confess Sin: If you are gluttonous, you must confess this sin. At the heart of this sinful behavior is a prideful desire to please and comfort yourself with food. You must recognize that if God has given you more resources than you need, it is not for your increased consumption but to share with those who have need (2 Cor 9:6-13; Eph 4:28; and Phil 2:4). (**Homework:** If this is true in your case, stop right now and confess this sin to God.)

Renew Your Mind through Scripture: God commands us to eat in ways that glorify Him (1 Cor 10:31). (**Homework:** Read the following biblical texts to understand how God sees and responds to gluttony: Proverbs 23:19-21; 1 Corinthians 6:12-13; and 19-20. Answer these questions from the biblical texts you just read: What did you learn about God? What did you learn about yourself? How do your thinking, feelings and actions need to change considering these truths?)

Obey God: Put off gluttony and put on self-control. (**Homework:** Spend time with God in His Word each day; attend worship at your church each week; ask God to help you learn to eat to live rather than living to eat; and ask family and friends to hold you accountable to eat for the glory of God rather than for your personal pleasure.)

Moderation is Key: Recognize the value of moderation in eating to ensure that food consumption does not become excessive or compulsive. (**Homework:** For a week, consciously stop eating when you are no longer hungry, not when you are full.)

Evaluate Priorities: Reflect on whether your physical consumption patterns indicate a spiritual void or misplaced priorities. This brings about your relationship with food and its potential to symbolize deeper spiritual needs. (**Homework:** Spend some time meditating on Philippians 3:19 and journal about your relationship with food and its place in your life.)

Savor; Don't Overindulge: Enjoy the good things in life like delicious food without overconsumption and/or without succumbing to excess. (**Homework:** Choose one meal this week where you will practice mindful eating: savoring each bite, appreciating flavors, and eating slowly.)

Physical and Spiritual Nourishment: Try to nourish your body with balanced meals and your spirit with God's Word. Be aware of this by pairing nourishment for the body with nourishment for the soul through Scripture and devotionals. (**Homework:** Pair each meal with a short Scripture reading or devotional, thus emphasizing spiritual nourishment alongside the physical.)

Have Accountability: Excess could be hard to define without seeking what is "normal" from others. (**Homework:** In the areas of your life that you are concerned have become gluttonous, ask three trusted friends or mentors what they would think would be "normal" or "excessive" related to your question. Example: What are excessive portion sizes at lunch? What is excessive spending on hobbies based on my income? What is excessive with _____?)

DISCUSSION STARTERS

1. **Satisfying Physical and Spiritual Hunger:** Reflecting on 1 Corinthians 6:13, how do you differentiate between physical hunger and a spiritual void in your life? How can finding spiritual sustenance in God's Word help you combat the urge to overindulge in food or other physical pleasures?

2. **The Perils of Excessive Pleasure:** Considering Solomon's wisdom in Proverbs 23:20-21, how do you recognize when indulgences, be it food or other pleasures, become excessive? How might grounding yourself in God's teachings help you exercise self-control and moderation, preventing the pitfalls of gluttony?

3. **Food, Body, and Service to the Lord:** Drawing from Philippians 3:19 where Paul warns against making our desires our ultimate priority, how do you ensure you are eating habits align with serving and honoring God? How can adopting a mindset of eating to nourish and fuel your body, God's temple, lead to a healthier relationship with food and prevent overconsumption?

GRIEF

G rief refers to an emotional response stemming from the depths of the human soul, precipitated by the experience of loss. This poignant emotion often manifests as intense sorrow, pain, and heartfelt lamentation. While grief is an inescapable aspect of the human condition, the Holy Scriptures offer invaluable wisdom, solace, and hope to those wrestling with the weight of their loss. By turning to biblical narratives and teachings, individuals can navigate through the shadows of mourning and find solace in God's unwavering love and promises.

> *He was despised and forsaken of men,*
> *a man of sorrows and acquainted with grief;*
> *And like one from whom men hide their face He was despised,*
> *and we did not esteem Him.*
> **Isa 53:3**

The Messiah in Isaiah 53 was a man who would be "acquainted with grief." Many Christians quickly agree that Jesus was the Messiah and died for their sins so that they might receive eternal life. While this is 100% true, it leaves out a convenient truth for you and me as we experience everyday grief. The truth is Jesus did not just die for our sins, but He lived a life as a man on this earth and tempted in every way so that He could respond obediently to the Father amid struggle as an example for us to follow. Jesus was intimately acquainted with grief, yet the Holy Spirit strengthened Him to respond obediently. You and I can find comfort amid grief by remembering that Jesus knows our hearts and is hurting with us. He is experienced more grief than we can comprehend. The Spirit that enabled the Son to endure grief while on this earth is the same Spirit that dwells within the Christians today to be a Helper to them in their time of need.

> *The Lord is near to the brokenhearted and binds up their wounds.*
> **Ps 147:3**

For someone grieving, the assurance of God's nearness to the brokenhearted can be incredibly comforting. Psalm 147:3 acknowledges the emotional pain and brokenness integral to the grieving process. It reassures those mourning that God is not merely a distant observer but actively involved in their healing, tending to their wounds with care and compassion. The imagery of binding up wounds conveys a personal, hands-on God ready to mend the broken pieces of a shattered heart. Turning to this verse encourages individuals to seek solace and restoration in God's love and healing power even in the depths of despair. Within biblical counseling for grief, Psalm 147:3 can serve as a crucial anchor offering comfort, hope and a tangible sense of God's presence during a time of loss. It functions as a spiritual affirmation and a therapeutic tool by fostering a deep connection between faith and recovery.

> *He will wipe away every tear from their eyes, and*
> *death shall be no more, neither shall there be*
> *mourning, nor crying, nor pain anymore.*
> **Rev 21:4**

The promise in Revelation 21:4 offers a future glimpse of heaven where pain and sorrow will be no more. This verse focuses on the ultimate hope and comfort of believing in Christ. In this future, sorrow and pain are entirely eradicated. It provides a forward-looking perspective for those in grief and offers hope and encouragement amid overwhelming sorrow. The powerful imagery of God wiping away tears and eliminating death, mourning, and pain communicates God's empathy and love which resonates deeply with those suffering a loss. It emphasizes the theological truth that death and sorrow are temporary and will be overcome in God's future kingdom. In the context of biblical counseling for grief, Revelation 21:4 can gently guide the individual towards a hope that transcends their current suffering by offering a vision of comfort and healing in the presence of God. This eternal perspective can be a source of strength and encouragement as it helps individuals process their grief through a lens of faith and hope in God's ultimate plan.

> *Blessed are those who mourn, for they shall be comforted.*
> **Matt 5:4**

Jesus' teaching in Matthew 5:4 is compelling and applicable for someone struggling with grief. This verse does not only acknowledge mourning but even calls those who mourn "blessed," a validation of the authentic and painful human experience of loss. It recognizes grief as a process where comfort from God is promised. In the context of grief, it is not a hollow sentiment but a spiritual truth that God sees the mourning and is near to provide comfort. In a counseling setting, it can be a gentle reminder that grief is a natural response to loss and that it is not a path one must walk alone. The presence and comfort of God are available for those who seek Him. The promise of comfort is not necessarily immediate but it is a firm assurance that there is hope and healing in God, even amid the most sorrow.

> *For I consider that the sufferings of this present time*
> *are not worth comparing with the glory that is to be revealed to us.*
> **Rom 8:18**

In his letter to the Romans, Paul offers a perspective that can provide solace to grieving people. He acknowledges the undeniable sufferings and pain experienced in the present world including the anguish of loss. Paul contrasts this temporal suffering with the incomparable glory awaiting believers in eternity. For those in grief, this verse can remind them that their pain, no matter how overwhelming, is temporary in the grand narrative of eternity. This perspective does not trivialize their pain but provides hope by pointing them to a future where overwhelming joy will overshadow their sorrow. Through this verse, biblical counseling can encourage grieving individuals to cling to the hope of what is ahead and to trust that the Creator has an eternal purpose that transcends our momentary afflictions. This verse reinforces that even in the face of overwhelming grief greater glory awaits those who trust in God.

Cast all your anxiety on Him because He cares for you.
1 Pet 5:7

Peter's exhortation in his first epistle can be incredibly comforting for those dealing with the weight of grief. The command to "cast" speaks of an active relinquishment and encourages believers to surrender their burdens, anxieties, and griefs to God. The reasoning behind this is not only the omnipotence of God but His deep, personal care for every individual. For people grappling with loss, the affirmation that God cares about their pain can be immensely healing. It is a reminder that they are not alone in their grief. The Creator of the universe is willing and eager to shoulder their pain. This verse can be a foundational component in biblical counseling for grief by enabling individuals to understand that there is a safe space with God where they can lay down their heavy burdens. Leaning on this scripture, counselors can help the grieving find solace in the truth that God is powerful enough to handle their grief and loving enough to care about their pain deeply.

PRACTICAL ADVICE + HOMEWORK

Confess Sin: Grief is a righteous emotion and a gift from God to help us with loss. Though it is painful, it is not sinful unless we begin to sorrow as those who have no hope (like an unbeliever—1 Thess 4:13). (**Homework:** If you are a believer and have begun to despair during loss, you must confess this sinful response to God. It is an indicator that you placed your hope in something other than Christ and have now lost that person or thing along with the hope you mistakenly placed there.)

Renew Your Mind through Scripture: God comforts us in our grief (Col 3:23). (**Homework:** Read the following biblical texts to understand how God sees and responds to grief: Psalm 34:15-22; 73:23-28; Romans 8:35-39; and Revelation 21:1-7. Answer these questions from the biblical texts you just read: What did you learn about God? What did you learn about yourself? How do your thinking, feelings and actions need to change considering these truths?)

Obey God: Grieve in God's presence. (**Homework:** Spend time with God in His Word each day; attend worship at your church each week; and use the words of the Psalms of lament to pour out your heart to God—Psalm 6; 42; and 130 are good places to begin.)

Find Comfort in God's Presence: Remember that God is near to the brokenhearted. This focuses on God's proximity and desire to heal as it resonates with Psalm 147:3 and the assurance of God's healing touch. (**Homework:** Meditate on Psalm 147:3 daily and journal your feelings and thoughts focusing on God's healing touch.)

Take Your Concerns to God: He knows your circumstances, but often we fail to cry out to Him. God's heart has been moved through prayer, and men have been molded by prayer amid grief. (**Homework:** Write down exactly what is causing you grief, and through prayer, cry out to God. Telling Him exactly what is happening and what you wish to happen.)

Anchor in Eternal Hope: Focus on the hope that assures us that pain and grief will eventually end. By linking our suffering with the promises of God, we are given an outlook that can offer comfort and solace in the long run. (**Homework:** Write down Revelation 21:4 and place it somewhere visible, reflecting on the eternal hope.)

Embrace Mourning with Hope: Recognize that grieving is a part of life and that Jesus assures us He will bring us solace. His perspective on mourning centers around the assurance of comfort from Him, which provides hope. (**Homework:** Reflect on Matthew 5:4 through quiet prayer and ask for Christ's comfort in grief.)

Create Memories and Honor the Loss: Participating in activities that pay tribute to and commemorate the departed individual provides a means of coping with sorrow and cherishing our departed loved ones. This demonstrates a compassionate attitude towards dealing with loss. (**Homework:** Consider creating a memory box or writing a letter to the departed in which you express your feelings and memories.)

DISCUSSION STARTERS

1. **Experiencing Grief Through Christ's Perspective:** Considering Isaiah 53:3 which speaks of the Messiah as "a man of sorrows and acquainted with grief," how does acknowledging that Jesus himself experienced deep grief impact your understanding of your own grief? How can reflecting on Christ's life, which was full of grief yet obedient to the Father, offer you a framework to navigate your sorrow?

2. **God's Intimate Care in Our Grief:** Psalm 147:3 emphasizes, "The Lord is near to the brokenhearted and binds up their wounds." How can you lean into this promise during times when grief feels overpowering? How might consciously acknowledging God's intimate involvement in your healing process influence your journey through mourning?

3. **Eternal Hope Amidst Earthly Grief:** Revelation 21:4 paints a picture of a future where God will eliminate all pain and sorrow. How can holding onto this promise anchor you in moments of grief and provide solace? How might envisioning this future, free of mourning and pain, help you navigate the challenges of the present grief?

GUILT

Within the biblical framework, guilt accompanies wrongdoing or a violation of God's righteous standards. When one sins, guilt is the consequence along with implications for both his or her emotional and spiritual state. This dual representation demonstrates humanity's inherent understanding of and reaction to breaches in divine law. Just as sin manifests through willful transgressions, the sensation of guilt is an inner testimony to one's deviation from God's path. Consequently, recognizing and addressing guilt is pivotal in repentance, redemption, and divine reconciliation.

> *According to Your knowledge I am indeed not guilty,*
> *yet there is no deliverance from Your hand.*
> **Job 10:7**

Sometimes, we feel and/or experience a state of guilt in our lives because we have committed a sin or wrongdoing towards God or others. However, sometimes we feel guilty or are made to feel guilty by misunderstanding Scripture or manipulating others. The reader of Job understands that Job was indeed innocent; however, Job's friends were convinced that Job was guilty of sin. During his pain, Job was trying to reconcile his innocence according to the will and ways of God with the appearance that his circumstances were punishment for sinful guilt and no deliverance. Just like Job, we must evaluate whether we are indeed guilty of sin so that we can confess it. If we think we are not guilty of sin yet are still experiencing feelings of guilt, we must seek biblical counsel to understand and continue to walk in obedience.

> *For God did not send his Son into the world to*
> *condemn the world, but to save the world through him.*
> **John 3:17**

One of the best benefits of the gospel is that we are forgiven for all our sins—past, present, and future. Jesus died to save us. All our sins have been washed away; therefore, we do not have to carry the weight of our sins. God sent His Son so we would not have to carry that weight. When we carry guilt, we carry something the Lord does not want us to bear. When we make decisions out of guilt, it will never lead to a good result. We cannot live in the past because God has already forgiven those sins. His continued promise is that His mercies renew every morning (Lam 3:22-23). Jesus came not to show us how horrible and helpless we are but to save us. Be free of your guilt and know you serve a God who did not come to condemn you but save you.

> *Then I acknowledged my sin to you and did not*
> *conceal my iniquity. I said, "I will confess my transgressions*
> *to the Lord," and you forgave the guilt of my sin. Selah.*
> **Ps 32:5**

The psalmist provides a reflection on the experience of guilt and the liberation that comes from confession. Unacknowledged sin can be a heavy and distressing burden. By choosing to confess, the psalmist demonstrates an understanding that genuine acknowledgment of one's sin is the pathway to restoration. It is an intimate portrayal of the human struggle with guilt that showcases the inner turmoil it brings, but its overarching message is one of hope and redemption. This verse is a poignant reminder that while guilt can be paralyzing, there is a way out through confession and seeking forgiveness. The emphasis is clear: openness and honesty before God leads to grace and peace.

Guilt

If we confess our sins, he is faithful and righteous to forgive
us our sins and to cleanse us from all unrighteousness.
1 John 1:9

John speaks directly to the issue of guilt and offers a transformative solution for those plagued by it. The verse emphasizes that when we admit our wrongdoings to God, He is not only faithful, but just in forgiving our sins. This assurance counters the stagnation that guilt can cause and reminds us that reconciliation is attainable. It underscores God's endless compassion and mercy, even when we falter. We are granted a clean slate by turning to Him and owning up to our sins. The verse is a beacon of hope for anyone weighed down by the remorse of past actions as it emphasizes the promise of renewal through confession. It affirms that no matter the depth of our guilt, God's capacity to forgive is greater.

Therefore, there is now no condemnation for those in Christ Jesus.
Rom 8:1

This passage offers relief to those burdened by guilt by asserting that no condemnation remains for those in Christ Jesus. This foundational statement reveals the transformative power of Jesus' sacrifice on the cross which frees believers from guilt. By being in Christ, individuals are placed in a new reality where their past mistakes no longer dictate their worth. The verse serves as a reminder of God's grace and mercy available to everyone and emphasizes the fresh start that faith offers. For those tormented by guilt, it provides a pathway to peace and assures them that their past is not an anchor. This message revitalizes hope and underscores the idea that in Christ a person's past does not have to define their future.

Therefore, confess your sins to one another and pray for one another, so that
you may be healed. The prayer of a righteous person is very powerful in its effect
James 5:16

James offers direct counsel on dealing with guilt that may stem from sin. The call to confess sins to one another emphasizes the importance of community and accountability in the Christian journey. By voicing our shortcomings, we make ourselves vulnerable and allow for genuine fellowship and support. James does not just stop at confession. He links it with the power of prayer by suggesting that they can bring healing together. This verse gives a blueprint for overcoming guilt: sincere confession followed by fervent prayer. It also underscores the potency of the prayers of the righteous, which is a comforting thought for those seeking restoration. This verse can guide individuals toward communal support and spiritual healing in counseling.

For I will be merciful to their wrongdoing,
and I will never again remember their sins.
Heb 8:12

This verse from Hebrews captures the essence of God's unparalleled mercy and His promise to believers. Rooted in the context of the New Covenant, it highlights God's commitment to be merciful to our sins. This powerful message can alleviate feelings of guilt. It paints a picture of a God who does not just forgive but completely removes our transgressions from His memory. This depth of forgiveness is a balm to the guilt-ridden soul and reassures that God's mercy truly eradicates the stain of sin. Within biblical counseling, this verse can serve as a reminder that no matter the magnitude of one's mistakes, God's mercy and forgetfulness are greater. Embracing this promise can pave the way for freedom from guilt as believers grasp the full extent of God's redemptive love.

PRACTICAL ADVICE + HOMEWORK

Confess Sin: If you are experiencing guilt, ask God to show you the sin behind this misery. This weight indicates sins in thinking and/or behavior that need to be confessed. (**Homework:** If this is true in your case, stop right now and confess sin to God. Guilt can only be alleviated when God forgives and cleanses sin.)

Renew Your Mind through Scripture: God teaches us that guilt and sin go together—the first is an indicator of the second (Ezra 9:6-15). (**Homework:** Read the following biblical texts to understand God's perspective on guilt and the remedy He has provided: Ezra 9:6-15 and Isaiah 53. Answer these questions from the biblical texts you read: What did you learn about God? What did you learn about yourself? How do your thinking, feelings, and actions need to change considering these truths?)

Obey God: Stop this sin and embrace freedom from its accompanying guilt. (**Homework:** Spend time with God in His Word each day, attend worship at your church each week, and keep a short sin list. Confess daily the behavior along with the prideful and selfish heart that produces that behavior. The prideful root must be put to death so the sinful behavioral fruit dies, too.)

Confession is Liberating: Recognize the freedom of confessing your wrongdoings and seeking God's forgiveness. This encourages personal reflection and openness before God that is grounded in the belief of the power of confession and redemption (James 5:16). (**Homework:** Set aside a quiet time to confess any known sins or transgressions to God, seeking His cleansing and forgiveness.)

Embrace God's Forgiveness: Once you have confessed, believing, and accepting that God's grace can cleanse you from guilt is essential. This highlights the undeserved grace that God offers. Drawing from 1 John 1:9, this foundation helps individuals acknowledge and embrace the reality of being forgiven. (**Homework:** Meditate on 1 John 1:9 and write down how it feels knowing God's promise to forgive and cleanse.)

Reflection and Freedom: When we feel guilty about something, it can be from many places. We might be prideful and think we should have done a better job. We could have acted on our selfish ambitions or feel embarrassed or ashamed. The root of your guilt might not be coming from a righteous place. You need to examine what you know about the situation you are feeling guilty about and then evaluate why you feel guilty. (**Homework:** In prayer, start by thanking God for sending His Son to die for us so we do not have to live in guilt and shame. Then, ask Him to bless your time reflecting on your situation. Get a journal and let out your feelings about your guilt. Go back through and highlight things that point to why you feel guilty about bringing it to your counselor next week.)

Identify Innocence: If you believe your guilt is manipulated or wrongfully inferred, seek to understand the truth of your situation. (**Homework:** Seek the help of a spiritual leader who is unbiased towards you to help you identify any actual sins you have committed, been accused of, or led to believe and compare them with Scripture.)

Release Self-Condemnation: Understand that you are free from the chains of guilt and condemnation in Christ. This invokes Romans 8:1 to provide assurance of freedom in Christ which helps to break the cycle of self-blame. (**Homework:** Reflect on Romans 8:1 and list any areas where you are still condemning yourself. Pray to be released from those feelings.)

DISCUSSION STARTERS

1. **Recognizing True Guilt vs. False Guilt:** Drawing from Job's experience in Job 10:7 where he feels the weight of accusation despite his innocence, have you ever felt similarly misunderstood or wrongfully accused? How can you discern between genuine guilt that arises from sin and false guilt induced by external pressures or misunderstandings? How does knowing the full context of Job's story help you navigate such feelings?

2. **Absorbing the Power of God's Grace:** Reflecting on John 3:17, which states that God did not send His Son into the world to con-

demn but to save, how can internalizing this truth reshape your view on self-worth and self-condemnation? Given that Jesus' sacrifice was made for our sin, how does this provide you with a sense of liberation from guilt? How does understanding God's purpose in sending His Son help in differentiating between conviction and condemnation?

3. **Path to Reconciliation and Peace:** With the words of Psalm 32:5 and 1 John 1:9 emphasizing the freedom found in confession and forgiveness, how have you experienced the healing that comes from genuine acknowledgment of wrongdoing? In what ways has confessing and seeking God's forgiveness transformed your personal relationship with Him?

HEALTH

Health is defined as the holistic state in which an individual experiences freedom from physical ailments or injuries. This physical state is also complemented by mental and social well-being. In biblical counseling, proper health is also interwoven with spiritual well-being. In this dual construct, a person's body and spirit are aligned with God's purpose and design as outlined in Scripture. This health perspective recognizes the inherent interconnectedness of our physical, mental, emotional, and spiritual facets which are all essential for living a life that brings glory and honor to God.

Dear friend, I pray that you are prospering in every way
and are in good health, just as your whole life is going well.
3 John 1:2

John provides insight into the holistic view of well-being, where spiritual prosperity is closely tied to physical health. This verse underscores the notion that God desires wellness for a person's soul and body. It serves as a reminder that one's spiritual well-being often manifests in one's physical condition. The connection between the soul prospering and overall health suggests that nurturing one's spiritual life can benefit the body. Furthermore, the verse emphasizes the importance of balance in one's life and urges believers to prioritize their spiritual and physical health. In today's fast-paced world, this Scripture is a timely reminder to care for one's body as a vessel and temple while nourishing the soul. Ultimately, it conveys that God's wish is for His children to thrive in every aspect of their lives.

> *A joyful heart is good medicine,*
> *but a broken spirit dries up the bones.*
> **Prov 17:22**

Our bodies are a temple of the Lord, and we are expected to treat them as such (1 Cor 6:19-20). Sometimes, we cannot help it when we get sick. Cancer, dementia, and ALS are all real things people must deal with that they might have never seen it coming. When we get a diagnosis of ourselves or a loved one that we were not ready for, it can make us question our faith. This verse talks about how a joyful heart is a good medicine. When walking through times of heartache and uncertainty, we need to have a joyful heart. This is only possible if you have a strong relationship with Christ. This means spending time with Him daily by reading His Word and praying.

> *Don't you know that your body is a temple of the*
> *Holy Spirit who is in you, whom you have from God?*
> *You are not your own, for you were bought at a price.*
> *So, glorify God with your body.*
> **1 Cor 6:19-20**

In Paul's letter to the church of Corinth, he offers a perspective on the significance of our bodies in the Christian faith. These verses emphasize that our bodies are not solely our own but are considered temples of the Holy Spirit. This Divine indwelling demands respect and care towards our physical selves and reinforces that our well-being is not only a personal matter but a spiritual one. Furthermore, the reminder that we were bought with a price highlights the invaluable worth and purpose God sees in us. Such a realization should motivate believers to treat their bodies respectfully and carefully. By viewing our bodies as sacred temples, we are called to make health-conscious decisions and understand that maintaining good health honors God. Ultimately, these verses provide both an incentive and a responsibility for Christians to prioritize their health again linking physical well-being with spiritual dedication.

Heal me, Lord, and I will be healed; save me,
and I will be saved, for you are my praise.
Jer 17:14

Jeremiah put forward a plea to the Lord for healing and salvation, which underlining the belief in God's power to restore both the body and the soul. This verse highlights the deep connection between spiritual well-being and physical health. It suggests that turning to God can result in holistic healing. The prophet Jeremiah's trust in God as the source of his restoration emphasizes the importance of faith as a component of well-being. Furthermore, his prayerful approach is a model for believers today. It shows that trusting God is pivotal in times of ailment or distress. Divine healing is not in opposition to and does not replace medical intervention; rather it complements it, thereby bringing peace. The verse reminds believers of the ultimate healer and the importance of faith in the journey to recovery. By integrating spiritual trust with practical health measures, one can seek a more comprehensive healing experience.

Therefore, I urge you, brethren, by the mercies of God,
to present your bodies a living and holy sacrifice, acceptable to God,
which is your spiritual service of worship.
Rom 12:1

Our entire being, body and soul, is designed and purposed to serve the Lord to accomplish His work on earth. Paul urges the Roman Christians to present their physical bodies to the service of the Lord for Kingdom purposes. Christians cannot serve the Lord in a fit manner if they have physically disqualified themselves due to poor health decisions or willful neglect of biblical principles related to their health. Believers ought to exercise their physical body, partake of nutritious meals, and avoid harmful activities or substances to be prepared for any service to which the Lord may call them.

Yet I will certainly bring health and healing
to it and will indeed heal them. I will let them
experience the abundance of true peace.
Jer 33:6

This promise from Jeremiah delivers hope to those struggling with health challenges. It conveys God's sovereignty over all health situations and affirms His capability to restore and heal. Jeremiah, speaking God's Word, promises physical healing and the peace that can only come from God. This holistic promise addresses the physical and emotional strains of poor health. By turning to God in trust and prayer, believers can seek His divine intervention and receive comfort in their health battles. This Scripture can provide solace, reminding those in poor health of God's continual presence and desire to heal and bring peace. This verse can encourage faith, patience, and hope in biblical counseling. It highlights God's enduring love and commitment to His children's well-being.

Come to me, all of you who are weary and
burdened, and I will give you rest.
Matt 11:28

In this verse, Jesus speaks directly to those exhausted from various burdens, including health challenges. He offers a refuge, a place of rest and rejuvenation for those wearied from life's hardships. This not only refers to spiritual or emotional burdens but also to physical ailments. Jesus presents Himself as the source of true comfort. In his presence, burdens are lightened, and souls find rest. These words can be a beacon of hope for someone struggling with health and reminds him or her that no one has to face their challenges alone. By leaning on Jesus, believers can find a unique rest that alleviates physical and emotional strain. In biblical counseling, this Scripture encourages a deep reliance on Christ, which will foster a relationship that can provide solace during trying health challenges. It reminds individuals that Jesus' invitation is ever-present. He is waiting to embrace and give rest to those in need.

PRACTICAL ADVICE + HOMEWORK

Confess Sin: God calls us to steward our bodies for Him. Following salvation, they no longer belong to us, and we manage them for Him as their Owner (1 Cor 6:19-20). We can neglect our bodies or inordinately focus on them. Each of these responses is sinful. (**Homework:** If this is true in your case, stop right now and confess your body's sinful mistreatment or idolatrous worship to God.)

Renew Your Mind through Scripture: God commands us to steward our bodies for His glory (1 Cor 6:19-20). (**Homework:** Read the following biblical texts to understand how God directs us in health: Proverbs 3:5-8; 1 Corinthians 6:19-20; and 1 Timothy 4:6-8. Answer these questions from the biblical texts you read: What did you learn about God? What did you learn about yourself? How do your thinking, feelings, and actions need to change considering these truths?)

Obey God: Cease either the neglect or the worship of health. (**Homework:** Spend time with God in His Word each day, attend worship at your church each week, redirect your focus from yourself to God by memorizing and meditating on 1 Corinthians 6:19-20.)

Holistic Health: Recognizing that God values our health and well-being is crucial. It highlights the significance of understanding that God cares for every aspect of our being, our body and spirit, as the Bible teaches us that they are intricately connected. (3 John 1:2). (**Homework:** Spend a few minutes daily checking in with yourself—physically and spiritually—and journal any observations or areas needing attention.)

Joyful Heart: A joyful heart is hard to sustain when walking through a challenging situation. It comes through a connection with God. When a loved one is sick, it is a terrifying situation. We must remember God has a plan for everyone, and it is not to harm but to prosper (Jer 29:11). We can have joy because we know God is the one who holds the future. The more you know God's Word, the more you will trust Him with your future. (**Homework:** With prayer for healing, ask God to give you a joyous heart through this journey. Spend time in the Word every day this week, going over a different Psalm each day.)

Respect Your Body: Acknowledge your form as a sanctuary where the Holy Spirit dwells and approach it with reverence and attentiveness. This principle reminds us that our bodies are a temple (1 Cor 6:19-20). (**Homework:** Identify one unhealthy habit you would like to change and plan to address it this week.)

Balanced Nutrition and Exercise: Honor God by making balanced food choices and keeping your body active. Doing so promotes responsible stewardship of the body and honors God through wise choices consistent with the biblical principles of self-control and discipline. (**Homework:** Plan three balanced meals daily and commit to a twenty-minute physical activity even if it is just a walk.)

Seek Medical Attention: Biblical counselors recognize the dichotomous nature of man. They recognize that medical professionals have studied the human body as God's creation and have made discoveries regarding how to help the body operate at its optimal potential. (**Homework:** Consult a medical expert who believes in Christ and share your concerns about your health and what steps you could take to address any underlying medical conditions.)

Discussion Starters

1. **The Interplay of Spiritual and Physical Health:** Given John's holistic view of well-being in 3 John 1:2 where spiritual prosperity

is closely tied to physical health, how do you see this connection manifesting in your own life? In moments where your spiritual life flourishes, have you noticed a direct impact on your physical health? Conversely, in moments of spiritual drought, how has your body responded?

2. **Navigating Health Challenges with Faith:** Considering Proverbs 17:22 and its emphasis on the therapeutic nature of a joyful heart, have you ever faced a significant health challenge that tested your faith and joy? How did you navigate this situation, and what role did your relationship with Christ play in your emotional and physical recovery?

3. **Body as a Sacred Temple:** Considering 1 Corinthians 6:19-20, where Paul emphasizes our bodies as temples of the Holy Spirit, how do you view your responsibility towards maintaining and respecting your physical health? Are there areas where you feel you could improve in honoring your body as a sacred vessel for the Spirit?

IMPOTENCE/
SEXUAL DYSFUNCTION

In biblical counseling, this issue refers to an individual's inability or diminished capacity to engage in or enjoy sexual intimacy as intended by God in the marital union. Rooted in various causes—whether physiological, psychological, or spiritual—this challenge underscores the interconnectedness of the human body, mind, and spirit. Addressing such concerns requires a compassionate, holistic approach grounded in understanding humanity's design and purpose as delineated in Scripture. This ensuring that the God-ordained gift of marital intimacy is experienced in a manner that glorifies Him.

Now the promises were spoken to Abraham and to his seed.
He does not say "and to seeds," as though referring to many,
but referring to one, and to your seed, who is Christ.
Gal 3:16
(for the man struggling with impotence)

Paul focuses on the promises given to Abraham and his offspring. They emphasize faith and the spiritual lineage of believers through Jesus Christ. A male struggling with impotence might find hope in this Scripture because it underscores God's faithfulness and the broader scope of the lineage that goes beyond physical constraints. Physical limitations or challenges do not limit God's plans and purposes for an individual. The emphasis on spiritual inheritance can provide comfort and remind the individual that their value and meaning extend beyond physical capabilities. Faith becomes a beacon of hope during personal trials, such as dealing with impotence. By leaning into faith, one can find deeper meaning, purpose, and identity that transcends physical issues. The verse is a testament to the idea that God's promises and purposes are unwavering even in the face of personal challenges.

He did not weaken in faith when he considered[a] his own body to be already dead (since he was about a hundred years old) and also the deadness of Sarah's womb. He did not waver in unbelief at God's promise but was strengthened in his faith and gave glory to God, because he was fully convinced that what God had promised, he was also able to do. Therefore, it was credited to him for righteousness. Now it was credited to him was not written for Abraham alone, but also for us. It will be credited to us who believe in him who raised Jesus our Lord from the dead. He was delivered up for our trespasses and raised for our justification.
Rom 4:19-25

We cannot rely on ourselves for anything but be reminded about the strength given to us through Christ. When we feel helpless, it is often because we have relied too much on ourselves to fix the problem or move forward. When we find our strength in Christ, our strength will never run out. Romans refers to Abraham and Sarah when they wanted a child. Abraham knew they could not rely on themselves alone because they were old, but He knew God kept His problems. If we focus more on the God than what we cannot do, we will be in a better mindset.

He gives the childless woman a household,
making her the joyful mother of children. Hallelujah.
Ps 113:9
(for the wife of a husband struggling with impotence)

For a woman whose husband is struggling with impotence, this verse offers hope and assurance of God's compassionate involvement in seemingly impossible situations. It is a testament to God's ability to bring joy and blessings from places of pain and waiting. While the verse speaks directly about barrenness, its broader message is about God's transformative power and the potential for miracles in all aspects of life. The woman can find comfort in the idea that God sees her pain, understands her desires, and can intervene in miraculous ways. Additionally, the verse can serve as a reminder that her identity and worth are not solely based on her circumstances but are deeply rooted in her relationship with God. By holding onto faith, she can navigate this challenging time with hope, grace, and the knowledge that God's plans often transcend our understanding.

> *Trust in the Lord with all your heart, and do not*
> *rely on your own understanding; in all your ways*
> *know him, and he will make your paths straight.*
> **Prov 3:5-6**

In times of personal and marital challenges, such as a husband struggling with impotence, Proverbs 3:5-6 offers wisdom and comfort for couples. The verses remind couples to wholeheartedly trust God's understanding rather than leaning solely on their insights. This can encourage a couple facing such challenges to approach the situation with faith when they know that God's perspective surpasses their immediate concerns. Additionally, by acknowledging God in every aspect of their lives, they can be directed toward solutions, peace, or understanding they might not have found on their own. Impotence can test a relationship's strength, patience, and understanding. By embracing the message of these verses, the couple can find strength in unity and ensure that their paths remain intertwined and supported in God's compassionate care. The verses call for a deep faith that can anchor the relationship in stormy times by encouraging resilience, hope, and mutual support.

> *Finally, be strong in the Lord and in the strength of His might.*
> **Eph 6:10**

This verse precedes the passage that explains "Armor of God" (6:13-17) and informs the believer that they are to "be strong," meaning, "be capable or made capable for service." When we feel we cannot do what God calls us to do, we are commanded to take action to be made capable. Paul encourages the believer to find his ability in God's ability which can be found in the right understanding and utilization of the armor of God in the proceeding verses. Christians often lack power not because God has failed them but because they have failed to utilize the power and tools via the Holy Spirit in a manner consistent with biblical instruction.

> *And we know that in all things God works for the good of those who love him, who have been called according to his purpose.*
> **Rom 8:28**

Dealing with impotence can lead many to question the "why" behind their trials. This verse reminds individuals that God has a sovereign plan working for their good despite adversity. This truth does not necessarily mean immediate relief or resolution but suggests a bigger picture—one we might not fully understand now. For a man struggling with impotence, it is a call to shift focus from the immediate struggle to the broader assurance of God's purpose for him. It may also encourage exploring other avenues of intimacy, connection, and communication in relationships, which shows understanding that God's "good" can manifest in multiple ways beyond physical healing.

PRACTICAL ADVICE + HOMEWORK

Confess Sin: While impotence can result from physical factors that can be diagnosed with medical tests, sometimes the problem is entirely spiritual. Prideful love of self and the use of pornography can lead to impotence, and this sin must be put off through confession (Eph 4:17-24). (**Homework:** If this is true in your situation, stop right now and confess the inward sin of pride and self-love and the outward sinful use of pornography. Confess this sin to God and to any you have mistreated because of this pattern of behavior.)

Renew Your Mind through Scripture: God commands us to be morally pure. (**Homework:** Read the following biblical texts to understand God's perspective on sexual immorality and moral purity: Proverbs 5; 1 Corinthians 6:13-20; Galatians 5:19-25; and Ephesians 4:17-24. Answer these questions from the biblical texts you read: What did you learn about God? What did you learn about yourself? How do your thinking, feelings, and actions need to change considering these truths?)

Obey God: Commit to put off a heart of pride and its outward expression in pornography use. (**Homework:** Spend time with God in His Word daily, attend worship at your church each week, and find a mentor or small group to hold you accountable for inner and outer transformation.)

Affirmation of Value: Physical limitations or abilities do not define your worth in the eyes of God. Your worth is intrinsic and grounded in our identity as children of the Highest which transcends physical abilities or limitations (Ps 139:13-16). (**Homework:** Spend time journaling about your intrinsic value as a child of God separate from any health issue.)

Trust in God's Plan: Remember that God has a unique plan for everyone. Challenges arise, but trust that He is with you. This fundamental truth emphasizes reliance on God's wisdom and guidance, as stated in Proverbs 3:5-6. Accepting challenges can be part of a greater biblical plan. (**Homework:** Meditate on Proverbs 3:5-6 and reflect on areas where you can further trust God's plan.)

Knowing God: We need to know who God is. To know God is to know His Word. Many rely on others to tell us what the Word says: preachers, teachers, influencers, mentors. We rarely pick up the Bible for ourselves and read it. We can hear from God just like anyone else. When we understand more about God, we realize we cannot rely on our strength. It is our strength that leaves us in a state of impotence. It is God's strength that gives us comfort. (**Homework:** Pray God would begin revealing places in your life where you are relying on yourself instead of God. Go back and read the story of Abraham and Sarah in Genesis 21. Highlight the times when they relied on God's strength instead of their own.

Pursue Medical Insight: The Bible does not discourage seeking medical help. It is wise to explore medical solutions while praying for healing. However, you should carefully consider the ethical implications of certain methods of help in this area. (**Homework:** Schedule a check-up or consultation with a healthcare professional to discuss your concerns.)

Embrace Other Forms of Intimacy: Intimacy is not solely about the physical act. Emotional and spiritual closeness is deeply fulfilling. (**Homework:** Dedicate time to bond with your partner non-physically through deep conversations, spiritual activities, or shared hobbies.)

DISCUSSION STARTERS

1. **The Spiritual Lineage of Faith:** Considering Galatians 3:16 which emphasizes the spiritual lineage of believers through Christ, how do you perceive your role and worth in the grand design of God's plan? How might a deep understanding of this verse provide hope and comfort when confronting physical limitations like impotence?

2. **Enduring Faith in God's Promises:** Romans 4:19-25 highlights Abraham's faith in God's promise despite the physical limitations of his and Sarah's bodies. How do you relate to Abraham's unwavering faith in the face of seemingly insurmountable odds? How can Abraham's story inspire you to trust God's promises and plans for your life even when faced with personal challenges?

3. **God's Transformative Power:** Reflecting on Psalm 113:9 which speaks of God giving joy to the childless woman, how do you understand God's ability to bring blessings from challenging situations? How can focusing on God's transformative power provide solace and hope, especially for a woman whose husband is grappling with impotence?

IN-LAWS

These are the relationships formed not merely by marriage but also by God's sovereign design. He intertwines lives for mutual edification, support, and care. The Scriptures frequently underscore the significance of family ties, both by blood and covenant. This connection encompasses not only immediate relations but also extends to broader members of the household, even those not bound by kinship. When rooted in love and understanding, these relationships testify to God's divine plan for community, familial unity, and a picture of God's spiritual family.

> *So, it came about in the morning that, behold, it was Leah! And he said to Laban, "What is this you have done to me? Was it not for Rachel that I served with you? Why, then have you deceived me?" But Laban said, "It is not the practice in our place to marry off the younger before the firstborn."*
> **Gen 29:25-26**

If every word from God is profitable for teaching, what can be learned concerning Laban's deception and Jacob's responses to his new father-in-law? Laban spoke a simple truth that is present in every family when he said, "It is not the practice in our place." Another way to phrase Laban's response would be to say, "This is not how our family does things." Every married couple must understand that their spouse's family is now theirs. Yet no matter how ethnically, socially, or economically similar the married couple's families are, each family and set of in-laws has an established culture/practice regarding how life ought to be lived. Before marriage, spouses should seek to understand each other's family dynamic and culture to better prepare for hidden struggles. The more diverse the family background, the more the spouses should converse to be on the same page in anticipating putting each other first and responding to in-law interactions.

> *"Haven't you read," he replied, "that he who created them in the beginning made them male and female, and he also said, 'For this reason a man will leave his father and mother and be joined to his wife, and the two will become one flesh'? So, they are no longer two but one flesh. Therefore, what God has joined together, let no one separate."*
> **Matt 19:4-6**

Depending on the situation, it could be hard for your spouse to part with his/her parents. When the Bible says, "leaving his father and mother," it does not mean never talking to them again only that priorities have shifted. The most crucial relationship, outside of your relationship with Christ, is with your spouse. No matter how much you love your in-laws, proper boundaries must be set. They can give you advice but cannot heavily influence your relationship because you are now building your own family.

> *But Ruth replied: "Don't plead with me to abandon you or to return and not follow you. For wherever you go, I will go, and wherever you live, I will live; your people will be my people, and your God will be my God. Where you die, I will die, and there I will be buried. May the Lord punish me, and do so severely, if anything but death separates you and me."*
> **Ruth 1:16-17**

The commitment displayed in Ruth 1:16-17, where Ruth pledges unwavering loyalty to her mother-in-law, Naomi. It is a poignant example of couples navigating complicated relationships with in-laws. Her dedication demonstrates the potential for love and devotion to transcend biological ties. It also suggests that forging solid bonds with in-laws is not just possible but can be deeply enriching. Even in the face of adversity, hardships, and the unknown; Ruth chose dedication over desertion. For modern couples, this can be a source of inspiration to approach in-law relationships with patience, understanding, and genuine commitment. A problematic start does not preclude the possibility of forging deep, meaningful relationships over time. Ruth's example emphasizes the importance of choosing love, understanding, and unity in family matters even when faced with complexities. Embracing this perspective can provide a foundation of mutual respect and commitment in the most challenging of familial relationships.

This is why a man leaves his father and mother
and bonds with his wife, and they become one flesh.
Gen 2:24

This passage underscores the fundamental shift when two individuals become one in marriage. They leave their families of origin to establish a new primary relationship. This foundational principle helps couples prioritize their marital bond above other familial ties, while also setting clear boundaries with extended families. While honoring and respecting one's parents remains essential, the autonomy and unity of the married couple take precedence. For couples facing difficulties with in-laws, this Scripture can remind them of the importance of establishing and maintaining boundaries to protect and nurture their marital relationship. This decision is not about severing ties but ensuring that the marriage remains the primary focus. By referencing this verse, couples can find strength and validation in prioritizing their relationship and working together to navigate in-law challenges. The scripture also serves as a reminder for parents to give their married children the space and freedom to cultivate their marriages.

With all humility and gentleness, with patience,
bearing with one another in love, making every effort
to keep the unity of the Spirit through the bond of peace.
Eph 4:2-3

Paul emphasizes the virtues of patience, humility, gentleness, and maintaining unity through the bond of peace. This verse encourages couples to approach situations with understanding and patience in challenging in-law relationships. It reminds them that the goal is to foster harmony and peace despite disagreements or differing viewpoints. For the married couple, applying these principles means standing united, communicating effectively, and working collaboratively to address any issues with in-laws. Paul prompts the reader to extend grace and understanding even when faced with difficult conversations or situations. By internalizing the teachings of this Scripture, couples can navigate the complexities of in-law relationships with love and unity. This verse not only provides guidance but also offers hope that, with effort, peaceful coexistence is achievable.

PRACTICAL ADVICE + HOMEWORK

Confess Sin: If you have dishonored your in-laws in your heart and through your actions, put off those sins in obedience to God. (**Homework:** If this is true in your case, stop right now and confess those sins to God and to them.)

Renew Your Mind through Scripture: God commands us to show love to all people even as He does (Matt 5:44-45). Even if your in-laws have been enemies to you, God calls you to love, speak blessing, do good and pray for them (Luke 6:27-28). (**Homework:** Read the following biblical texts to understand how God asks you to treat those He has placed in your life: Leviticus 19:18; Matthew 5:38-49; and Matthew 22:34-40. Answer these questions from the biblical texts you just read: What did you learn about God? What did you learn about yourself? How do your thinking, feelings and actions need to change considering these truths?)

Obey God: Treat your in-laws with honor and respect—the way you wish to be treated (Luke 6:31). (**Homework:** Spend time with God in His Word each day; attend worship at your church each week; and ask your mate to hold you accountable for your heart attitudes and behaviors toward his or her parents. Memorize Luke 6:27-28 and put it into practice in the way you relate to your in-laws).

Boundaries: If you or your spouse are clinging too tightly to your parents, you must set clear boundaries. You or your spouse cannot run to your parents every time you get into a fight; this is not what marriage is about. You have entered a covenant relationship with God and this other person. (**Homework:** Start by praying with your spouse and asking God to bless your relationship. Then, have a relationship about where you think your in-laws are too involved in your relationship, and begin to work on a plan together to set boundaries.)

Study Your Family: Learn what cultural expectations or habitual patterns each family engages in and adjust accordingly. (**Homework:** Sit down with your spouse and discuss what each of the in-laws think about a topic, and together, pray how you as a married couple can honor God first, your spouse second, your kids third, and your parents fourth with your mutually agreed upon decision as to how you will handle the topic.)

Prioritize Your Immediate Family: While respecting and loving extended family is crucial, prioritizing your immediate family's needs and boundaries echoes the biblical injunction to leave father and mother and unite with one's spouse. Focus on highlighting the balance between honoring extended family and nurturing the immediate family unit (Gen 2:24). (**Homework:** Discuss limitations with your spouse/partner and ensure you agree.)

Patience and Humility: Approach in-law relationships with patience, humility, and understanding. It is a perfect time to live out what Jesus said about loving one another and treating others with kindness (Eph 4:2). (**Homework:** Think of an in-law you've had difficulty with and commit to a specific act of kindness toward them this week.)

Open Communication: Establish clear communication lines with in-laws, ensuring that expectations and boundaries are mutually understood, which goes with the biblical encouragement for honest, loving communication (Eph 4:25). (**Homework:** Schedule a family chat or dinner where everyone can openly communicate their feelings and expectations thus promoting understanding.)

DISCUSSION STARTERS

1. **Setting Boundaries in Marriage:** Genesis 2:24 emphasizes the importance of a married couple forming their own unit. How have you and your spouse established boundaries with in-laws to protect your marital relationship? In instances where these boundaries might have been crossed, how can you approach these situations biblically and ensure that your marriage remains the primary focus while still respecting and honoring your extended family?

2. **Embracing Cultural Differences and Practices:** Laban's statement in Genesis 29:25-26 points to the unique practices and cultures within families. How have you and your spouse navigated and reconciled the cultural or habitual differences between your in-law families? How can you find a middle ground that considers both families' traditions and ensures your relationship with God and each other remains central?

3. **Cultivating Love and Loyalty in In-Law Relationships**: Ruth's loyalty to Naomi in Ruth 1:16-17 highlights the potential depth of in-law relationships. Have you experienced moments where you have felt a strong bond or faced challenges with your in-laws? How can Ruth's dedication inspire you to approach these relationships with patience, understanding, and a commitment to unity even amidst potential conflicts or misunderstandings?

LAZINESS

A lack of motivation for work or necessary tasks leads to inaction. At its core, laziness can be a spiritual issue and reflect a heart misaligned from God's purpose for mankind. The Bible consistently portrays work as a task that serves and glorifies God. Laziness is not just a reluctance to engage in physical labor but can be seen as a resistance to fulfilling the God-given mandate to labor and be fruitful. It is vital to differentiate between the genuine need for rest, as God modeled on the seventh day, and the habitual avoidance of responsibility. When counseling, it is essential to discern the heart behind the inaction and guide individuals to line up with God's purpose and find joy in their labor for His glory.

Go to the ant, you slacker! Observe its ways and become wise.
Without leader, administrator, or ruler, it prepares its provisions in summer;
it gathers its food during harvest
Prov 6:6-8

Using Proverbs 6:6-8 as a guide, we can draw lessons from the diligent ant emphasizing foresight and hard work. Without any overseer, this tiny creature gathers food during harvest preparing for less plentiful times. This proactive behavior showcases the significance of initiative and planning. In contrast, laziness can result in unpreparedness and ensuing hardship. Emulating the ant's work ethic promotes the value of consistent effort and highlights the drawbacks of procrastination. It is a reminder of the importance of staying active and planning. The message is clear: preparing today can prevent potential challenges tomorrow.

> *The slacker does not plow during planting season;*
> *at harvest time, he looks, and there is nothing.*
> **Prov 20:4**

This verse provides an insightful observation about the consequences of avoiding work when it is due. This scripture points to a person unwilling to plow during the season, which illustrates the shortsightedness of laziness. Consequently, they need something to reap at harvest time. This teaches that avoiding responsibilities in the present can result in a lack of benefits in the future. The wisdom conveyed is about understanding the relationship between effort and reward. Laziness might offer momentary comfort but results in missed opportunities in the long run. Embracing diligence and foresight can help prevent future regrets and losses.

> *In fact, when we were with you, this is what we commanded you:*
> *"If anyone isn't willing to work, he should not eat."*
> **2 Thess 3:10**

This passage addresses the issue of idleness, declaring that those who do not work should not eat. Such a critical principle emphasizes the importance of individual responsibility and the idea that effort should precede reward. It encourages personal initiative and discourages dependency without genuine need. Essentially, it warns against the pitfalls of becoming complacent or expecting undeserved entitlements. Such teachings act as a deterrent against laziness and highlight the consequences it can bring both in spiritual and practical terms. The underlying message is clear: Hard work and diligence are virtuous and should be integral to one's character. Through such teachings, the scripture prompts reflection on the value of work in one's life.

Laziness

Then the Lord God took the man and put him into
the garden of Eden to cultivate it and keep it.
Gen 2:15

God created man to work, be productive, and manage His creation. Work was pleasant before the Fall of Man, but after the Fall, work became difficult (Gen 3:17-19). Christians need to understand that while work is challenging due to sin in the world, we were designed to work even before sin entered it. When mankind is productive, contributing to society, earning an income, and doing his best unto the Lord; he is fulfilling part of his purpose on earth. Laziness is the opposite of working hard unto the Lord and is sinful. While other passages can address the attitude we serve with, the relationships we serve, and the overall work ethic of a Christian; this passage addresses the bottom line that mankind was created with the capacity and God-given command to work from the beginning.

A little sleep, a little slumber, a little folding of
the arms to rest, and your poverty will come
like a robber, your need, like a bandit.
Prov 24:33-34

In his characteristic wisdom, Solomon presents a vivid depiction of the outcome of repeated laziness. The imagery he uses of slowly giving in to the temptation to rest excessively is something to which many can relate. The consequences of such behavior are stark: unexpected poverty and need. This Scripture is not a call to avoid physical sleep but a broader warning against the dangers of complacency. By heeding this counsel, one recognizes that repeated inaction can lead to unforeseen difficulties. It is an invitation to remain vigilant, to be proactive, and to understand that laziness has real-world implications. This passage should motivate individuals to break out of the idleness cycle and pursue diligence with a renewed sense of purpose.

Whatever you do, do it from the heart,
as something done for the Lord and not for people.
Col 3:23

This New Testament admonition by Paul serves as an excellent antidote to laziness. The verse underscores that our work is not merely for earthly purposes or recognition but is a form of worship unto God. By viewing even the most mundane tasks as acts of service to the Lord, the motivation to be diligent increases manifold. This scripture serves as a reminder that our primary audience is God. Our perspective shifts when we work with Him in mind. Instead of succumbing to laziness due to a lack of immediate gratification or acknowledgment, one finds purpose in even the most minor tasks. It is a call to elevate our work ethic because we know that our labor is never in vain when done for the Lord. This mindset can inspire individuals to replace complacency with a sense of purpose and spiritual responsibility.

PRACTICAL ADVICE + HOMEWORK

Confess Sin: If you are lazy, you must confess this sin. At the heart of this sinful behavior is a selfish desire to serve yourself and your own desires rather than God and others. (**Homework:** If this is true in your case, stop right now and confess the sin to God and to any you have wronged through your selfish attitude and its behavioral expression in idleness.)

Renew Your Mind through Scripture: God commands us to work diligently for Him (Col 3:23). (**Homework:** Read the following biblical texts to understand how God sees and responds to laziness: Proverbs 6:6-11; Proverbs 24:30-34; Colossians 3:22-25; and 2 Thessalonians 3:6-10. Answer these questions from the biblical texts you just read: What did you learn about God? What did you learn about yourself? How do your thinking, feelings and actions need to change considering these truths?)

Laziness

Obey God: Put off laziness and putting on diligence. (**Homework:** Spend time with God in His Word each day, attend worship at your church each week, in whatever work God gives you to do, do it diligently so that He is glorified, memorize Colossians 3:23-24 to correct your thinking about personal laziness.)

Value Preparation: Understand the importance of preparing and working ahead, ensuring future success, and avoiding last-minute panic. It features the biblical truth that promotes planning and foresight (Prov 21:5). (**Homework:** Plan out your upcoming week, breaking them into manageable daily goals.)

Commit to Responsibility: Recognize that your responsibilities and the consequences of neglecting them reverberates with the biblical principle that everyone is accountable for their actions and must uphold their responsibilities (Gal 6:5). (**Homework:** List responsibilities you have been avoiding and tackle at least one each day for the next week.)

Find Meaningful Work: Engage in projects you find meaningful and fulfilling to ignite your passion and drive and connect with the scriptural emphasis on doing work wholeheartedly as unto the Lord (Col 3:23-24). (**Homework:** Dedicate some time to a passion project or hobby you have been putting off due to laziness or procrastination.)

Seek Accountability: Share your goals with a trusted friend or family member who can encourage your progress. This reflects the Christian notion of fellowship and mutual encouragement (Heb 10:24-25.) (**Homework:** Share your weekly plan with someone close and ask them to check in on your progress throughout the week.)

Serve Others and Give: Serving the needs of others is a function of the Church. Finding ways to give of our time, energy, and resources to help another is both a command and fulfilling as a Christian. (**Homework:** Ask your pastor or a church leader how you can serve the local body this week and do it. This might be cutting grass for a widow, babysitting a child for a single mom, or even cleaning the church bathrooms—all for no pay.)

DISCUSSION STARTERS

1. **Cultivating Diligence in a World of Distraction:** Given the proverbial call to examine the diligent ant in Proverbs 6:6-8, how do you see modern distractions contributing to the rise of laziness in society? How might the lessons from the ant teach us to overcome these distractions and prioritize our God-given tasks?

2. **Consequences of Avoiding Responsibility:** Drawing from Proverbs 20:4 where the slacker finds nothing at harvest time due to avoiding his duties, how have you personally experienced the results of neglecting responsibilities? How can these real-life experiences, paired with Scripture motivate you to change your behavior and serve God and others diligently?

3. **Recognizing the Spiritual Implications of Laziness:** Considering the strong directive in 2 Thessalonians 3:10 on work and the right to eat, do you feel that sometimes laziness is not just a personal flaw but can have spiritual ramifications? How can understanding this deeper dimension of laziness inspire a more fervent commitment to diligence?

LONELINESS

Derived from the biblical understanding that it is not suitable for man to be alone, loneliness is the sense of isolation and disconnection from others. As sheep are safest under the vigilant watch of their Shepherd, so too are believers safeguarded in the fellowship of the Body of Christ. Straying from this communal fold can leave one vulnerable, akin to a solitary house susceptible to robbery or a lone vessel on turbulent waters prone to the perils of the adversarial pirate, Satan. In biblical counseling, addressing loneliness requires comforting the afflicted and guiding them toward godly fellowship and reminding them of the strength of collective worship and shared faith.

God provides homes for those who are deserted.
He leads out the prisoners to prosperity,
but the rebellious live in a scorched land
Ps 68:6

This Psalm speaks to God's heart for those who feel isolated by emphasizing that He places the lonely in families. It serves as a reminder of God's unceasing love and desire to see every individual integrated into a community. Loneliness can be a harrowing experience, but this verse reassures us that God is both aware of and cares about the lonely state of individuals. The imagery of God placing solitary souls into families underscores His commitment to relational healing and connection. Furthermore, the verse encourages individuals to seek out spiritual communities or churches where they might find familial bonds and overcome feelings of isolation. This scripture beautifully showcases God's intent that he does not desire anyone to walk through life alone. He seeks instead to envelop them in love and community.

> *Do not fear, for I am with you; do not be afraid,*
> *for I am your God. I will strengthen you; I will help*
> *you; I will hold on to you with my righteous right hand.*
> **Isa 41:10**

This verse is a powerful testament to God's promise of presence and support especially during moments of loneliness. It assures individuals that God stands steadfastly beside them even in solitude. God's commitment remains unwavering even when human relationships falter or fail to provide the necessary companionship. The call not to fear emphasizes God's role as a protector and comforter. By highlighting God's strength and help, the verse suggests a divine fortification against the pangs of isolation. Those battling loneliness can find solace in knowing they are never truly alone with God. This Scripture is a beacon of hope as it reminds individuals of God's constant companionship amid life's lonely stretches.

> *Even if my father and mother abandon me, the Lord cares for me.*
> **Ps 27:10**

King David comforts those who are lonely by emphasizing that God's love remains steadfast even when familial and human connections falter. The verse speaks directly to the fear of abandonment, which can be a robust root of loneliness. Its assertion that God will take care of the forsaken confirms that no one is ever truly alone. This idea can incredibly comfort individuals who have been rejected or feel isolated from their families or communities. It highlights the connection between the individual and God that transcending human relationships. By reflecting on this verse, those grappling with loneliness can foster a deeper spiritual connection and know they are cared for by Christ. It serves as a spiritual anchor providing hope and solace in solitude.

Jesus came near and said to them, "All authority has been given to me in heaven and earth. Go, therefore, and make disciples of all nations, baptizing them in the name of the Father and of the Son and of the Holy Spirit, teaching them to observe everything that I have commanded you; and remember, I am with you always, to the end of the age."
Matt 28:18-20

This passage, often referred to as the Great Commission, concludes with Jesus telling the disciples that He is with them even until the end. Ministering in a dark world is difficult. Teaching others what God desires from them and seeing people turn away from Christ and abandon His teachings hurts. Still, we must take hold of the truth that even if others turn from us, HE is with us! We are not only serving the Lord but serving with Him. The local church body is where we serve and find like-minded relationships where we never walk the Christian walk alone. Regardless of how we feel, we are never alone, even if we are sent out to make disciples alone.

A friend loves at all times, and a brother is born for adversity.
Prov 17:17

This proverb highlights the importance and value of friendship and familial bonds during trying times. It signifies that genuine relationships stand firm through life's peaks and valleys. For those grappling with loneliness, this Scripture serves as an encouragement to seek and nurture such steadfast relationships. The verse also underscores the value of being part of a faith community where one can find brothers and sisters in Christ. Grounded in mutual faith, these relationships can offer companionship and understanding. It also suggests that such faith-based friendships can provide much-needed solace and connection in times of loneliness.

Two are better than one because they have a good reward for their efforts.
For if either fall, his companion can lift him up;
but pity the one who falls without another to lift him up.
Eccl 4:9-10

This passage from Ecclesiastes highlights the tangible benefits of companionship. At its core, Ecclesiastes is a commentary on the human need for connection and the advantages of mutual support. Those battling loneliness can be encouraged by the understanding that God acknowledges our need for fellowship. It is a Scripture that endorses seeking companionship and the importance of being there for others. Having someone by your side can make all the difference in life's challenges. This verse also encourages individuals to actively seek out community through church groups, bible studies, or outreach programs. In that community, they might find the companionship that upholds and supports just as the scripture describes.

PRACTICAL ADVICE + HOMEWORK

Confess Sin: If you have sinned in your loneliness by failing to turn to God for comfort and are looking to be satisfied with human companionship only, you must confess this sin. (**Homework:** If this is true in your situation, stop right now and confess the sin of neglect and idolatry to God and to any you have mistreated because of this sinful pattern of worship.)

Renew Your Mind through Scripture: God commands us to worship Him only (Ex 20:3). (**Homework:** Read the following biblical texts to understand how God sees and responds to loneliness: Psalm 25:8-18; Psalm 68:3-6; and Romans 8:35-38. Answer these questions from the biblical texts you just read: What did you learn about God? What did you learn about yourself? How do your thinking, feelings, and actions need to change considering these truths?)

Loneliness

Obey God: Use the distress of loneliness as a cause to seek Him. (**Homework:** Spend time with God in His Word each day, attend worship at your church each week, join a small group for fellowship and accountability, and serve others so that your focus is not on your loneliness but on their needs).

God's Presence: In times of solitude, remember that God is always there. Embrace your connection with Him. Find comfort in the promises in scripture like Deuteronomy 31:6, which assures us of God's presence by our side. (**Homework:** Dedicate ten minutes each morning to quiet reflection or meditation, focusing on God's presence in your life.)

Service to Others: Serving others can alleviate isolation and create connections. It would help if you were proactive in getting out of your bubble and doing something. One of the best ways to overcome a pity party is to help others. This goes hand in hand with Christ's teaching of loving and serving our neighbors (Gal 5:13-14), promoting a sense of connection and purpose. (**Homework:** Volunteer for a local charity or community service activity in the upcoming month.)

Stay Connected: Reach out to friends or family even if it's been a while. Relationships require effort and nurturing. Your network of friends is not what you have on social media platforms. It is the living, breathing individuals with who you can spend time. (**Homework:** Call or message someone with who you have not recently spoken and reconnect.)

Serving Alone to Music: If your job or ministry involves extended times of isolation (*e.g.,* a truck driver, homeschool teacher, single adult working from home), utilize Christian music that is uplifting with lyrics that encourage. (**Homework:** When feelings of loneliness hit you, have a music playlist available to get your mind on the truth of His presence.)

DISCUSSION STARTERS

1. **Finding Family in Faith:** Psalm 68:6 talks about those who have been deserted. Considering God's heart for the isolated and how He places the lonely in families, how do you perceive the church or faith community's role in providing solace during isolation? How have you experienced God's love and intention for connection in your spiritual community?

2. **Assurance of God's Constant Companionship:** Isaiah 41:10 provides a powerful affirmation of God's presence during moments of loneliness. How can you anchor your heart in this truth when feelings of isolation seem overwhelming? Reflecting on this verse, what steps can you take to cultivate a daily awareness of God's unwavering companionship?

3. **The Enduring Nature of God's Love Amidst Human Rejection:** In Psalm 27:10, David emphasizes that even when familial and human connections fail, the Lord's care remains. How does this assurance impact your perspective on loneliness or feelings of rejection? How might leaning into this truth your relationship with God and others?

LUST

Lust is a sinful desire emanating from the heart, characterized by an intense longing that often leads individuals away from God's righteous path. It is the inner genesis of transgressions. It anchors itself in the heart, which is the epicenter of moral discernment and spiritual vigor. Lusts are the very entities that captivate our desires and diver a person's focus from divine purpose and truth. If left unchecked, such overpowering urges can disrupt one's relationship with the Lord and the pursuit of His righteousness.

> *But I tell you, everyone who looks at a woman lustfully*
> *has already committed adultery with her in his heart.*
> **Matt 5:28**

Jesus delves into the complex issue of lust by going beyond mere physical actions to consider even a lustful look akin to adultery. The gravity of this statement emphasizes the seriousness with which the matter should be taken and highlights that purity of thought is as essential as purity of action. This verse pushes individuals to reflect on the nature of desire and recognizes that unchecked lust can lead to harmful thoughts and actions. Encouraging self-awareness and conscious control of one's thoughts serves as a call to cultivate inner integrity. It promotes a broader understanding of faithfulness and commitment and urges believers to be mindful indeed and thought. For someone struggling with lust, meditating on this verse can be a challenging yet transformative exercise that underscores the need for personal growth and spiritual maturity. This passage helps to guide individuals towards a more disciplined and thoughtful approach to relationships and personal conduct.

I have made a covenant with my eyes.
How then could I look at a young woman?
Job 31:1

Job 31:1 speaks to the commitment to setting boundaries for oneself particularly in lust. It highlights the importance of personal integrity and self-control even in the privacy of one's thoughts. In a culture that often minimizes or normalizes lustful desires, this passage serves as a reminder to be intentional about guarding one's heart and mind. This verse provides conviction and encouragement for someone struggling with lust to take proactive steps to manage his/her behavior. It emphasizes personal responsibility while also acknowledging the complexity of human desire. One may find strength and guidance to combat lustful tendencies by aligning oneself with this scriptural principle. Ultimately, it offers a timeless and powerful insight into how a person might live with integrity and honor in this critical aspect of life.

Flee sexual immorality! Every other sin a person commits is outside the
body, but the person who is sexually immoral sins against his own body.
Don't you know that your body is a temple of the Holy Spirit who is in you,
whom you have from God? You are not your own, for you were bought
at a price. So, glorify God with your body.
1 Cor 6:18-20

Paul states that our bodies are not our own but are temples of the Holy Spirit. For someone struggling with lust, this teaching emphasizes the sacredness of the human body and urges a perspective that sees sexual purity not just as a moral ideal but as a form of worship. Understanding one's body as something sacred that belongs to God can be a powerful motivator to pursue purity and honor in all sexual matters. The passage also provides a broader context by connecting physical actions with spiritual consequences. It offers encouragement for those seeking to live a life in alignment with spiritual principles. By recognizing the body as a vessel for the Divine, a person may find new strength and perspective in the struggle against lust. This approach to understanding the human body leads to more respect for oneself and others while offering a unique and compelling reason to strive for purity.

> *Among them, we too all formerly lived in the lusts of our flesh,*
> *indulging the desires of the flesh and of the mind, and were by nature*
> *children of wrath, even as the rest. But God, being rich in mercy,*
> *because of His great love with which He loved us, even when we were*
> *dead in our transgressions, made us alive together with Christ*
> *(by grace you have been saved), and raised us up with Him, and*
> *seated us with Him in the heavenly places in Christ Jesus,*
> *so that in the ages to come He might show the surpassing riches*
> *of His grace in kindness toward us in Christ Jesus.*
> **Eph 2:3-7**

As unsaved people, our lives were defined by sinful living, speaking, and thinking. We sought every source of happiness, pleasure, and want of which we could take hold. However, those sins we passionately desired are the marks against us that had us heading for wrath (Rom 6:23). When Jesus saved us, he saved us *from* a life of sin *to* a life of holiness. Our desires changed the more we focused on the changes brought about as a result of our salvation. We began to crave the things of God and choke out the former desires replacing them with Godly ones. As Christians, we have no right to lust or long for sinful pleasure.

> *Keep your heart with all vigilance,*
> *for from it flow the springs of life.*
> **Prov 4:23**

A Biblical Handbook for Counseling Heart Issues

Solomon's wise words in this proverb highlight the significance of guarding one's heart, the epicenter of all emotions and desires, from lust. This Scripture emphasizes that what we allow into our hearts can influence our entire lives. It serves as a stark reminder to remain vigilant against lustful thoughts and desires by considering the impact these negative things can have on our lives. For someone grappling with lust, this verse encourages a proactive stance in guarding the mind and heart against inappropriate or harmful desires. It underscores the reality that purity does not just involve avoiding explicit external actions and maintaining inner sanctity. Reflecting on this Scripture can guide individuals to prioritize emotional and spiritual health. Acknowledging that our inner life directly influences our outward behavior is an excellent first step. A disciplined heart leads to a righteous life.

> *Let your fountain be blessed, and rejoice with the wife of your youth,*
> *a lovely deer, a graceful doe. Let her breasts satisfy you always;*
> *may you be captivated by her love forever*
> **Prov 5:18-19**

Solomon provides a beautiful portrayal of marital love and intimacy in these verses. True satisfaction can be found within the bounds of a committed relationship. The bond of marriage serves as an alternative vision to the fleeting pleasures of lustful pursuits. For individuals struggling with lust, these verses offer a perspective that values deep, committed, and enduring love over transient passions. It encourages cultivating and appreciating genuine, loving relationships and emphasizes their capacity to bring true joy and contentment. Such love is to be cherished and celebrated, offering a fulfilling alternative to the temptations of lust. By refocusing on this biblical ideal of love and marital intimacy, one can be guided towards more wholesome desires and away from the snares of lustful enticements. It is a reminder that true satisfaction is found in genuine love and commitment.

PRACTICAL ADVICE + HOMEWORK

Confess Sin: The sin of lust must be put off through confession (Eph 4:17-24). (**Homework:** If this is true in your situation, stop right now and confess the sin of lust to God and to anyone you mistreat because of this sinful response pattern.)

Renew Your Mind through Scripture: God commands us to be morally pure (1 Thess 4:3-5). (**Homework:** Read the following biblical texts to understand how God sees and responds to lust: Matthew 5:27-28; 1 Corinthians 6:13-20; 1 Thessalonians 4:3-8; James 1:13-15; and 1 John 2:15-17. Answer these questions from the biblical texts you read: What did you learn about God? What did you learn about yourself? How do your thinking, feelings, and actions need to change considering these truths?)

Obey God: Put off lust immediately (Eph 4:17-24). (**Homework:** Spend time with God in His Word each day, attend worship at your church each week, flee from things (places, people, movies, music, etc.) that elicit lustful responses (1 Cor 6:28).

Guard Your Heart and Mind: Be conscious of what you allow into your mind through media, conversations, and daily interactions. This echoes Jesus' teachings on the purity of thought, acknowledging that sin can start within the mind (Matt 5:28). (**Homework:** Avoid movies, series, or songs that may promote or glorify lustful behaviors and note any changes in your thoughts for one week.)

Value and Respect: Cultivate a mindset that values and respects everyone as individuals not objects of desire, and emphasizes seeing others through a Christ-like lens, which honors their intrinsic worth as beings created in God's image. (**Homework:** Write down and reflect on the inherent value of individuals. Consider their personalities, contributions, and worth outside of physical attraction.)

Engage in Spiritual Practices: Nurturing your spiritual life can help you face and overcome temptations. It allows you to deepen your connection with God and strengthen your determination. This is seen in the teachings of Paul regarding self-discipline (Gal 5:22-23). (**Homework:** Dedicate fifteen minutes daily to prayer, meditation, or reading spiritual literature focusing on purity and self-control.)

Seek Biblical Wisdom: Consider seeking counseling and pastoral care if lustful thoughts and actions are overwhelming. Reaching out for help further ensures a well-rounded approach by utilizing spiritual guidance to conquer temptation. (**Homework:** Research local counseling services or join Biblical Wisdom Groups.)

Starve the Flesh: Paul said as lost people, we "indulged the flesh" (Eph 2:3-7); therefore, as Christians, when we find ourselves desiring sin, we must not fall into temptation. (**Homework:** Identify the sinful desires or lusts that you are struggling with and identify two or three practices that you engage in that feed these desires. Develop a plan to cease feeding the lust with practices in your life that feed holiness instead.)

DISCUSSION STARTERS

1. **Understanding Personal Boundaries:** Considering Job's commitment mentioned in Job 31:1 where he made a covenant with his eyes not to look lustfully, have you considered setting specific boundaries for yourself? How do these boundaries reflect your commitment to honor God and maintain personal integrity, especially in the face of pervasive societal influences?

2. **Valuing the Temple of the Holy Spirit:** With 1 Corinthians 6:18-20 emphasizing our bodies as temples of the Holy Spirit, how do you view and value your body in this context? How can this per-

spective shape your choices and behaviors, especially regarding sexual purity and honoring God with your actions?

3. **The Journey from Lust to Love:** Drawing from Proverbs 5:18-19, which highlights the beauty and satisfaction of marital love, how can you redirect lustful desires towards building and cherishing genuine love and intimacy? How does understanding and appreciating the biblical portrayal of love guide you to find fulfillment and contentment in your relationships?

MARRIAGE

Sometimes referred to as "holy matrimony," marriage represents a union God instituted. This sacred bond, designed for one man and one woman, is oriented towards procreation and is underscored by a covenantal promise. It is a lifelong commitment reflecting Christ's unwavering love for the Church. In this relationship, couples are called to love, honor, and cherish one another. This relationship mirrors God's steadfast love and faithfulness for them and for others.

Husbands, love your wives, just as Christ
loved the church and gave himself for her.
Eph 5:25

Paul calls husbands to love their wives just as Christ loved the church and gave himself up for her. For couples experiencing marriage issues, this verse can be a reminder of the sacrificial, selfless love required in a relationship. It encourages partners, especially husbands, to prioritize the needs and well-being of their spouse even above their own desires or comfort. By applying this principle, couples can work towards fostering an environment of mutual respect, compassion, and understanding. The love described here is not based on fleeting emotions but on a deliberate choice to act lovingly regardless of circumstances. In the context of marriage difficulties, this call to Christ-like love can provide both a challenge and an inspiration by guiding couples towards reconciliation and deeper connection. This verse serves as a significant touchstone for couples seeking to align their marriage with spiritual principles and find healing amid conflict.

A man who finds a wife finds a good thing
and obtains favor from the Lord.
Proverbs 18:22

This proverb offers wisdom regarding the value of finding a good spouse, comparing it to finding favor with the Lord. For couples struggling with marriage issues, this verse can serve as an essential reminder of the intrinsic value of their relationship and the potential for it to be a source of blessing. Seeing marriage as something positive and God-ordained can inspire couples to invest time and effort into nurturing their relationship. This verse may also prompt couples to reflect on the qualities that initially drew them together and consider how they might foster those qualities anew. Emphasizing the value of a good spouse might lead them to seek pastoral counseling to address and resolve their issues. It is a gentle encouragement to view marriage not merely as a social contract but as a spiritual covenant with significant worth. Ultimately, this perspective can foster a sense of commitment and optimism which will guide couples to work on their problems rather than abandon the relationship.

Love is patient, love is kind. Love does not envy, is not boastful, is not arrogant,
is not rude, is not self-seeking, is not irritable, and does not keep a record of
wrongs. Love finds no joy in unrighteousness but rejoices in the truth. It bears
all things, believes all things, hopes all things, endures all things.
1 Cor 13:4-7

1 Corinthians 13:4-7 is often cited in the context of love and is particularly relevant for couples facing marital difficulties. This passage defines love as patient, kind, and enduring. By providing this detailed definition, it offers couples a blueprint to assess and develop their behavior toward one

another. These principles can encourage a more compassionate and empathetic approach for those struggling with conflicts or misunderstandings. The emphasis on love's perseverance can be a reminder that every relationship encounters challenges, and working through them with grace can lead to growth and deepened connection. By applying these principles, couples can shift focus from their problems to the potential of their love. This focus shift fosters a more positive and nurturing environment within the relationship. These verses provide a valuable framework to help couples understand what love should look like and how they might strive to embody these qualities in their relationship.

Let your fountain be blessed and rejoice in the wife of your youth.
As a loving hind and a graceful doe, let her breasts satisfy you at all times;
Be exhilarated always with her love. For why should you, my son,
be exhilarated with an adulteress and embrace the bosom of a foreigner?
Prov 5:18-20

Solomon writes these words to warn the reader of an adulteress woman; however, there is still an encouraging point for married couples in this passage. The marriage relationship is supposed to be exhilarating. Men and women are often attracted to each other based on shared interests, the excitement of getting to know someone new, and even their physical appearance. The temptation to divorce or be unfaithful in marriage can come from the desire to find something exhilarating. While not every day will be a romantic fairy tale, Christian spouses should nurture intimacy in their marriages to encourage an exciting life together that is mutually enjoyed. Additionally, this lessens the temptations of lust spouses may face.

Therefore, what God has joined together, let no one separate.
Mark 10:9

In Mark 10:9, Jesus speaks about the sanctity and permanence of the marital bond. For couples encountering difficulties in their marriage, this verse serves as a crucial reminder that God orchestrated their union. Each marriage carries a divine seal of commitment. Recognizing that marriage is not just a personal contract but a covenant before God can instill a sense of reverence and responsibility in husbands and wives to uphold the marriage covenant. This Scripture challenges couples to resist external influences or transient emotions that might push them towards separation and instead seek God's guidance in preserving and nurturing their relationship. Drawing strength from this divine affirmation, couples find encouragement to face challenges head-on by embracing the potential for restoration and growth. This verse reinforces the idea that marriages are meant to be lasting commitments. Understanding the sanctity attached to marriage should urge spouses to rely on God's wisdom and grace in their journey together.

PRACTICAL ADVICE + HOMEWORK

Confess Sin: Marriage is designed to picture Christ and His relationship to His people (Eph 5:22-33). If your personal sin obscures the picture He intends to paint through your marriage, put off that sin for the sake of all in this relationship—your God, your spouse, and you. (**Homework:** If this is true in your situation, confess your sins to God and your spouse.)

Renew Your Mind through Scripture: God commands us to conduct ourselves in our marriages according to His plan and purpose. (**Homework:** Read the following biblical texts to understand God's directives for marriage: Genesis 2:18-25; Ephesians 5:22-33; and 1 Peter 3:1-7. Answer these questions from the biblical texts you read: What did you learn about God? What did you learn about yourself? How do your thinking, feelings, and actions need to change considering these truths?)

Obey God: Make a commitment, with God's help, to make your marriage the picture God designed it to be (Eph 5:22-33). (**Homework:** Spend time with God in His Word each day, attend worship together each week, and find a couple with a solid marriage to mentor you and your spouse as you grow together in your love for God and each other.)

Selfless Love: Model your love in marriage after Christ's selfless love for the church, reflecting Christ's love for the church (Eph 5:25), encourages spouses to act selflessly and with compassion. (**Homework:** Write a letter or talk with your spouse about a recent time they showcased selfless love and express your gratitude.)

Practice Patience and Kindness: Embrace the qualities of love described in 1 Corinthians in your marriage as it sets the standard for interaction between spouses. (**Homework:** For a week, consciously avoid reacting in anger or frustration to your spouse. Instead, respond with patience and understanding.)

Open Communication: Always be transparent, honest, and kind in your communication because it reflects the biblical principles of loving your neighbor as yourself (Mark 12:31) and speaking the truth in love (Eph 4:15). This approach nurtures trust and unity, embodying the oneness and mutual respect that God intends for the marital relationship (Gen 2:24). (**Homework:** Set aside time each week for uninterrupted conversations, discussing both joys and challenges.)

Seek Wisdom Together: Regularly study scriptures and pray to ground your marriage in biblical truth. Couples who spend time together in the Word, nurturing spiritual growth and unity, are following the psalmist's wisdom that blessed are those who meditate on God's law (Ps 1:1-2). (**Homework:** Begin a weekly Bible study or devotional reading with your spouse. Focusing on marriage-related verses or topics.)

Date Night/Event: Think back to things you did together early in marriage before kids, careers, or anything else that may have stifled the excitement of the marriage intimacy. Plan how to rekindle those passions with each seeking to serve the other.

DISCUSSION STARTERS

1. **Sacrificial Love in Action:** Reflecting on Ephesians 5:25, which calls on husbands to love their wives as Christ loved the church, how can you see this form of sacrificial love play out in your day-to-day interactions? How might embodying this Christ-like love transform the dynamics of your relationship, especially during moments of tension or disagreement?

2. **Rediscovering the Value of Your Union:** Proverbs 18:22 speaks of the blessing and favor one obtains from the Lord when finding a good wife. Can you recall moments when you truly felt this favor in your relationship? How can you both actively recognize and cherish the worth of your partnership, especially in challenging times? How can you draw strength from the belief that your union is God-ordained?

3. **Defining Love in Your Marriage:** Based on the attributes of love described in 1 Corinthians 13:4-7, how do you view love's role in your marriage? As you assess your behavior and interactions, which attributes come naturally and which need more intentional effort? How might embracing these characteristics shape your relationship into a more compassionate and enduring bond?

MOODINESS

Moodiness refers to disposition characterized by abrupt shifts in emotional states often transitioning swiftly from contentment to anger or sadness. While mood fluctuations are a natural part of the human experience, consistent patterns of moodiness may indicate underlying heart issues that need addressing through godly wisdom, self-examination, and the application of biblical truths. In biblical counseling, the goal is not merely to suppress or regulate emotions but to understand their root cause and align one's heart with the transformative power of God's Word.

Why, my soul, are you so dejected? Why are
you in such turmoil? Put your hope in God,
for I will still praise him, my Savior, and my God
Ps 42:11

The pertinence of Psalm 42:11 to moodiness lies in its call to self-examination and trust in God. Amid emotional turmoil, this verse addresses one's soul by asking why it is downcast. This reflective question encourages people to confront and understand their feelings, promoting self-awareness. The verse also directs the soul to hope in God because faith and trust in God can provide stability and perspective during emotional ups and downs. A moody or downcast individual may find a source of comfort and direction by focusing on a spiritual connection. Despite feelings of hopelessness, the instruction to praise God can also serve as a tool to shift focus away from temporary emotions toward eternal truths. In this way, Psalm 42:11 provides both a method of self-inquiry and a spiritual solution. It offers wisdom and comfort to those dealing with moodiness.

When I was a child, I used to speak like a child,
think like a child, reason like a child; when I
became a man, I did away with childish things.
1 Cor 13:11

As we mature in Christ, the customary practice of obedience in our lives transforms much of our thinking, speaking, and acting. Moodiness is often described as an oscillation of emotions ranging from pleasant to raging at the flip of a switch. It can also be described as easily triggered into fits of whining, irritability, or aggressiveness. When very young, children learn to develop and regulate their emotions. Children meltdown over seemingly nothing, get excited over the simplest things, and turn around and act out when irritated. Mature believers in Christ must understand that God expects us to grow past the baby stages and into maturity. This growth also assumes we will learn to think like adults, process our emotions and feelings like adults, and then live our daily lives with self-control rather than moodiness.

Now we have this treasure in clay jars, so that this
extraordinary power may be from God and not from us.
We are afflicted in every way but not crushed; we are
perplexed but not in despair; we are persecuted but
not abandoned; we are struck down but not destroyed.
2 Cor 4:7-9

Paul speaks to the resilience of the human Spirit in the face of trials, which is a message that should resonate with those struggling with moodiness. These verses depict how fragile we are and liken people to earthen vessels containing a divine treasure. The emphasis on being struck down but not destroyed acknowledges that life may be filled with challenges and emotions that are difficult to navigate. This metaphorical language invites an understanding that while moodiness may arise from life's hardships, it does not define or control one's existence. Through these verses, we recognize that God's strength is revealed in our weakness. By faith, individuals can persevere through the ups and downs of their moods. Thus, 2 Corinthians 4:7-9 offers empathy and empowerment to those grappling with moodiness when it points to a spiritual perspective that transcends temporary emotional states.

> *You will keep the mind that is dependent*
> *on you in perfect peace, for it is trusting in you*
> **Isa 26:3**

This verse offers insight into finding peace and stability even in moodiness. It underscores the importance of focusing on God and promises that those who keep their minds steadfast on Him will experience perfect peace. This principle can be applied to someone struggling with moodiness as it suggests that a close relationship with God can bring emotional balance. Turning one's attention to faith can give us a perspective that transcends immediate emotional reactions. The verse encourages a deep trust in God which can help moderate mood swings and develop a more consistent emotional state. It is a reminder that God's unchanging nature can provide a steadying influence on our ever-changing emotions. Isaiah 26:3 offers a spiritual path to address moodiness by emphasizing the importance of trust in God and rely on him.

> *The Lord is my shepherd; I have what I need.*
> *He lets me lie down in green pastures; he leads me beside quiet waters.*
> *He renews my soul; he guides me along the right paths for his name's sake.*
> **Ps 23:1-3**

David's poetic depiction of God's pastoral care is a meditation for anyone navigating the tumultuous waters of moodiness. This Psalm, steeped in imagery of peace and restoration, paints a vivid picture of a God actively involved in the well-being of His children. For those overwhelmed by their emotions, the tranquil scenes of green pastures and quiet waters serve as a powerful metaphor for rest and rejuvenation in God's presence. The verse also speaks to the soul's renewal, which can be deeply resonant for someone seeking emotional balance. According to the Psalm, this restoration and guidance is not due to our merit but is rooted in God's character and purposes. Psalm 23 provides a scriptural balm to those experiencing moodiness by emphasizing God's intimate care and tranquility.

PRACTICAL ADVICE + HOMEWORK

Confess Sin: Emotional volatility is a sign that you yield to your emotions instead of the Holy Spirit. God instructs His children to be filled with and controlled by Him only (Gal 5:16-24). (**Homework:** If this is true in your situation, stop now and confess the sin of yielding to your emotions instead of God.)

Renew Your Mind through Scripture: God commands us to submit to Him rather than to our emotions. (**Homework:** Read the following biblical texts to understand God's perspective on the problem: Mark 14:32-36; Galatians 5:16-24; Ephesians 5:15-20; and Colossians 3:1-15. Answer these questions from the biblical texts you read: What did you learn about God? What did you learn about yourself? How do your thinking, feelings, and actions need to change considering these truths?)

Obey God: Yield to His Spirit instead of to your emotions (Gal 5:26-24). (**Homework:** Spend time with God in His Word each day, attend worship at your church each week, and memorize Galatians 5:19-24 to help you think truth when you are tempted to give into emotions. Ask family members and friends to hold you accountable to be emotionally controlled by confronting you when you are ruled by your emotions instead of by God's Spirit.)

Consult a Doctor: There are some cases where moodiness could be biologically and/or chemically instigated, such as side effects of a medical condition or medications taken. (**Homework:** In extreme cases of moodiness or when all else leaves you stumped, consult a medical doctor to determine if there may be an identifiable underlying biological or medicinal cause to the moodiness.)

Self-awareness and Reflection: Before reacting, take a moment to understand and address the root of your emotional response. (**Homework:** When moody, take ten minutes to sit quietly, breathe deeply, and reflect on what triggered the emotion. Write it down and consider ways to address it. Pray about your emotional volatility.)

Praise and Hope: In moments of emotional distress, focus on gratitude and praising God. This simple act resonates with the Psalms' exhortation to give thanks in all circumstances (Ps 34:1), turning attention away from distress and towards gratitude. (**Homework:** List five things you are grateful for each day and recite them when you feel moody.)

Seek Wise Counsel: Discussing your feelings with someone trustworthy can provide perspective and comfort. This echoes the wisdom of seeking guidance from others (Prov 19:20), which provides perspective and encouragement. (**Homework:** Set up a time to talk with a mentor, pastor, or friend about patterns in your moodiness and gain insights.)

Immerse Yourself in the Scriptures: Dive into biblical stories where individuals faced emotional turmoil and learned from their responses and outcomes. Learn from biblical characters who have faced emotional challenges like the psalmists who poured out their hearts to God. (**Homework:** Read and reflect on the Psalms. Note how the psalmists navigate their emotional highs and lows while keeping faith in God.)

DISCUSSION STARTERS

1. **Self-Reflection and God's Restoration:** Psalm 23:1-3 vividly describes God as a shepherd providing for and restoring His people. How do you see God's hand amid your mood swings? How might meditating on His role as the shepherd, leading you to quiet waters, provide stability during your emotional highs and lows?

2. **Navigating Emotional Turbulence with Scripture:** The Bible is filled with individuals who faced emotional challenges exhibited in part by the psalmists' raw expressions of God. How can their experiences guide or encourage you in navigating your own moodiness? In what ways can their faith journeys inspire you to anchor your emotions in God's truth?

3. **Transformation in Maturity and Dependence:** 1 Corinthians 13:11 highlights the growth from childish ways to maturity in Christ. How do you see your emotional responses aligning with this journey of spiritual growth? How can deepening your trust in God and daily immersion in Scripture guide you toward more stable emotional reactions and a greater sense of inner peace?

OVERWHELMED / STRESS

Stress often arises from innate tendencies. In these moments of feeling overwhelmed, believers must remember to turn their gaze to the ultimate Shepherd. God is not just any shepherd but one characterized by compassion, unwavering care, and remarkable courage. In facing life's challenges, trusting in this Shepherd provides us solace and direction based on biblical truths.

I call to you from the ends of the earth when my heart is without strength.
Lead me to a rock that is high above me.
Ps 61:2

This Psalm can be particularly relevant for those feeling overwhelmed as it expresses a cry for help and a desire to find refuge in something greater than oneself. People often feel overwhelmed when facing problems beyond their control or understanding. In this verse, calling out to God from the "ends of the earth" signifies a sense of desperation and need. The imagery of the rock that is higher where one can stand symbolizes a stable, secure place above the chaos. For those overwhelmed by life's demands, seeking God's support provides a pathway to safety and assurance. The verse encourages the belief that a source of strength and stability is available no matter how impossible a situation might seem. In essence, Psalm 61:2 offers solace and perspective, which reminds us that we are not alone in our struggles. God can help us rise above what overwhelms us.

But he himself went a day's journey into the wilderness and came and sat down under a juniper tree; and he requested for himself that he might die, and said, "It is enough; now, O Lord, take my life, for I am not better than my fathers." He lay down and slept under a juniper tree; and behold, there was an angel touching him, and he said to him, "Arise, eat." Then he looked and behold, there was at his head a bread cake baked on hot stones, and a jar of water. So, he ate and drank and lay down again. The angel of the Lord came again a second time and touched him and said, "Arise, eat, because the journey is too great for you." So, he arose and ate and drank, and went in the strength of that food forty days and forty nights to Horeb, the mountain of God.

1 Kgs 19:4-8

Elijah was a prophet of God who was on the run from Jezebel because she had promised to kill him. However, Elijah's response was not confidence in God's protection but to run. He then asked God to go ahead and kill him now. Under extreme stress, God sent an angel to minister to Elijah. He was instructed to rest and eat a meal. The angel of the Lord specifically said, "Arise, eat" because our bodies need nutrition and rest to respond to overwhelming stress. Physical ailments can affect our Spirit, and spiritual struggles can cause physical ailments. As dichotomous creatures, we must understand this simple connection and ensure we care for both. When under stress, we need rest and food.

"Come to me, all of you who are weary and burdened, and I will give you rest. Take up my yoke and learn from me, because I am lowly and humble in heart, and you will find rest for your souls. For my yoke is easy and my burden is light."

Matt 11:28-30

Jesus speaks so clearly with this passage for those who feel overwhelmed and offers an invitation to find rest and relief. It acknowledges our heavy burdens due to personal struggles, work, relationships, or other stressors. The text extends a gentle call to come to Christ, the one who promises rest and ease from these burdens. The metaphor of a yoke is often used to symbolize oppression or burden in the Bible. The Lord's yolk is described here as easy and His burden as light, suggesting a transformation of what we carry. The overwhelmed individual can find renewed strength and purpose by following Christ's ways and learning from Him. This passage reassures us that support and comfort are available amid life's challenges. Overall, it provides hope and encouragement for those feeling overburdened by emphasizing that they are not alone and that God's assistance is available.

> *We are afflicted in every way but not crushed;*
> *we are perplexed but not in despair; we are*
> *persecuted but not abandoned; we are*
> *struck down but not destroyed.*
> **2 Cor 4:8-9**

We all experience feeling overwhelmed at times. 2 Corinthians 4:8-9 addresses this feeling by showcasing resilience through faith. In this passage, the Apostle Paul not only acknowledges the difficulties and pressures he and others faced but also emphasizes that they were never ultimately defeated. The juxtaposition of being "hard-pressed" but not "crushed," and "perplexed" but not in "despair" portrays a picture of enduring strength despite circumstances. It assures believers that even when life's situations feel unbearable, there is an underlying strength rooted in faith that sustains them. This passage serves as a reminder that difficulties and overwhelming problems do not have the final say. There is resilience and power through faith in Christ. These words can inspire hope and encouragement for anyone feeling overwhelmed. They emphasize that people are not alone in their struggles and that faith makes triumph possible. The passage delivers a strong message; people can persevere even in the face of seemingly insurmountable obstacles.

The Lord is near to the brokenhearted and
saves those who are crushed in spirit
Ps 34:18

Feelings of being overwhelmed can often result in emotional despair which results in one feeling brokenhearted or crushed in spirit. This Psalm serves as a balm to that pain because it emphasizes God's closeness during the most challenging times. It is a potent reminder that God's presence is strongest when we are weakest. He does not just observe our pain. He actively seeks to save and comfort those who reach out to Him. This verse is a beacon of hope. It offers assurance of God's ever-present help and the promise of salvation for those who feel at the end of their rope. God's loving embrace is always available even in deep distress.

PRACTICAL ADVICE + HOMEWORK

Confess Sin: The sense of being stressed must be put off through confession since God has not asked more of us than He can do through us (Phil 2:12-13). (**Homework:** If this is true in your situation, stop right now and confess the sin of not trusting God to work in you to provide the desire and the ability to do what pleases Him.)

Renew Your Mind through Scripture: God commands us to work as He directs. (**Homework:** Read the following biblical texts to understand how God sustains us as we hope in Him and walk forward in obedience: Isaiah 40:28-31; Philippians 2:12-13; and Philippians 4:11-13. What did you learn about God? What did you learn about yourself? How do your thinking, feelings, and actions need to change considering these truths?)

Obey God: Commit to work diligently in your service to Him (1 Cor 15:58). (**Homework:** Spend time with God in His Word each day and attend worship at your church each week. List your responsibilities and ask God to enable you to carry them out with His help and for His glory. Ask spouses, mentors, and Spirit-filled believers to help you assess your list to see if you are taking on more than God has asked you to do. Go to God with that list and ask Him the same question while seeking His direction through Scripture. Memorize 1 Corinthians 15:58 to help you think truth about the responsibilities God has asked you fulfill.)

Seek Refuge in God: Whenever feeling overwhelmed, visualize God as a rock. See Him as a stable foundation to rely upon. The biblical metaphors of God as our rock and fortress are found in Psalm 18:2 and in this context accentuate reliance on a stable foundation. (**Homework:** Write down three challenges you are facing. To each challenge, jot a prayer entrusting that situation to God.)

Rest in Christ: Remember Jesus' call to the weary and burdened. Reflecting on the concept of His yoke as light should remind you of Jesus' gentle invitation to the weary. Matthew 11:28-30 underscores the restorative power of following His words. (**Homework:** Dedicate twenty minutes of quiet time daily to rest, be still, and meditate on Jesus' invitation in Matthew 11:28-30.)

Take a Nap and Eat: Analyze your schedule and diet and ensure you get adequate sleep and a healthy diet. (**Homework:** Write out a weekly schedule and meal plan from the previous week. Have a friend or medical professional review it to give you honest feedback about any recommended changes you need to make for the upcoming week.)

Share with Others: Sharing feelings can lighten your load and provide a fresh perspective. This is the biblical principle of bearing one another's burdens and receiving support from your church. (**Homework:** Talk to a trusted friend or mentor about a situation that overwhelms you and seek their insights and prayers.)

Remember Past Victories: Reflect on situations where God guided you through overwhelming times. This instills a sense of gratitude and confidence. It reminds you of God's faithfulness in past challenges and reso-nating with the Bible's recounting of God's character. (**Homework:** Cre-ate a list of past challenges and note how each was resolved or how you grew from it. Refer to this list in future moments of feeling overwhelmed.)

DISCUSSION STARTERS

1. **Seeking God as Your Fortress:** Considering the imagery in Psalm 61:2, where God is likened to a rock and refuge, how does visu-alizing God as a steadfast protector help you when feeling over-whelmed? How can acknowledging God as your fortress help you find strength and stability amidst the chaos?

2. **Physical Restoration and Spiritual Renewal:** Reflecting on Eli-jah's experience in 1 Kings 19:4-8, where he felt extreme stress and was provided both rest and sustenance by an angel, how do you see the connection between physical health and spiritual well-being in your own life? How can prioritizing rest and proper nutrition help bolster your spiritual resilience when facing overwhelming situations?

3. **Embracing Jesus' Offer of Rest:** In Matthew 11:28-30, Jesus in-vites those weary and burdened to find rest in Him. How can you practice leaning into this divine invitation daily? How might in-ternalizing the concept of Jesus' light yoke alter your perspective on your burdens, transforming them into moments of growth and deeper trust in Him?

PERFECTIONISM

Perfectionism is an incessant pursuit of faultlessness, often rooted in a desire for human approval or a misguided understanding of one's worth. The relentless pursuit of flawlessness can be spiritually crippling and can lead one to rely on their own strength rather than God's grace. Just as every day has its night, every soul has its struggles. In pursuing perfection, believers must remember that true completeness is found not in personal efforts but in Christ's redemptive work. When His children surrender their imperfections to Him, they are transformed not into worldly standards of perfection but into His likeness.

Be perfect, therefore, as your heavenly Father is perfect.
Matt 5:48

Jesus calls for believers to be perfect as their heavenly Father is perfect which can be challenging and illuminating for those struggling with perfectionism. While it sets a high standard, the underlying message is not about attaining flawlessness in human terms but seeking spiritual maturity and integrity. The call to perfection here is rooted in love, mercy, and grace, reflecting God's character rather than human achievement. This passage can help reframe the idea of perfection for those who grapple with it and direct their focus toward inner growth and alignment with biblical principles rather than external validation or self-imposed pressure. It is an invitation to cultivate a heart that mirrors God's love rather than obsessing over worldly perfection. Therefore, this verse can offer a balanced perspective emphasizing wholeness, compassion, and spiritual development rather than exacerbating the struggle with perfectionism. It invites a shift from a self-centered pursuit of perfection to a God-centered pursuit of growth and love.

> *Not that I have already reached the goal or am already perfect,*
> *but I make every effort to take hold of it because I also have been taken*
> *hold of by Christ Jesus. Brothers and sisters, I do not consider myself to*
> *have taken hold of it. But one thing I do: Forgetting what is behind and*
> *reaching forward to what is ahead, I pursue as my goal the prize*
> *promised by God's heavenly call in Christ Jesus.*
> **Phil 3:12-14**

This passage speaks to the human condition of not having reached perfection but continually striving toward the goal. These verses emphasize the pursuit rather than the attainment. This mindset can resonate powerfully with those struggling with perfectionism as it acknowledges human imperfection and emphasizes the importance of focusing on the future not past mistakes or failures. This passage encourages readers to press on toward their spiritual goals and embrace growth rather than flawless achievement. For those trapped in the relentless pursuit of perfection, it offers a perspective that values effort, persistence, and the journey over the result. The apostle Paul's humility in admitting that he has not reached perfection but is still continually striving can be a source of comfort and inspiration. These verses provide a liberating framework for understanding perfection not as an impossible standard but as an ongoing spiritual development and fulfillment process in Christ.

> *And he said to Him, "Teacher, I have kept all these things from my*
> *youth up." Looking at him, Jesus felt a love for him and said to him,*
> *"One thing you lack: go and sell all you possess and give to the poor,*
> *and you will have treasure in heaven; and come, follow Me." But at*
> *these words he was saddened, and he went away grieving, for he was*

Perfectionism

one who owned much property.... . They were even more astonished
and said to Him, "Then who can be saved?" Looking at them,
Jesussaid, "With people it is impossible, but not with God;
forall things are possible with God"
Mark 10:20-22, 26-27

The young rich man wanted to know what he needed to do to be saved. He was 100% confident that he had kept the Law of Moses to perfection. He even prided himself on such. However, Jesus pointed out one imperfection that the man did not want to address. His perfection was indeed imperfect, and that revelation caused him distress. People who struggle with perfectionism often exhibit legalistic tendencies or struggle to give and receive grace and mercy when they or others fail to live up to certain expectations. Jesus addresses the disciples who were perplexed at His response that no one who is imperfect can enter the Kingdom. He told them that it has more to do with God's ability to perfect us than for us to be perfect before Him in our strength. We cannot be perfect and earn our salvation, but we can strive for excellence without perfection becoming an idol we seek to obtain in this life.

But he said to me, "My grace is sufficient for you,
for my power is perfected in weakness." Therefore,
I will most gladly boast all the more about my
weaknesses, so that Christ's power may reside in me.
2 Cor 12:9

Paul addresses embracing weakness by recognizing that perfection is found in Christ's strength, not in our abilities. For those who struggle with perfectionism, this can be a reminder that our weaknesses do not define failure but are an opportunity for grace. It illustrates that true strength comes from acknowledging our limitations and relying on God's power. This shift in perspective from self-reliance to dependence on God can alleviate the pressure to perform perfectly and the accompanying fear of failure. The verse teaches that God's perfect strength is manifested in our imperfections, which highlights that our worth is not in our flawless performance but in Christ's love and grace. By embracing this understanding, those striving for perfection can find freedom in knowing that they do not have to be perfect as God's grace is sufficient for them. The passage offers a compassionate perspective that can encourage a healthier approach to personal growth and achievement focused on grace rather than unrealistic perfection.

> *That He might present to Himself the church in*
> *all her glory, having no spot or wrinkle or any such*
> *thing; but that she would be holy and blameless.*
> **Eph 5:27**

In this passage, Paul paints a picture of the Church, the collective body of believers, as being presented to Christ in all her glory, spotless and without blemish. For those grappling with perfectionism, this verse offers a deeper understanding of perfection in God's eyes. It is not about human standards of flawlessness but about being purified, refined, and sanctified through Christ. The focus is not on individual achievements or an absence of mistakes but on the collective holiness and blamelessness that come from Christ's work in believers. For perfectionists, this can shift perspective from personal perfection to a communal and Christ-centered understanding of holiness. Instead of individual striving, it is about being a part of a body that Christ is purifying. Recognizing this can bring relief and purpose when one realizes that perfection is a work Christ does in us and not something we achieve on our own. In counseling, this verse can offer a transformative lens, redirecting the focus from self-perfection to participation in Christ's redemptive work for the whole Church.

PRACTICAL ADVICE + HOMEWORK

Confess Sin: To believe we are without sin and to center our lives around the pursuit of perfection rather than of Christ is an expression of a heart of pride (1 John 1:8). In the pursuit of this goal, we may set unreachable standards for ourselves and live in constant self-condemnation. We may perform for others seeking their approval so that we can believe we are reaching this goal, or we may condemn others for their failure to meet the standard we have set for them. (**Homework:** If this is true in your life, stop right now and confess the sin of pride and the pursuit of perfectionism rather than God. Make this confession to Him and to any you have mistreated because of these sinful attitudes and actions.)

Renew Your Mind through Scripture: God commands us to die to self and seek Him (Luke 9:23). (**Homework:** Read the following biblical texts to understand how God sees and responds to the pride of perfectionism and how it is He who perfects us: Proverbs 6:16-19; Proverbs 21:4; John 17:20-23; 1 John 3:1-3. Answer these questions from the biblical texts you just read: What did you learn about God? What did you learn about yourself? How do your thinking, feelings, and actions need to change considering these truths?)

Obey God: Put off pride and put on humility in Christ. (**Homework:** Spend time with God in His Word each day and attend worship at your church each week. Memorize Proverbs 21:4 to help you see your pride and perfectionism as God sees it.)

Pursue Heart Perfection: Understand that Christ's call to perfection is about love and heart purity not flawless performance. This points to Matthew 5:43-48 and redefines perfection as love and compassion instead of flawless achievement. (**Homework:** Reflect on Matthew 5:43-48 and identify one way to show love to an enemy this week.)

Embrace Progress, Not Perfection: Recognize that spiritual growth is a journey and perfection is not about being flawless but pressing toward God's calling. This reflects the biblical narrative of spiritual growth, where Paul emphasizes pressing toward the goal rather than achieving immediate perfection. (**Homework:** Read Philippians 3:7-14 and journal about an area in which you have grown recently and an area where you still hope to grow.)

Seek Forgiveness from Others: Ask those closest to you if you have been demanding perfection out of them or have been showing little grace or patience. (**Homework:** Identify areas of demanded perfection related to others and encourage them for their efforts. Intentionally tell them that you recognize their desires to learn and grow. Ask for forgiveness where you have been too hard.)

Let Go of Unrealistic Standards: Our righteousness comes through our faith in Christ, not by our achievements. (**Homework:** Write a list of self-imposed standards, pray over them, and consciously choose to release at least one.)

DISCUSSION STARTERS

1. **The Pursuit of Spiritual Perfection:** Given Jesus' call in Matthew 5:48 to "be perfect," how have you understood this command concerning your struggles with perfectionism? How might shifting your perspective from worldly perfection to spiritual maturity rooted in love, mercy, and grace impact your approach to personal growth and your interactions with others?

2. **The Journey Over the Destination:** Reflecting on Philippians 3:12-14, Paul discusses the ongoing pursuit of spiritual goals rather than attaining immediate perfection. Can you identify moments when you have been too focused on a flawless result rather than valuing the growth process? How can this scripture guide you to find balance and peace in your journey with Christ by emphasizing effort over perfection?

3. **Perfection Through Christ's Grace:** In 2 Corinthians 12:9, Paul

speaks about the power of Christ being perfected in our weaknesses. How do you view your weaknesses or imperfections considering this Scripture? Will embracing Christ's grace and strength in your moments of vulnerability shift your understanding of perfectionism and offer you solace?

PORNOGRAPHY

Pornography derives from the Greek words *porne* (prostitute) and *graphos* (writing). It has historically referred to writings about prostitutes or fornication. In contemporary contexts, pornography is defined as any material—in the form of pictures, videos, or text—created to arouse the viewer or reader sexually. The Bible, while not explicitly using the term "pornography," speaks unequivocally about lust and immoral sexual behaviors.

> *Charm is deceitful and beauty is vain,*
> *but awoman who fears the Lord, she shall be praised.*
> **Prov 31:30**

Research has shown that men/women who engage in the use of pornography begin to lose interest, especially sexual interest, in their spouses. Spiritually speaking, their hearts are forsaking their first love and yearning after another. Even if the "another" is an unknown image or form of pornography and the illusion of excitement or arousal is shallow, that desire is only seeking to satisfy a biological urge rather than a biblically-blessed expression of sexuality. Proverbs 31:30 could be interchanged for either gender in principle to communicate that sexual attraction and satisfaction gained through the appeal of the eyes or emotional charm is inferior to the spiritual condition of the relationship. Sexuality is to be fully expressed and enjoyed in marriage, not through the lust of the flesh or mind.

But I tell you, everyone who looks at a woman lustfully has already committed adultery with her in his heart.
Matt 5:28

This verse speaks to lustful thoughts and how they equate to adultery in the heart. For those struggling with pornography, this verse is a poignant reminder that purity is not just about physical actions but also about the desires and thoughts within the mind. It emphasizes the importance of controlling one's thoughts and understanding that mental events have spiritual significance. By recognizing that even a lustful glance can be sinful, individuals are encouraged to reflect on their internal world and how it aligns with their spiritual beliefs. This can motivate them to seek support, guidance, and practical strategies to overcome this struggle. Moreover, the verse's clear statement can serve as a wake-up call to take this issue seriously and to approach the issue with a committed and proactive attitude. Jesus' teaching in Matthew 5:28 thus offers both a challenge and an invitation to pursue integrity and holiness in all aspects of life. This includes the seemingly private realm of personal thoughts and desires.

Flee sexual immorality! Every other sin a person commits is outside the body, but the person who is sexually immoral sins against his own body. Don't you know that your body is a temple of the Holy Spirit who is in you, whom you have from God? You are not your own, for you were bought at a price. So, glorify God with your body.
1 Cor 6:18-20

The passage of 1 Corinthians 6:18-20 exhorts believers to flee sexual immorality and recognize that the body is a temple of the Holy Spirit. For those struggling with pornography, this passage offers practical and spiritual wisdom. It emphasizes that our bodies are not our own. They have been bought at a price, which underscores the importance of treating them with respect and purity. Engaging with pornography is seen as being at odds with this sacred responsibility. The call to flee sexual immorality is strong and unmistakable, reinforcing that this is not a minor issue but one requiring severe and immediate attention. The understanding that our bodies are dwelling places for the Holy Spirit provides both a motivation and a framework for seeking healing and wholeness. This passage, therefore, not only clarifies the gravity of sexual impurity but also inspires a positive, respectful, and sanctified view of the body. This mindset drives individuals to seek higher standards for their actions and thoughts.

No temptation has come upon you except what is common to humanity. But God is faithful; he will not allow you to be tempted beyond what you are able, but with the temptation he will also provide the way out so that you may be able to bear it.
1 Cor 10:13

What Paul writes can be incredibly relevant for those who struggle with pornography because it deals with temptation and the assurance a way to overcome it exists. The verse promises that every temptation that has overtaken a person is common to all other believers. With each temptation, God will provide a way for them all to endure it. This promise is assurance to everyone battling with the lure of pornography that they are not alone in their struggle and that their situation is not unique or insurmountable. The promise that God will provide a way out encourages a belief that He will help overcome this challenge. It reframes the struggle with pornography not as a failing but as a life-dominating sin that can be conquered. The emphasis on God's faithfulness and provision offers a hopeful perspective for those seeking to change their behavior. It turns the focus from shame and guilt to a reliance on Christ, who understands human frailty and offers strength to overcome it.

I have made a covenant with my eyes; why then would I focus on a young woman?
Job 31:1

Job's declaration in this verse sheds light on the proactive steps taken by righteous individuals to safeguard themselves against temptations. For those grappling with pornography, this verse serves as a guidepost. It underscores the notion that genuine change begins with a decision, a commitment to oneself and God, to avoid circumstances or triggers that lead to sin. The "covenant with my eyes" signifies an active, deliberate choice to guard what one allows to enter one's mind through the eyes. In a world inundated with sexual imagery, this covenant becomes ever more crucial. It is a personal pledge to uphold purity, not just an arbitrary set of rules. By making such a covenant, an individual acknowledges the gravity of the issue and takes responsibility for their actions and choices. The verse suggests that intentionality coupled with God's grace, can act as a potent shield against the pervasive lure of pornography.

Practical Advice + Homework

Confess Sin: The sin of seeking sexual satisfaction through pornography use which is rooted in pride and self-love must be put off through confession (Eph 4:17-24). (**Homework:** If this is true in your situation, stop right now and confess the inward sin of pride and self-love as well as the outward sinful use of pornography. Confess this sin to God and to any you have mistreated because of this pattern of behavior.)

Renew Your Mind through Scripture: God commands us to be morally pure. (**Homework:** Read the following biblical texts to understand God's perspective on sexual immorality and moral purity: Proverbs 5, 1 Corinthians 6:13-20, Galatians 5:19-25, and Ephesians 4:17-24. Answer these questions from the biblical texts you just read: What did you learn about God? What did you learn about yourself? How do your thinking, feelings and actions need to change considering these truths?)

Obey God: by Repent of your heart's pride and its outward expression in pornography use. (**Homework:** Spend time with God in His Word each day and attend worship at your church each week. Find a mentor or small group that will hold you accountable for inner and outer transformation).

Pornography

Guard Your Heart and Eyes: Recognize the weight and implications of Jesus' words about lust and understand that mental acts are as significant as physical ones. The moral weight of mental acts elevates the need for mental purity. (**Homework:** Memorize Matthew 5:28 and recall it whenever tempted to view explicit material.)

Value Your Body as God's Temple: Reflect on the sanctity of your body as the dwelling place of the Holy Spirit and the need to honor it. Much like our physical body, of which we need to be aware of what we put in it, we must also be conscious of what we are watching and reading. (**Homework:** Write a letter to yourself about why your body is valuable and the importance of keeping it pure.)

Make a Commitment for Purity: Inspired by Job's words, make a personal covenant with your eyes and heart. Forge a tangible and personal pledge that aligns with Biblical values. (**Homework:** Draft a personal commitment or covenant on sexual purity and place it somewhere you can see daily.)

Spiritual War: There is a spiritual war of sexual temptations all around. Ask yourself why you are susceptible to the temptation of pornography right now. (**Homework:** Journal what happens when you are tempted to view pornography. With a trusted believer of the same gender, analyze the underlying drive for you to engage in sexually stimulating materials. Pray through how to obey the Lord to resolve those issues.)

Replace Negative Inputs: Substitute harmful content with wholesome and edifying materials not only provides a practical tool for avoidance but encourage a positive and constructive response, reflecting the Bible's teachings on renewing the mind and focusing on what is pure and noble. (**Homework:** List three positive activities or resources you can turn to when tempted, such as reading a spiritual book, listening to uplifting music, or engaging in a hobby. Commit to choosing one of these the next time temptation arises.)

DISCUSSION STARTERS

1. **Recognizing True Beauty and Worth:** Proverbs 31:30 emphasizes the value of a woman who fears the Lord suggesting that true beauty and worth are found in a relationship with God. How does this perspective contrast with the fleeting allure presented in pornography? In what ways can you cultivate a deeper appreciation for the spiritual over the physical, focusing on the eternal beauty that God values?

2. **Reflection on Lustful Thoughts:** Matthew 5:28 cautions against viewing others with lust and equates such thoughts with adultery in one's heart. How has this verse challenged your understanding of purity? Can you identify moments when you have allowed such thoughts to fester? What steps can you take to align your mind more closely with Christ's teaching on this matter?

3. **Stewardship of Our Bodies:** 1 Corinthians 6:18-20 reminds us of our bodies' sacredness as temples of the Holy Spirit. Given this divine perspective, how does engaging in pornography affect your view of yourself and others? How can this understanding motivate you towards sanctity and respect for your body and those of others?

PROCRASTINATION

The act of willfully delaying the doing of something that should be done is the definition of procrastination. For many, it becomes a consistent and habitual response to significant and minor tasks. Though procrastination is not explicitly mentioned in the Bible, the Word offers wisdom that speaks against the spirit of delay and complacency. In biblical counseling, procrastination can be seen as a lack of trust in God's provision and strength or resistance to His calling. Overcoming this desire to delay requires seeking God's wisdom and relying on His strength while regularly reflecting upon our stewardship of the time and resources He has given us.

> *He who watches the wind will not sow*
> *and he who looks at the clouds will not reap.*
> **Eccl 11:4**

Solomon uses a simple farming example to teach the reader about procrastination. Procrastination, or the putting off action until another time or day, will leave a person wanting in life. The farmer who sits and watches the wind blow through the field every day rather than planting seeds in that field can never expect a harvest. The farmer who watches the clouds blow by on the day of harvest rather than harvesting will watch his fields rot or be destroyed by pestilence since he has not correctly pulled them from the field. The individual who has a task before him or her but chooses to defer action may find himself or herself in dire need without the time or opportunity to complete the task. Believers need to discipline themselves to manage their time wisely. Part of this discipline is getting the work that needs to be accomplished when the time for work is at hand instead of waiting. Procrastination leads to many other issues, such as stress, anxiety, chaos, conflict, financial troubles, and other issues that might have been avoided by simply sowing and reaping at the proper time.

> **The slacker does not plow during planting season;**
> **at harvest time, he looks, and there is nothing**
> **Prov 20:4**

This passage can be seen as highly relevant to the issue of procrastination as it speaks metaphorically about the consequences of laziness and the lack of preparation. This passage warns that just as a farmer who refuses to plow in the right season will have no harvest, procrastinators will also face the consequences of their inaction. It emphasizes the importance of timely effort and highlights that a right time exists for everything. Delaying necessary responsibilities can lead to failure or lack of success. The imagery of the farmer's actions and the resulting harvest provides a vivid picture of the cause-and-effect relationship between effort and reward. For those struggling with procrastination, this message can be a powerful reminder that putting off necessary duties will eventually lead to unwanted outcomes. It teaches the value of diligence and the importance of seizing opportunities when they arise. Ultimately, it serves as both a warning and a motivator as it urges individuals to act responsibly and promptly to achieve their goals.

> **The slacker craves, yet has nothing,**
> **but the diligent is fully satisfied**
> **Prov 13:4**

This verse provides a poignant lesson about procrastination by contrasting the desires of the diligent with the results of laziness. It illustrates that those who are diligent and proactive in their endeavors achieve satisfaction and success, while the lazy are left wanting. This highlights the significance of timely action and persistence in pursuing goals. This proverb serves as a cautionary tale and a call to action for individuals struggling with procrastination. The contrasting outcomes presented in the passage are a vivid reminder of the potential rewards of diligence and the emptiness that comes with inaction. The wisdom contained in this verse can be used as a motivational tool. This inspires individuals to overcome procrastination and engage in productive efforts. The encouragement to be diligent and the warning against laziness make this passage a powerful teaching tool for those seeking to conquer procrastination.

> *Pay careful attention, then, to how you walk—not as unwise people but as wise—making the most of the time, because the days are evil.*
> **Eph 5:15-16**

Paul emphasizes the importance of living wisely and maximizing every opportunity. This appeal calls for careful consideration of time spent and encourages intentional living. These verses apply to those who struggle with procrastination as they challenge the believer to evaluate their time use and seize opportunities rather than put them off. The urging to walk wisely and redeem time provides a biblical basis for pursuing goals promptly and not letting procrastination hinder progress. By highlighting the fleeting nature of time, these verses push individuals to take immediate action and not delay in fulfilling responsibilities. This wisdom can guide those seeking to overcome procrastination and lead a more disciplined and purposeful life. The connection between wisdom, time management, and intentional living found in this passage offers both a challenge and an encouragement to take control of procrastination.

> *A little sleep, a little slumber, a little folding of the hands to rest, and poverty will come upon you like a robber, and want like an armed man*
> **Prov 6:10-11**

This Scripture uses illustrative language to underscore the dangers of complacency and inactivity which often result from procrastination. The repetitive phrasing of "a little" emphasizes how seemingly insignificant amounts of delay or negligence can accumulate into substantial adverse outcomes. The imagery of poverty approaching "like a robber" reinforces the sudden and often unexpected consequences that can arise from chronic procrastination. For those wrestling with procrastination, these verses warn sternly about the long-term consequences of repeatedly delaying tasks. It stresses that, over time, what might seem like harmless moments of rest can lead to significant setbacks in life. This verse is a call for vigilance and proactive behavior. It teaches believers the value of timely action and the importance of avoiding the temptations of idleness.

Do not boast about tomorrow,
for you do not know what a day may bring
Prov 27:1

The proverb warns against presuming the future, which is a foundational issue for those who procrastinate. It reminds readers of life's unpredictability and how today's opportunities might not be present tomorrow. By taking this verse to heart, one can recognize that postponing tasks relies on the false assumption that future circumstances will be more favorable. The message here is a sobering reminder that now is the best time to act because tomorrow is not guaranteed. For individuals grappling with procrastination, this verse can provide a sense of urgency to address tasks in the present moment and serves as a call to prioritize and seize the day as delays can result in missed opportunities. It encourages a mindset of immediacy and a conscious choice to act on what can be done today rather than assuming the future will offer a better moment.

PRACTICAL ADVICE + HOMEWORK

Confess Sin: The sin of procrastination must be put off through confession (James 4:17). Sometimes, we procrastinate because we are lazy, feel inadequate, or have forgotten that God is our resource in all that He commands us to do. (**Homework:** If this is true in your situation, stop right now and confess the sin of procrastination to God and to any you have mistreated because of this sinful pattern of behavior.)

Renew Your Mind through Scripture: God commands us to be diligent. (**Homework:** Read the following biblical texts to understand how God sees and responds to procrastination: Proverbs 24:3-34; Ephesians 5:15-17; Colossians 3:23-24; and James 4:13-17. Answer these questions from the biblical texts you read: What did you learn about God? What did you learn about yourself? How do your thinking, feelings, and actions need to change considering these truths?)

Obey God: Work diligently to serve Him (Col 3:23-24). (**Homework:** Spend time with God in His Word each day and attend worship at your church each week. Make your list of God-given responsibilities and ask Him to enable you to carry them out with His help and for His glory. Memorize Colossians 3:23-24 to help you think truth when you are tempted to procrastinate.)

Recognizing Wisdom: It is essential to take timely action and not let procrastination hinder your progress toward fulfilling responsibilities and achieving goals. This timely action is rooted in Proverbs and emphasizes the biblical warning against laziness. (**Homework:** Identify one area in your life where procrastination is an obstacle, set specific deadlines related to that area, and create a plan to meet those deadlines. Journal reflecting on the insights from Proverbs 20:4.)

Create a Schedule: Create a weekly schedule broken into thirty-minute time slots daily. (**Homework:** Create a schedule for every thirty-minute timeslot each day and keep it with you. Check off each task as completed. Each day, reevaluate the time managed wisely versus wasted as you establish the new habits of time management rather than procrastination.)

Self-Reflect on Desires and Outcomes: Recognize the difference in results between diligent and procrastination. Focusing on personal desires and outcomes, connect these to the spiritual importance of diligence, and contrast it with procrastination's fruitlessness. (**Homework:** List three personal goals and the immediate actions needed to make progress towards them.)

Value Time as a Limited Resource: Understand that time is fleeting and should be used wisely. This understanding is tied to biblical truth as it instills a respect for time as a gift from God and urges individuals not to waste what God has given them. (**Homework:** Reflect on Ephesians 5:15-16. Based on that reflection, create a schedule for a week, allocating time intentionally to priorities.)

Act Now: Instead of waiting for perfect conditions, start with what you have and where you are. Promote immediate action and responsibility in your life. This is the biblical value of stewardship over our talents and resources. (**Homework:** Identify one thing you have been avoiding and commit to starting it within the next twenty-four hours.)

DISCUSSION STARTERS

1. **Timeliness and Stewardship in Actions:** Ecclesiastes 11:4 uses the imagery of a farmer to depict the pitfalls of procrastination. How have you experienced the repercussions of "watching the wind" or "looking at the clouds" in your own life? How can internalizing Solomon's teachings help you act diligently, seeing every opportunity as a God-given chance to sow seeds for a fruitful harvest in the future?

2. **Confronting the Temptations of Inaction:** Proverbs 6:10-11 vividly warns about the dangers of complacency and how even a short delay can have severe consequences. Can you recall when a slight delay snowballed into a more significant setback? Reflecting on the imagery of poverty coming like a robber, how does this motivate you to act immediately and diligently in tasks God places before you?

3. **Value of the Present Moment:** Proverbs 27:1 cautions against relying too heavily on the future. How often do you put off tasks until tomorrow? How can embracing the unpredictability of life as mentioned in this proverb inspire you to act with urgency today and truly seize the day for God's glory?

PTSD
(POST-TRAUMATIC STRESS DISORDER)

PTSD is an emotional and mental response stemming from direct or indirect exposure to traumatic events that leads to manifestations such as intense anxiety, intrusive memories, and distressing dreams. While the Bible does not have a definition of PTSD, the Bible does not shy away from acknowledging the depths of human suffering. For those wrestling with PTSD, the Bible becomes a source of comfort and restoration and affirms that God understands pain, is present in suffering, and offers hope for healing based on His unfailing love and faithfulness.

> *The Lord is my shepherd; I have what I need. He lets me lie down*
> *in green pastures. He leads me beside quiet waters. He renews my life;*
> *he leads me along the right paths for his name's sake.*
> **Ps 23:1-3**

For someone grappling with PTSD, the metaphor of the Lord as a Shepherd who leads him/her to green pastures and quiet waters paints a picture of guidance, protection, and peace. For someone grappling with PTSD, life may feel chaotic and scarred by trauma. This image provides a reassuring symbol of restorative calm. The notion of God refreshing the soul connects deeply with the need for inner healing and renewal that PTSD often demands. These verses offer a scriptural foundation for meditation and reflection and guiding the mind away from traumatic memories and toward a peaceful, spiritually nourishing space. By focusing on God's presence and care through Psalm 23:1-3, a person with PTSD can find solace and encouragement in their healing journey. This Psalm grounds him/her in the promise that he/she is not alone because a loving Shepherd is guiding him/her toward recovery.

> *When I pondered to understand this, it was troublesome*
> *in my sight until I came into the sanctuary of God...*
> *My flesh and my heart may fail, but God is the*
> *strength of my heart and my portion forever.*
> **Ps 73:16, 26**

The psalmist expressed throughout Psalm 73 a traumatic perception that he has experienced throughout his life as he has watched sin prevail and his hard work towards holiness persecuted and neglected. PTSD is referred to as a "perception disorder" by some biblical counselors. In this circumstance, a victim perceives a reality based on his/her belief that he/she is constantly in danger of some future, unknown threat or continued trauma even though the past attack is over and he/she is now safe. Reliving his/her trauma through dreams, intentional thoughts, or even uncontrollable triggers when he/she sees, smells, or hears things that remind him/her of his/her trauma all affect his/her entire body. The psalmist recognized thousands of years ago that the strength needed to overcome such perceived danger, as well as for someone to endure trauma's effects on him/her, is a moot point considering the fact that God is his/her internal strength. His/her mind may be scared and sensitive to anxiety, nightmares, or perceived threats. Still, God is the strength within the soul to overcome and respond holistically to life's circumstances even in the face of PTSD.

> *You will keep the mind that is dependent*
> *on you in perfect peace, for it is trusting in you.*
> **Isa 26:3**

PTSD can often disturb mental peace and control. This verse centers on the notion of perfect peace God gives those who remain steadfast in their trust. For someone battling PTSD, trust may be challenging, and peace might seem unattainable. This Scripture offers an anchor in God's unwavering steadiness and suggests that healing can come through reliance on Him. The promise of perfect peace resonates deeply with the desire for tranquility and stability amid the tumultuous aftermath of trauma. By meditating on and absorbing the truth found in Isaiah 26:3, an individual with PTSD can cultivate a sense of trust and reliance on God's loving control. This can ultimately lead to a peace that transcends understanding and promotes healing from the traumatic experiences that precede PTSD.

Humble yourselves, therefore, under the mighty hand of God, so that he may exalt you at the proper time, casting all your cares on him, because he cares about you. Be sober-minded, be alert. Your adversary the devil is prowling around like a roaring lion, looking for anyone he can devour.
1 Pet 5:6-8

This Scripture speaks of humility, reliance on God, vigilance, and an understanding that spiritual battles are at play. For someone with PTSD, the call to cast anxiety on God emphasizes surrendering control and trust in God's loving care. This action is absolutely crucial for his/her healing. The warning to be alert and sober-minded may resonate with the heightened awareness often associated with PTSD and transform it into a call for spiritual vigilance. Acknowledging a spiritual enemy who seeks to devour parallels the inner battles an individual with PTSD faces, giving him/her a framework for understanding his/her struggle. The assurance that God's mighty hand can lift him/her up offers hope and a promise of restoration that is grounded in His love and strength. Overall, this passage provides a multifaceted approach that acknowledges the complexity of PTSD while offering spiritual principles for healing and resilience.

He heals the brokenhearted and binds up their wounds.
Ps 147:3

For those dealing with PTSD, the fabric of their heart and minds can feel torn and shattered by the echoes of traumatic events. This Scripture from Psalm 147 speaks directly to the brokenhearted by assuring them of God's healing nature. When a person feels that the fragments of his/her past experiences are too heavy to bear, this verse emphasizes that God comes close, mends his/her hurt, and patches up his/her emotional and psychological wounds. The image of God binding up wounds is powerful. It implies God's closeness, His tender touch, and His personal involvement in the healing process. This Scripture can be a comforting affirmation for any individual with PTSD, as it reminds him/her that healing is possible. It is a promise rooted deeply in God's love and care for His creation.

> *Do not fear, for I am with you; do not be dismayed,*
> *for I am your God. I will strengthen you and help you;*
> *I will uphold you with my righteous right hand*
> **Isa 41:10**

Fear is an everyday companion for a person grappling with PTSD. The traumatic memories, triggers, and anxiety can bring about an overwhelming sense of dread and apprehension. In this verse from Isaiah, God speaks directly into that fear by offering a comforting and steadfast presence. The phrase "do not fear" is not just a command but a promise anchored in God's presence. This verse can be a beacon of hope for someone with PTSD. It reminds him/her that he/she is not alone in his/her struggles. God's promise to uphold, strengthen, and help is an assurance of His active involvement in his/her journey toward healing. Embracing this Scripture can help that person with PTSD lean into God's strength and find solace in the knowledge that he/she is held, supported, and cherished by a loving God, even amid his/her deepest fears.

PRACTICAL ADVICE + HOMEWORK

Confess Sin: PTSD is not a term found in Scripture, so it needs to be described in biblical terms to find biblical solutions. The distress associated with this clustering of physical sensations can be understood in biblical terms as fear. Turning to God in this kind of distress is essential. (**Homework:** If you have turned away from God because of your distress, stop now and confess this sin to God.)

Renew Your Mind through Scripture: God comforts fear with His presence and His Word. (**Homework:** Read the following biblical texts to understand how God comforts His people: Psalm 23 and Psalm 27. Answer these questions from the biblical texts you read: What did you learn about God? What did you learn about yourself? How do your thinking, feelings, and actions need to change considering these truths?)

Obey God: Turn to and trust God every moment of your life. (**Homework:** Spend time with God in His Word each day and attend worship at your church each week. Memorize Psalm 23 to help you remember the truth that God is with you and is protecting you in moments of distress.)

Find Comfort in God's Guidance: Lean on the understanding that God leads you to peace like a Shepherd. As a Shepherd, He leads, protects, and nurtures His sheep. For someone with PTSD, recognizing God in this role can provide a sense of security and guidance. Comfort comes from knowing that God leaves none of his children alone in their struggles. (**Homework:** Reflect on Psalm 23:1-3 daily, imagining yourself in the green pastures and quiet waters God provides.)

Identify Triggers and Prepare Responses: Our flesh and spirit affect each other. Sometimes, we cannot control how the body reacts to certain stimuli that remind us of past trauma. (**Homework:** Identify things that trigger traumatic thoughts of danger or threats. Develop a plan to perceive the current reality considering Scripture. Trust the Lord to carry you through the moment with God-honoring responses.)

Build Trust in God's Peace: Focus on keeping your mind steadfast and trusting in God's promise of peace. Trusting in God's peace provides a stable anchor in distress and chaos. It is a reminder that God's control surpasses our understanding, and His care for us is unwavering. (**Homework:** Write out Isaiah 26:3 and place it somewhere visible. Reflect on this verse when anxiety strikes.)

Release Anxiety to God: Practice casting your fears and anxieties on God, knowing He cares for you. For someone dealing with PTSD, this practice can be a comforting and healing way to alleviate stress. Put your trust in God knowing that He loves you and is willing to shoulder your burdens. (**Homework:** Spend a few minutes each day praying specifically about giving your anxieties to God based on 1 Peter 5:7.)

Develop Healthy Strategies: Incorporate healthy, positive activities that complement the spiritual focus. Doing so allows you to experience God's love and grace practically, which fosters emotional resilience and strengthens the connection to biblical truth. (**Homework:** Explore hobbies or activities that make you feel relaxed and peaceful, integrating them into your routine.)

DISCUSSION STARTERS

1. **The Shepherd's Leading**: Psalm 23:1-3 paints a vivid image of the Lord as a Shepherd guiding His flock to places of rest and renewal. How have you experienced or longed for this shepherding care amid PTSD? Reflecting on the idea of God as the one who leads you beside calm waters and green pastures, how might embracing this guidance help you navigate the turbulent waters of trauma and find moments of restoration?

2. **Perception and Reality:** Psalm 73 showcases the psalmist's struggle with the seeming prosperity of the wicked. PTSD can similarly skew our perceptions, making us feel trapped in the past. Reflect on the statement, "My flesh and my heart may fail, but God is the strength of my heart." How can this truth clarify when PTSD threatens to distort your present reality? How can you rely on God to strengthen your heart when trauma memories resurface?

3. **God's Peace Amidst Storms:** Isaiah 26:3 speaks of the peace God grants to those who trust in Him. Considering the inner turbulence PTSD often brings, what challenges or hesitations might you have in fully trusting God to maintain peace in your mind? How can grounding yourself in this promise help you move from a state of distress to one of trust especially during the unexpected triggers of PTSD?

REBELLION

Rebellion is ultimately an act of defiance against God. God's tolerance for rebellion is limited because it is akin to brazenly challenging Him directly. It is a willful and obstinate resistance to God's sovereign authority. When people rebel, they are not merely rejecting human ordinances but directly opposing the Almighty Himself. As believers seeking to orient their lives with biblical truths, understanding rebellion's gravity is crucial in returning their hearts to a humble submission under God's loving dominion.

> *For rebellion is like the sin of divination,*
> *and defiance is like wickedness and idolatry.*
> *Because you have rejected the word of the Lord,*
> *he has rejected you as king.*
> **1 Sam 15:23**

This verse provides insight into the grave nature of rebellion against God by particularly equating rebellion with the sin of divination. In this passage, the prophet Samuel rebukes King Saul for his disobedience. This occurrence sheds light on how rebellion reflects a conscious choice to disregard God's commands. It serves as a warning to those who choose their own way over God's way. Rebellion leads to rejection by God. Furthermore, the passage illustrates that obedience to God is better than sacrifices, showing that mere ritualistic compliance is not enough. This truth can be a sobering reminder for those in rebellion to align one's will with God's will. Understanding the spiritual gravity of rebellion can lead to a sincere examination of one's heart and a return to a path of obedience. Lastly, it stresses not merely following religious customs or personal desires but the need for humility and submission to God's authority.

> *Obey your leaders and submit to them, for they*
> *keep watch over your souls as those who will give*
> *an account. Let them do this with joy and not with*
> *grief, for this would be unprofitable for you.*
> **Heb 13:17**

Leaders, especially spiritual leaders, are tasked with soul care and will answer to God for how they either minister to or abuse those under their authority. At the same time, those under the leadership of pastors must understand that these leaders have a weighty task. Rebellious servants or individuals under pastoral leadership are a drain on those entrusted to care for their souls, which makes spiritual leadership jobs more difficult. Rebellion is the push against authority, and if that authority is God-honoring, rebellion is a sin that brings grief to the one leading. Christians should be a source of joy and encouragement to their soul-care leaders rather than a cause of grief. This does not discount the biblical accountability of leaders, but rebellion should be avoided and leadership honored when possible.

> *An evil person desires only rebellion:*
> *a cruel messenger will be sent against him.*
> **Prov 17:11**

The proverb offers an understanding of the nature of rebellion and the consequences that follow. It conveys that those intent on rebellion seek only evil. This saying suggests that rebellion is not a passive or accidental state but an active pursuit contrary to what is good. It warns of the innate connection between rebellion and evil intentions, which leads to deliberate actions that counter God's will. The proverb further emphasizes that a cruel messenger will be sent against the rebellious individual. This truth symbolizes the inevitable consequences or judgments that befall those who act in defiance. In practical terms, this passage serves as a stern warning against choosing a path that disregards moral and biblical order. The wisdom found in these words encourages reflection and self-examination by prompting individuals to consider their actions and attitudes. Ultimately, this verse clearly shows that rebellion against God does not go unnoticed or unpunished. This reality fosters a deep understanding of the importance of obedience and alignment with biblical principles.

Remind them to submit to rulers and authorities, to obey,
to be ready for every good work, to slander no one, to avoid fighting,
and to be kind, always showing gentleness to all people.
Titus 3:1-2

The verses found in Titus 3:1-2 address the principles of submission, obedience, and the proper conduct that believers should exhibit. They emphasize the importance of being submissive to rulers and authorities by extoling believers to live a life that is obedient and ready for every good work. This truth serves as a clear counterpoint to rebellion especially rebellion against God. It provides a roadmap to a more righteous life. These verses remedy the defiant attitude that often accompanies rebellion by highlighting the value of showing perfect courtesy toward all people. The teachings in this passage encourage self-reflection and a transformation from rebelliousness to a life of humility and grace. Moreover, they underscore that rebellion against earthly authorities often mirrors a more rebellion against God. Titus 3:1-2 calls to abandon the path of rebellion and embrace a life marked by obedience, goodness, and respect for God and His plan.

PRACTICAL ADVICE + HOMEWORK

Confess Sin: The sin of rebellion is identifiable by its outward manifestations of complaining speech, wrong thoughts about God, and blame-shifting of personal sin (Deut 1:26-28). (**Homework:** If this is true in your situation, stop right now and confess the sin of rebellion to God.)

Renew Your Mind through Scripture: God condemns rebellion. (**Homework:** Read the following biblical texts to understand how God sees and responds to rebellion: Deuteronomy 1:26-28; 1 Samuel 15 [focus particularly on verses 10-23]; and Isaiah 30:1-5. Answer these questions from the biblical texts you just read: What did you learn about God? What did you learn about yourself? How do your thinking, feelings and actions need to change considering these truths?)

Obey God: Make a commitment to submit to Him each day. (**Homework:** Spend time with God in His Word each day and attend worship at your church each week. Memorize Proverbs 3:5-6 to help you submit to God rather than to your own understanding.)

Seek to Understand Leadership: We are often tempted to rebel because we do not understand where or why we are being led. (**Homework:** Before you rebel against your authority especially pastoral leadership, sit down with the leadership and seek to understand the direction and reasons for their decisions.)

Understand the Gravity of Rebellion: Recognize that rebellion against God's Word is a grave matter that Scripture equates with serious sins. (**Homework:** Reflect on 1 Samuel 15:23 and journal about times when rebellion might have steered you away from God's plan for your life.)

Avoid Cultivating a Rebellious Heart: Understanding that continuous rebellion can lead to further estrangement from God. Additionally, His blessings should encourage believers against acting rebelliously any longer and encourage them to conduct a personal evaluation of areas in which they do not bring God praise, glory, and honor. (**Homework:** List ways or areas in your life where you might be rebelling against biblical or worldly authority and seek reconciliation.)

Seek God's Wisdom: When you doubt an authority, seek biblical wisdom. God's wisdom in this regard encourages those practicing rebellion to search the Bible, which offers them a stable and trustworthy sense of direction. Reading and obeying the Word will convince them of their need to align their thoughts and actions with biblical principles. This kind of behavior results from seeking biblical wisdom, which leads to a God-honoring life. (**Homework:** Spend time in prayer asking God to help you discern and submit to righteous authorities in your life.)

Seek Wise Counsel: When struggling with feelings of rebellion, confide in a trusted believer or mentor to gain perspective. It is hard to remain in rebellion when you are actively seeking help from others. Your natural tendency will be to reject the authority over you, but you need to be held accountable by a godly authority figure. (**Homework:** Discuss your feelings and actions with a spiritual mentor or trusted individual to gain wisdom and truth.)

Discussion Starters

1. **Grasping the Weight of Rebellion:** Considering the weight of the message in 1 Samuel 15:23, how do you perceive rebellion in your life? Does understanding its comparison to divination provide a clearer picture of its severity? How can we draw parallels from King Saul's actions to moments when we may have prioritized our desires over God's commands?

2. **Reflecting on Leadership and Submission:** Considering Hebrews 13:17, what are your feelings toward the leaders God has placed in your life? Do you find it easy or challenging to submit to them? How might recognizing their burdens and responsibilities shape your understanding and reactions toward their leadership?

3. **Examining the Heart's Intent:** Proverbs 17:11 depicts rebellion as more than just a one-off act but as a deep-seated intention

of the heart. Can you identify times when your intentions have strayed from God's will? How might leaning into the wisdom of Proverbs steer you away from rebellion and closer to obedience?

REJECTION

Rejection is an emotional experience marked by feelings of isolation, abandonment, and a deep-seated sense of unworthiness. Many biblical figures felt rejection and their stories provide valuable insight into how faith can offer comfort and guidance in seasons like this. Throughout the Bible, numerous individuals faced rejection like Joseph being sold by his brothers, David being pursued by King Saul, and Jesus being denied by Peter. When someone feels the sting of rejection, it is crucial that he/she remember that his/her personal worth is not defined by the acceptance of others but by his/her identity in Christ.

Do not cast me off in the time of old age;
Do not forsake me when my strength fails.
Ps 71:9

The psalmist writes about how God has made him a marvel to many through God's miraculous work in and around his life. This led the writer to a life of praise and adoration of the Lord and of declaring so to all around him. The writer's enemies have taken notice of the trouble in his life and are seeking an opportunity to destroy him because they think God has forsaken him. The psalmist's prayer is that God would not leave him alone and in need during his old age (*e.g.*, time of vulnerability) or when his strength fails (*e.g.*, when he is weakest). God would never do such a thing, so the writer is just expressing his heart by bringing his needs before the Lord. Christians must understand that even though they *know* the Lord will never reject or forsake them, it is okay for them to bring those things to the Lord in prayer. The practice of asking God to keep His Word is a statement of faith in Him. God delights when His children depend on Him.

> *Fear not, for I have redeemed you; I have called you by name, you are mine.*
> **Isa 43:1**

For someone grappling with rejection, the feeling of abandonment can be overwhelming. This passage particularly applies to someone dealing with rejection because it addresses personal worth and belonging. Rejection often leads to feelings of unworthiness and a painful sense that he/she does not belong or is not valued. This verse directly counters that perception by stating that God has redeemed the individual. God calls him/her by name and affirms that he/she belongs to Him. The assurance that God knows and claims him/her can provide a sense of acceptance that transcends human relationships. It shifts the focus from the rejection by people to the embracing love and approval of God. An individual grapples with rejection, he/she may find comfort, affirmation, and a restored sense of self-value rooted in his/her relationship with God by meditating on this truth. Isaiah 43:1 is a powerful reminder of his/her intrinsic worth and eternal acceptance in the eyes of his/her Creator.

> *For the Lord will not reject his people; he will never forsake his inheritance.*
> **Ps 94:14**

Psalm 94:14 serves as a powerful reminder that rejection is not a final decision for those who belong to God's family. Unlike failed human relationships that can lead to feelings of rejection and abandonment, God's commitment to His people is unbreakable and eternal. This verse can be a source of comfort for those who feel rejected as it redirects their focus from being rejected by others to their becoming steadfast in believing God has accepted them. It asserts a divine promise that no matter how isolated or forsaken believers might feel as a result of others' actions, God will never reject or forsake them. In the context of rejection, this verse serves as a reminder that Christians' true worth and belonging are found in their relationship with God, not in human acceptance or approval. The unchanging nature of God's love expressed in this verse offers a stable foundation for them to rebuild their sense of self-worth and identity. This truth becomes a powerful tool for healing and overcoming the painful experience of rejection.

Cast your burden on the Lord, and he will sustain you;
he will never allow the righteous to be shaken.
Ps 55:22

Dealing with rejection often involves carrying a heavy emotional burden. Psalm 55:22 is beneficial for someone who feels rejected because it addresses the emotional burden he/she carries. "Cast your burden on the Lord, and he will sustain you; he will never allow the righteous to be shaken" is a reassuring invitation for him/her to lay the heavy weight of rejection before God. It acknowledges that the feelings associated with rejection are not insignificant. The emotions that result from rejection are burdensome and can deeply shake the dejected person. Nevertheless, this verse also offers a divine solution because it promises that God will receive and sustain the one who turns to Him. It emphasizes that God's support is steadfast and unshakeable. God provides stability, even when rejection makes everything else uncertain. The verse encourages a trusting relationship with God, whereby his/her pain can be shared and his/her healing can begin. By casting the burden of rejection on the Lord, the hurting person can find a source of strength and resilience rooted in biblical truth rather than human validation.

Let all bitterness and wrath and anger and clamor
and slander be put away from you, along with all
malice. Be kind to one another, tenderhearted,
forgiving one another, as God in Christ forgave you.
Eph 4:31-32

In the throes of rejection, the emotional turbulence a dejected person feels can quickly devolve into bitterness, wrath, and anger. Ephesians 4:31-32 speaks directly to those feelings, urging him/her to put away such negative emotions and reactions. The hurt and pain of rejection can overwhelm him/her, leading him/her to harbor resentment and/or speak ill of those who caused his/her pain. The Scripture prescribes a Christ-like response to rejection. A rejected individual is asked to be kind, tenderhearted, and forgiving. Doing so is a reflection of the love and forgiveness the person who has been hurt has received from God through Christ. By meditating on these verses, he/she can be reminded that the ultimate standard of his/her reactions to life's hurts is anchored in the grace he/she has been given. This grace-centered perspective offers a roadmap for navigating rejection. Even in the most hurt, he/she can choose kindness, compassion, and forgiveness, which leads to healing. This decision mirrors God's heart. Paul's writing serves as a foundational Scripture for the individual battling the pain of rejection by reminding him/her of the transformative power of Christ's love and forgiveness.

> *But whoever has doubts is condemned if he*
> *eats because the eating is not from faith. For*
> *whatever does not proceed from faith is sin.*
> **Rom 14:23**

Navigating rejection requires a heart anchored in faith. Paul highlights the importance of acting from a place of faith and conviction. For people facing rejection, the pain might tempt them to respond or act in ways that do not align with their faith. This verse serves as a reminder that actions taken without the backing of faith are not only futile but also sinful. It emphasizes the need to remain rooted in their beliefs even when experiencing feelings of inadequacy or abandonment. When counseling those who grapple with rejection, this verse can be a tool to help them reflect on their actions and ensure all actions align with their faith. Even in the face of rejection, individuals can maintain integrity, find strength, and remain aligned with God's will when they act out of faith. This passage is an essential cornerstone for those seeking to navigate rejection biblically as it urges them to act from a place of faith and trust in God's plan.

PRACTICAL ADVICE + HOMEWORK

Confess Sin: Even if those who have an obligation to love you the most reject you, the Lord does not. Sometimes, you will be tempted to ascribe the actions of those who have sinned against you to God. Doing so is not an accurate picture of what he does or who He is (Ps 27:10). You may occasionally feel like He is far away; however, that feeling is also not true (Ps 145:17-19). (**Homework:** If you are guilty of ascribing sinful human nature to a holy God, stop right now and confess that sin to Him.)

Renew Your Mind through Scripture: God promises that He does not leave us or forsake us, and we must accept this truth by faith. (**Homework:** Read the following biblical texts to understand God's promises to you: Psalm 145:17-19; John 10:27-30; John 14:15-21; and Romans 8:35-39. Answer these questions from the biblical text you just read: What did you learn about God? What did you learn about yourself? How do your thinking, feelings, and actions need to change considering these truths?)

Obey God: Commit yourself to believing that He is with you even when you feel rejected and alone. (**Homework:** Spend time with God in His Word each day and attend worship at your church each week. Meditate on the truths of these biblical texts, and memorize Romans 8:35-39 to help you think truth when you feel alone.)

Embrace Your Identity in God: Know that you are God's child, and that human rejection does not define you. Find your worth in being God's child rather than seeking man's approval. (**Homework:** Reflect on Isaiah 43:1 daily. Write down how it makes you feel and how it shapes your understanding of yourself.)

Pray Scripture's Promises: God will never reject us, and we must remind ourselves of such. Praying Scripture back to God builds our confidence in His acceptance of us as His children. (**Homework:** Find several scriptural promises that speak to your circumstances and heart in this time. Pray those Scriptures to the Lord daily, asking Him to honor His Word while giving you strength and faith to endure while you wait on Him.)

Find Security in God's Acceptance: Rest in the truth that God accepts His people, and you belong to Him. God's love is unwavering and steadfast. (**Homework:** Memorize Psalm 94:14 this week. Repeat it to yourself when feelings of rejection impose on your thoughts.)

Lay Your Burdens Before God: When feeling overwhelmed by rejection, surrender your burdens to God in prayer. Trusting Him to sustain you. Daily surrender the pain of rejection to God and be assured of His supportive presence. (**Homework:** Spend ten minutes in prayer each evening. Focusing on Psalm 55:22 and cast your burdens on Him.)

Engage in Service: Focusing on others can shift your perspective and alleviate feelings of rejection. When you are focused on helping others, your mindset will move from self and instead puts your mind on helping those in need. (**Homework:** Volunteer or find ways to serve others. Reflect on Christ's love to those around you, as well as to yourself.)

Discussion Starters

1. **Wrestling with Feelings of Abandonment:** Considering the deep yearning and plea in Psalm 71:9 of "Do not cast me off in the time of old age; Do not forsake me when my strength fails," have you ever felt this sincere call to God during times you experienced rejection and/or abandonment? How can grounding your worth and identity in God's eternal acceptance, as emphasized in Isaiah 43:1, reshape your understanding of your value, especially when you feel most forsaken by others?

2. **The Assurance of God's Acceptance:** Psalm 94:14 declares, "For the Lord will not reject his people; he will never forsake his inheritance." How does this truth speak to the areas where you have felt the most rejected? As you meditate on the promise of God's unwavering acceptance and your place as His inheritance, how does this reshape your perspective when faced with the fleeting approval of man?

3. **Navigating the Emotional Weight of Rejection:** The encouragement in Psalm 55:22 is to "Cast your burden on the Lord, and he will sustain you; he will never allow the righteous to be shaken." What burdens do you need to lay before God in your journey of handling rejection? How might surrendering these feelings of abandonment and seeking solace in His sustaining power guide you to a more sense of peace and resilience?

RELATIONAL IDOLATRY

Relational idolatry occurs when individuals prioritize their desires and relationships over their relationship with God, leading them to isolate themselves from God and others in pursuit of self-satisfying desires.

One who isolates himself pursues selfish desires;
he rebels against all sound wisdom.
Prov 18:1

This Scripture highlights that in such a context, isolation is not merely a state of being alone but an active rebellion against godly wisdom. This form of isolation stems from a self-centered mindset where the individual becomes the sole determiner of his/her path by disregarding God's counsel and the wisdom of others. Such a mindset can cause him/her to drift away from the truth and expose him/her to various dangers and temptations. Furthermore, the Scripture makes it evident that the isolation borne from relational idolatry is not only self-destructive but also counter to God's design for community and mutual edification. This verse becomes a mirror in counseling as it reflects the dangerous path of the one ensnared in relational idolatry. By meditating on this wisdom, an individual can be encouraged to shift focus from himself/herself to God. By doing so, he/she will recognize the value of godly relationships along with the importance of seeking wisdom outside of his/her own understanding.

> *Do nothing out of selfish ambition or conceit,*
> *but in humility consider others as more*
> *important than yourselves. Everyone should*
> *look not to his own interests, but rather*
> *to the interests of others.*
> **Phil 2:3-4**

Philippians 2:3-4 presents a counter-narrative to the pitfalls of relational idolatry. At the heart of relational idolatry lies a skewed perception that seeks to elevate human relationships above one's relationship with God. This understanding is oftentimes rooted in selfish desires or a deep-seated need for validation and approval. Such tendencies can lead an individual to place an unhealthy emphasis on another person's opinions, affirmations, or desires, which effectively replaces God's sovereign place in his/her life. These verses advise a different approach. They call for a heart posture of humility by urging the believer to prioritize the well-being and interests of others above his/her own. This is not a call to seek validation but to genuinely care for and serve others selflessly. By encouraging this mindset, the Scripture directly confronts the essence of relational idolatry by emphasizing that relationships should not be avenues for selfish gain or validation. Instead, relationships should be platforms for selfless love that mirrors Christ's love. Furthermore, the directive to "do nothing out of selfish ambition or conceit" is a potent reminder of the dangers of allowing pride or personal desires to govern our relationships. Such motivations can easily blur the boundaries of healthy interactions and lead to patterns of codependency or relational idolatry.

> **You shall have no other gods before Me.**
> **Ex 20:3**

At its essence, this directive from the Book of Exodus establishes the priority of God first above all else. The command is clear, straightforward, and devoid of ambiguity. The sin of relational idolatry emerges when our reverence, dedication, or obsession with another individual precedes our commitment to God. Such misplaced adoration can manifest in many ways: an excessive reliance on someone for emotional sustenance; an overwhelming desire for approval; or a drive to base our self-worth on our relationship status. In elevating a person to this pedestal, we inadvertently grant them divine attributes they neither possess nor can fulfill. A dangerous action that sets both parties up for disappointment. This commandment is a reminder that only God with His unending love and eternal nature should occupy the highest throne in our hearts. Individuals can recalibrate their relationships by internalizing this truth. Doing this ensures that our relationships are rooted in healthy dynamics and mutual respect rather than a toxic cycle of dependency and idolization.

> ***Anyone who loves their father or mother more than me is not worthy of me; anyone who loves their son or daughter more than me is not worthy of me.***
> **Matt 10:37**

We fall into the trap of relational idolatry when we allow a human relationship whether with parents, children, or anyone else, to surpass our love for God. This distorts our relationship with the person and detracts from our relationship with God. By placing someone else in God's rightful position in our hearts, we risk compromising the principles and commandments He has set for us. This potentially leads to harmful decisions and outcomes. Moreover, no human relationship can provide the eternal security, love, and fulfillment that God can. By seeking in others what can only be found in God, we inadvertently set ourselves up for heartbreak and dissatisfaction. In these verses, Jesus guides us to a healthier balance which ensures our love for God remains supreme. This ultimately leads to healthier, more grounded human relationships undergirded by divine love and guidance. He is cautioning against putting finite humans in the infinite space only God should occupy. This teaching serves as a potent antidote to relational idolatry because it reminds believers of the primacy of their relationship with God and the dangers of substituting any earthly relationship in its place.

Indeed, I count everything as loss because of the surpassing worth of knowing Christ Jesus my Lord. For his sake I have suffered the loss of all things and count them as rubbish, in order that I may gain Christ.
Phil 3:8

The Apostle Paul provides a clear and potent reflection of the value he places on his relationship with Christ in these verses by emphasizing its supremacy over all else. This passionate proclamation stems from a transformative encounter with Jesus on the road to Damascus which reshaped his worldview and value system. It is evident that for Paul, no earthly accolade, status, or relationship could compare to the "surpassing worth of knowing Christ Jesus." At the heart of relational idolatry is the misplacement of priority. This prioritization is where we elevate or pursue human relationships above our relationship with God. Such idolatry can manifest in a variety of ways from seeking validation, love, or security primarily from other humans to being overly devastated by the loss or challenges in relationships. Paul's words in Philippians remind us that no matter how meaningful our earthly relationships might be, they should never overshadow our relationship with Christ. Paul's use of the term "rubbish" to describe everything else compared to Christ is particularly striking. It is a vivid metaphor that underscores the transient and perishable nature of worldly gains and human relationships, particularly compared to Christ's eternal and unchanging love. Paul's perspective offers an antidote to relational idolatry by encouraging reevaluating where we find our true worth and identity.

PRACTICAL ADVICE + HOMEWORK

Confess Sin: Pride lies behind independence and codependence. You must recognize that truth as you humbly confess these personal sins. Knowing that God is faithful to forgive and cleanse your heart following confession encourages this humble and obedient action. (**Homework:** Stop right now and confess known sins.)

Relational Idolatry

Renew Your Mind through Scripture: All proper relationships begin with God's dependence. A proper view of man incorporates acknowledging his desperate need (Ps 40:17) and receiving the discerning counsel of God (James 1:5). These truths come from Scripture and are essential for correcting unbiblical thinking about ones' self. (**Homework:** Read the following biblical texts to understand God's dependence: Proverbs 121:1-8; Matthew 6:25-34; and Matthew 11:28-30. Answer these questions from the biblical text you just read: What did you learn about God? What did you learn about man (yourself)? How do your thinking, feelings, and actions need to change considering these truths?)

Obey God: Put God first in your mind and heart. Demonstrate your obedience through your faithful attendance to corporate worship. (**Homework:** Spend time with God in His Word each day and attend worship at your church each week. Participate in small groups if they are available for needed fellowship and accountability.)

Prayerful Inventory: Before bed, spend five minutes talking to God about the relationships you navigated during the day. Ask for wisdom to keep Him first. (**Homework:** Make this a nightly routine.)

Confess the Sinful Heart of Pride: Pride results from sinful independence and codependence. You must recognize this truth as you humbly confess these personal sins. Knowing that God is faithful to forgive and cleanse your heart following confession encourages this humble and obedient action. (**Homework:** Stop right now and confess your sins.)

Measure Your Loss: If the idea of losing a particular relationship troubles you more than the idea of losing your relationship with God, it is a red flag. (**Homework:** Take a heart inventory by listing relationships and how much emotional weight you give them. Compare this list to the emotional and spiritual weight you give your relationship with God. Rebalance as needed.)

Accountability Partner: Find someone who can serve as a spiritual mentor to hold you accountable in avoiding relational idolatry. (**Homework:** Schedule a monthly catch-up with this person to discuss your challenges and victories in this area.)

Scriptural Anchor: Pick a verse, like Psalm 118:8, that helps you combat relational idolatry and then memorize it. (**Homework:** Repeat this verse to yourself whenever you are tempted to place human relationships higher than your relationship with God.)

DISCUSSION STARTERS

1. **Relational Priorities in the Eyes of God:** Reflecting on Proverbs 18:1 and Exodus 20:3, have you ever found yourself placing a relationship above God either knowingly or unknowingly? How can understanding the true essence of these verses help redirect our priorities and ensure God remains preeminent in all relationships?

2. **Sacrificial Love vs. Selfish Desires:** Philippians 2:3-4 speaks of valuing others above oneself, which contrasts sharply with the concept of relational idolatry. How can you identify signs of selfish ambition in your relationships? What steps can you take to cultivate a heart that genuinely prioritizes others and reflects Christ's love?

3. **Measuring the Weight of Relationships:** In light of both Philippians 3:8 and Matthew 10:37, consider the various relationships in your life. Which relationships consume most of your emotional energy, and how do they compare to the weight you give to your relationship with Christ? How might re-evaluating and recalibrating these emotional investments align better with God's design for your relationships?

SEXUAL IMMORALITY

The term "sexual immorality," derived from the Greek word *porneia*, predominantly refers to fornication, which is the act of engaging in sexual relations between individuals who are not united in the covenant of marriage. The Bible is clear regarding the sacredness of the marital bond and the sanctity of the sexual union within that bond. To act as though married outside this divine institution is to tread outside the boundaries God has lovingly set for our protection and well-being. Embracing God's design for sexuality within the confines of marriage fosters a pure relationship that honors both our Creator and the sanctity of our own bodies.

> *Flee sexual immorality! Every other sin a person commits is outside the body, but the person who is sexually immoral sins against his own body. Don't you know that your body is a temple of the Holy Spirit who is in you, whom you have from God? You are not your own, for you were bought at a price. So, glorify God with your body.*
> **1 Cor 6:18-20**

Paul speaks directly to sexual immorality by commanding believers to flee from it and explaining why it is distinct from other sins. These verses emphasize the sacredness of the human body as a temple of the Holy Spirit. For someone struggling with sexual immorality, the passage provides a solid rationale for pursuing purity by reminding him/her that Jesus bought him/her with a price. This transaction alludes to

Christ's sacrifice. Furthermore, the connection between the body and the Holy Spirit emphasizes the importance of honoring God with one's body. This act of honoring includes one's sexuality. The passage also provides hope and direction for the person who is struggling by pointing him/her toward God's standards for sexual conduct. Overall, these verses create a compelling argument against sexual immorality by drawing attention to the spiritual significance of the body and calling for a life that aligns with God's design and purpose. This call serves as both a warning and an encouragement as it steers those who read them towards a path of integrity and   holiness in their sexual conduct.

Let us behave properly as in the day, not in carousing and drunkenness,
not in sexual promiscuity and sensuality, not in strife and jealousy.
But put on the Lord Jesus Christ and make no provision for
the flesh in regard to its lusts.
Rom 13:13-14

Paul tells the church that sexual promiscuity and sensuality are not proper behavior for believing Christians. Sexual promiscuity refers to the casual acceptance and viewing of sexual relationships with various individuals such that sexual encounters would be viewed no different than just a casual date. Sexual sensuality refers to the loosening of moral restraints and seeking to gratify the fleshly appetite for sex. Such behaviors are viewed as fleshly living and as succumbing to the lusts of the flesh. Paul tells the Christians to make no provision for such behaviors. This means that believers are to actively avoid partaking in these activities and desires and conversely seek to honor God's vision for sexuality as a pure practice only carried out in a marriage relationship.

For this is God's will, your sanctification: that you keep away
from sexual immorality, that each of you knows how to control his
own body in holiness and honor, not with lustful passions,
like the Gentiles, who don't know God.
1 Thess 4:3-5

Sexual Immorality

This passage addresses the issue of sexual immorality directly by defining God's will for believers which includes their sanctification and avoidance of sexual impurity. Paul emphasizes that living in holiness and honor is a calling from God and contrasts with unfortunately common lustful passion among those who do not know God. This instruction sets clear boundaries and provides a spiritual and moral framework for understanding sexuality. For those struggling with sexual immorality, these verses offer guidance and purpose. Pursuing purity is not only about personal morality but also about aligning with God's will. Furthermore, the passage reassures believers that they have the Holy Spirit's empowerment to live out this calling. By underscoring the link between sexual behavior and one's relationship with God, the text serves as a compelling reminder of the spiritual implications of one's physical actions. 1 Thessalonians 4:3-5 offers both challenge and comfort to those seeking to overcome sexual immorality and live in a way that honors God.

> *Marriage is to be honored by all and the*
> *marriage bed kept undefiled, because God*
> *will judge the sexually immoral and adulterers*
> **Heb 13:4**

Paul places a high value on the sanctity of marriage, stating that the marriage bed should remain undefiled and warning that God will judge those who engage in sexual immorality. This verse serves as a strong directive for those struggling with sexual misconduct because it emphasizes the importance of maintaining purity within the bounds of marriage. This a clear guideline for acceptable behavior for someone grappling with these issues as it aligns sexual behavior with the broader Christian ethical framework. It is not simply a rule but an affirmation of a worldview that sees sexual relations within marriage as honorable and sacred. It provides a sobering incentive to seek help, accountability, and personal transformation by presenting sexual immorality as something that will face judgment. The context of Hebrews encourages readers to live lives pleasing to God and sexual integrity is a vital part of a God honoring life. Altogether, this passage encourages the pursuit of holiness by aligning one's actions with a faith-centered understanding of sexuality.

> *For out of the heart come evil thoughts, murders, adulteries,*
> *sexual immorality, thefts, false testimony, and blasphemies.*
> **Matt 15:19**

In this verse, Jesus addresses the root of sexual immorality. He traces it back to the heart and its intentions. This implies that the actions of sexual misconduct are not just random occurrences but arise from deep-seated desires and thoughts within an individual's heart. For someone seeking counsel on sexual impropriety, this revelation is vital as it shifts the focus from external behavior modification to a transformative heart change. Addressing the issue at its core requires a genuine relationship with Christ who is the only one capable of changing the heart. By understanding that the heart is the wellspring of these actions, one can take the necessary steps towards genuine repentance though seeking God's transformative power. Including sexual immorality alongside other sins such as murder, theft, and blasphemy underscores its seriousness in God's eyes. This verse serves as both an insightful diagnostic tool and a guide to the path of renewal and redemption.

> *But I tell you that anyone who looks at a woman lustfully*
> *has already committed adultery with her in his heart.*
> **Matt 5:28**

In the Sermon on the Mount, Jesus intensifies the understanding of sexual sin by asserting that even a lustful look is tantamount to adultery. This verse emphasizes the idea that purity is not only about actions but also about the intentions and desires of the heart. It broadens the perspective on sexual immorality by noting that it is not just physical actions but also mental and emotional engagements that God is concerned about. Jesus underscores the seriousness of maintaining mental and emotional purity by equating lustful thoughts with adultery. For someone struggling with sexual misconduct, this verse is a powerful reminder to guard their actions and thoughts. It challenges believers to maintain a higher standard of purity that aligns with the holistic and encompassing nature of God's commandments. By internalizing the teachings of this verse, one can work towards creating a safeguard against temptations and recognize the value of purity in all facets of life.

Practical Advice + Homework

Confess Sin: Sexual immorality is the result of misplaced worship. When we worship the creature instead of the Creator, it always has a sexual expression (Rom 1:18-32). (**Homework:** If this is true in your situation, stop right now and confess the sin of idolatry as well as its outward sexual expression to God.)

Renew Your Mind through Scripture: God's Word explains the cause of sexual immorality and gives the remedy. (**Homework:** Read the following biblical texts to understand the cause and the solutions for sexual immorality: Romans 1:18-32; 1 Corinthians 5:13-20; and Colossians 3:1-5. Answer these questions from the biblical text you just read: What did you learn about God? What did you learn about yourself? How do your thinking, feelings, and actions need to change considering these truths?)

Obey God: Decide you will worship Him rather than anyone or anything else. (**Homework:** Spend time with God in His Word each day and attend worship at your church each week. Confess your sin to God and to others you have sinned against sexually. Participate in small groups within your church for accountability as extoled in James 5:16.)

Value Your Body: Remember that your body is a temple of the Holy Spirit and treating it respectfully honors God. This concept of the body as a temple is repeated often which shows its importance. (**Homework:** Reflect on 1 Corinthians 6:18-20 and journal how to honor God with your body.)

Avoid Situations and Circumstances: Avoid situations and circumstances that feed your lusts or make promiscuity readily available to engage in. (**Homework:** Identify the locations, times of day, and circumstances/stimuli that trigger desires or thoughts of sexual immorality. Journal these. Meet with a trusted friend to develop a plan of how to avoid them and respond to them in a way that honors God, so you are prepared to win rather than fall to temptations.)

Practice Self-Control: Cultivate a spirit of self-control and distance yourself from situations that might lead to temptation. Honoring God with their body as instructed in 1 Corinthians 6:18-20. (**Homework:** Identify potential triggers or conditions that might lead to sexual temptation and develop strategies to avoid or combat them.)

Honor Marriage: If you are married or considering marriage, treat the institution with the respect God intends. If you are single, respect the marriages of others. For someone dealing with sexual immorality, adhering to this principle can guide them towards living in alignment with biblical values by fostering healthy relationships and personal integrity. (**Homework:** Reflect on Hebrews 13:4 and consider ways to uphold the sanctity of marriage in your own life and community.)

Seek God's Will: Strive to align your desires with God's design for purity and sanctification., Individuals find fulfillment, healing, and peace that honors the Creator's intentions through pursuing a life according to God's plan. (**Homework:** Dedicate a specific time each day for a week to pray and seek God's Wisdom on maintaining purity.)

DISCUSSION STARTERS

1. **The Body as a Temple:** 1 Corinthians 6:18-20 speaks to the sacredness of our bodies as the temple of the Holy Spirit. How does understanding your body as a dwelling place for the Spirit of God

shape your perspective on sexual purity? Considering this truth, how can you actively make choices that honor God with your body, recognizing its immense value in His eyes?

2. **God's Vision for Purity:** Romans 13:13-14 and 1 Thessalonians 4:3-5 draw a clear distinction between the desires of the flesh and God's call to sanctification. Can you identify moments or situations where you have felt the pull of these fleshly desires? How can the practice of "putting on the Lord Jesus Christ" daily transform your responses to temptations and align your actions more closely with God's vision for purity?

3. **Heart's Intention and Actions:** Jesus' words in Matthew 15:19 and 5:28 emphasize that our actions, especially those in the realm of sexuality, originate from the heart's intentions. What steps can you take to cultivate a heart that desires God's righteousness? How can understanding that even lustful thoughts are equivalent to adultery encourage you to guard not just your actions but also your thoughts and emotions?

SLEEP/INSOMNIA

Sleep issues, including insomnia, cannot be reduced merely to a medical inconvenience or the restless tossing of a weary body; they are often windows into the soul's unrest before the Lord. While our Creator designed sleep as a gift of restoration and trust, an embodied reminder that He alone sustains the world, sleepless nights frequently reveal anxieties, misplaced confidences, or burdens we have struggled to yield to Him. They expose the tension between our frailty and our reluctance to rest in God's care. From a biblical perspective, insomnia is not simply about brain chemistry or disrupted patterns, but about the heart's struggle to find peace in the presence of the One who neither slumbers nor sleeps.

And He said to them, "Come away by yourselves to a secluded place
and rest a while" (For there were many people coming and going,
and they did not even have time to eat).
Mark 6:31

Jesus highlights the importance of rest and retreat, offering a biblical solution to those grappling with insomnia and the resultant weariness. The disciples were so engrossed in their work that they did not even have time to eat. They had overlooked the basic human need for rest in their passionate zeal. Jesus, being fully God and fully man, perfectly understood human limitations and the intrinsic need for rejuvenation. By inviting His disciples to a secluded place, He emphasized the significance of detachment from ceaseless activity and the clamor of life. This act was not only about physical relaxation but also a time of spiritual renewal, reflection, and intimacy with the Father. Jesus, amidst His earthly ministry, saw the need for sleep. For someone struggling with insomnia, this verse is a potent reminder to prioritize rest and self-care through understanding that rest is divinely sanctioned. Furthermore, this Scripture teaches that genuine rest is not merely physical but also involves drawing near to God. An individual can find peace in God's presence and thereby let go of worldly anxieties. It serves as a gentle reminder that he/she is not designed to operate ceaselessly. In moments of exhaustion, God provides him/her with an invitation to find rest and renewal in Him.

> *In vain you get up early and stay up late, working hard to*
> *have enough food—yes, he gives sleep to the one he loves.*
> **Ps 127:2**

The psalmist speaks to the futility of anxious toil and highlights that rest is a gift from God. This passage can comfort someone struggling with sleep, reassuring him/her that relentless worry and work are unnecessary. It emphasizes that true rest and peace come from trusting in God's provision and care rather than relying solely on his/her efforts. For the person plagued by insomnia or anxiety at night, the verse encourages him/her to shift his/her perspective. By doing so, the individual may find solace in relinquishing control and allowing faith to guide his/her rest. The message of this psalm promotes a balanced lifestyle and underscores the importance of trust in God, which leads to a more peaceful state of mind conducive to sleep. Overall, this passage can serve as a spiritual guide and comfort for the one struggling with sleep by encouraging him/her to rely on biblical wisdom rather than human anxiety and effort.

> *When you lie down, you will not be afraid;*
> *you will lie down, and your sleep will be pleasant*
> **Prov 3:24**

This verse provides wisdom that can be deeply comforting for those struggling with sleep as it promises that those who find wisdom and understanding will sleep without fear. The verse suggests that peace of mind and security come from trusting in biblical wisdom not in human strength or understanding. People struggling with insomnia or anxiety can find solace in the idea that aligning themselves with God's wisdom will lead to peaceful sleep. This connection between spiritual alignment and physical rest highlights that the state of their souls is deeply connected to their bodily well-being. Additionally, the assurance of safety and rest emphasizes the importance of surrendering control and trusting God. For those who find sleep elusive, this passage can encourage a shift in focus from worry to faith. Proverbs 3:24 can be a source of comfort and encouragement by promoting trust in God to achieve peaceful sleep.

> **The sleep of the worker is sweet, whether he eats little or much,**
> **but the abundance of the rich permits him no sleep.**
> **Eccl 5:12**

The insight found in this passage speaks about the relationship between contentment and restful sleep. It contrasts the rest of a laborer who is tired and therefore sleeps well with the restless sleep of the rich who are burdened with worries. This passage teaches that contentment and a clear conscience can lead to better sleep, while anxiety and greed can disrupt rest. It encourages individuals to find satisfaction in their daily work and not to be consumed by the pursuit of wealth or constant worries. People facing sleep difficulties can reflect on the underlying causes, such as stress or dissatisfaction, and seek to address these issues. By promoting an attitude of contentment and trust, this verse points to better mental and emotional well-being. Ultimately, it underscores the importance of a balanced life and the cultivation of inner peace as pathways to restful sleep.

> **It is in vain that you rise up early and go late to rest,**
> **eatingthe bread of anxious toil; for he gives to his beloved sleep.**
> **Ps 127:2**

A Biblical Handbook for Counseling Heart Issues

The psalmist addresses the futility of restless work and worries by shedding light on the delicate balance between human responsibility and divine provision. First, he cautions against an excessive reliance on one's own efforts to the point of neglecting rest, which illustrates that such tireless endeavors might not yield the desired outcomes. The one who suffers from insomnia does so because of an overactive mind that is consumed with his/her worries, plans, or fears about the future. The psalmist recognizes this issue and suggests that such constant labor and anxiety can be fruitless. The verse emphasizes the idea that genuine rest and the restoration that comes from sleep is a divine gift given by God to those He loves. The person who suffers from insomnia is encouraged to reflect upon and understand that while he/she might do his/her part in seeking solutions, ultimately God Himself is the true giver of peaceful sleep. This realization can lead to a change in his/her perspective. Rather than seeing sleep as something to be anxiously pursued, it can be viewed as a gracious gift to be received. In the context of biblical counseling for insomnia, this verse serves as a prompt for someone to evaluate the root causes of his/her sleeplessness. Is he/she overly preoccupied with tasks or anxieties? Is he/she trying too hard in his/her own strength without looking to God? By understanding and embracing the teachings of this psalm, such a person can begin the journey to a peaceful night's rest grounded in the knowledge that God, in His loving care, desires to gift him/her the rest he/she desperately seeks.

> *In peace I will both lie down and sleep;*
> *for you alone, O Lord, make me dwell in safety.*
> **Ps 4:8**

David illuminates the juxtaposition of peace and safety with God as its source. For individuals plagued with insomnia, the night can often be a haunting reminder of physical and mental unrest. This Scripture reframes that narrative by suggesting that their solace does not hinge on external circumstances but on God's unwavering presence. The assuring statement, "for you alone, O Lord, make me dwell in safety," reiterates that safety and peace are found in God's presence not just in the absence of threats or concerns. In counseling, Psalm 4:8 becomes a grounding Scripture that urges individuals to shift their focus from the anxieties that keep them awake to the encompassing safety of God's arms. Meditating on this verse can become a spiritual lullaby as it reminds sleep-deprived souls that rest is not just shutting their eyes, but leaning into the embrace of a protective God. By embedding this truth into their hearts, those battling insomnia can transition from seeking mere sleep to seeking God's peace, which ultimately provides the rest for which they yearn.

> *When I am afraid, I put my trust in you.*
> **Ps 56:3**

Insomnia often arises not just from physical conditions, but also from emotional and spiritual unrest. Whether about past mistakes, future uncertainties, or present challenges; deep-seated fears can relentlessly churn in our minds during the night hours. The verse from Psalm 56:3 offers a direct response to these anxieties. It points out that trusting in God can remedy fear-driven sleeplessness. Having faced numerous life-threatening situations, David found solace by redirecting his focus from his fears to his faith in God. When we struggle with insomnia because of our anxieties, meditating on this Scripture can be a gentle reminder that we have a divine source of comfort and assurance. This shift of focus helps cultivate a mental environment conducive to sleep. Grounding ourselves in the certainty of God's sovereignty and care allows us to release our grip on our worries. Instead, we can embrace the peace and safety that comes from trusting in a God who neither slumbers nor sleeps. Overall, this verse emphasizes the concept that true spiritual and physical rest can be found when we shift our trust from our own abilities and understanding to the ever-watchful care of God.

PRACTICAL ADVICE + HOMEWORK

Confess Sin: If you are keeping yourself awake with worry, the heart of the problem lies in a lack of trust in God. (**Homework:** If this is true in your situation, stop right now and confess the sin of worry and lack of trust in Him to God.)

Renew Your Mind through Scripture: God promises to give His beloved sleep (Ps 127:2). Even when they trouble themselves with worries, He visits them in the night to meet with them (Ps 17:3). (**Homework:** Read the following biblical texts to understand how God works in the nighttime hours: Psalm 16; Psalm 17; and Psalm 63:1-8. Answer these questions from the biblical text you just read: What did you learn about God? What did you learn about yourself? How do your thinking, feelings and actions need to change considering these truths?)

Obey God: Trust Him no matter the day's worries. (**Homework:** Spend time with God in His Word each day and particularly before going to bed at night. Attend worship at your church each week. Put on the full armor of God [Eph 6:10-18] before sleeping so that even as you may feel vulnerable in sleep, you remember God is protecting you. Do not forget that you are in a relationship with a God who neither slumbers nor sleeps [Ps 121:3-4], but who attentively watches over you as you rest [Ps 4:8]).

Trust in God's Provision: Avoid excessive worry through knowing God provides for and watches over you. Trusting in God's provision alleviates anxiety and stress as it recognizes that God is in control. Knowing this, allow your mind to find peace. This peace of mind can translate into a more relaxed state, which makes falling and staying asleep easier. (**Homework:** Before bedtime, list your worries. Then, pray and release them to God. Trust in His care to take care of them and you.)

Seek Quality Rest: Prioritize getting good sleep as it is both a gift from God and necessary for well-being. Addressing sleep issues with a focus on quality rest can strengthen the body and mind. Align your sleeping rhythm with biblical principles that reflect the truth that your body is a temple of the Holy Spirit. (**Homework:** Set a consistent weekly bedtime and minimize screen time thirty minutes before sleeping.)

Sleep/Insomnia

Peaceful Environment: Creating a peaceful and quiet sleeping environment aligns with the biblical principle of rest and tranquility. This type of atmosphere allows your mind and body to relax in accordance with God's design. It not only honors the Lord by recognizing the importance of rest but also directly aids you in falling and staying asleep. It combats issues like insomnia by promoting overall well-being. (**Homework:** Tidy up your sleeping area. Consider soft background music or white noise. Read one of the Psalms from this chapter before bed. Memorize one of the verses shared in this chapter so that you can recite it to yourself when struggling with insomnia.)

Acknowledge God's Sovereignty: Remember God remains vigilant while you sleep. Sleep issues can be good because they force you to trust in God's control. Even in rest, He watches over you. This trust can bring peace and relaxation which eases the stress, which may hinder your falling or staying asleep. Align yourself with biblical teachings about God's care and omnipotence. (**Homework:** As a nightly practice, thank God for the day and affirm your trust in His protection as you sleep.)

Below are helpful instructions from a Sleep RN. (***These suggestions are not medical advice and should not be considered such. Make sure to consult your own medical doctors. The following list are the items that helped the author during his episodes of insomnia.***)

Are you having difficulty initiating sleep or maintaining sleep?

1. *Try to stay awake during the day. If you must nap, do so before 2:00 pm and limit naps to thirty minutes. If you nap longer, you will get REM sleep, which will delay your sleep onset at night.*
2. *No matter what, develop a consistent wake-up time even on days off. You cannot control falling asleep, but you can control wakefulness. This kind of schedule helps strengthen sleep drive throughout the day.*
3. *Limit caffeine to nothing past 11:00 am or noon.*

4. *Maintain appropriate sleep hygiene steps: First, no blue light for one hour before bed (e.g., no phone or television). It throws off your sleep drive as the brain perceives the light as time to wake up. Second, your bed is solely for sleep and nothing else. If you wake up during the night, do not stay in bed longer than thirty minutes. Get out of bed and do something in another room until you are sleepy again. Third, your bedroom should be dark. Use black-out curtains, if necessary. Fourth, keep your bedroom cool and quiet.*

5. *If you are stressed, set aside worry time to think. Write out thoughts, then put them away.*

6. *Expose yourself to light as soon as you awake.*

7. *Utilize prayer, meditation, and relaxation techniques.*

8. *Exercise early in the morning.*

9. *Get out of bed as soon as you awake. No lounging in bed in the mornings.*

10. *Consider buying a weighted blanket.*

DISCUSSION STARTERS

1. **Seeking Solace in God's Design for Rest:** Reflecting on Mark 6:31, where Jesus calls the disciples to rest, how do you see the importance of balancing work with rejuvenation in your life? How can a closer adherence to this divine rhythm of rest and activity relieve your struggles with sleep or restlessness?

2. **Wisdom Over Worry:** Proverbs 3:24 promises peaceful sleep. In what ways have your anxieties or fears potentially impeded your ability to rest? How can lean into God's wisdom, rather than your own understanding, usher in a more restful sleep?

3. **Contentment and Sleep:** Ecclesiastes 5:12 provides a poignant reflection on contentment and its relation to rest. How do you see

the relationship between your contentment and your sleep quality? How might finding contentment in God rather than worldly possessions or achievements pave the way for deeper, more restorative sleep?

SPOUSE ABUSE

NOTE:

If you or someone you know is being abused, seek help immediately from local authorities (law enforcement) and your church leadership. As a counselor and/or church leader, you must take allegations of abuse just as seriously as suicide attempts. Involve law enforcement immediately. Also get the local church leadership involved immediately. Use wisdom regarding the safety of all involved, but do not hesitate in reporting and proactively responding to these situations.

Spousal abuse starkly contrasts with the divine design for marital relationships. Spouse abuse, often termed "domestic violence" or "intimate partner violence," manifests as a pattern of behavior intended to rule over a partner. Such behavior contradicts the biblical command for husbands to love their wives as Christ loves the church and for wives to respect their husbands. Be it physical, sexual, economic, or psychological; abuse represents a gross deviation from God's commandment to love your neighbor as yourself. Believers are called to uphold relationships marked by love, respect, and self-sacrifice. Doing so reflects Christ's love for His church. The act of abusing one's spouse not only harms the victim but it also breaks the sacred covenant of marriage.

Seek the LORD, all you humble of the earth, who carry out what
he commands. Seek righteousness, seek humility; perhaps you
will be concealed on the day of the LORD's anger.
Zeph 2:3
(for the abuser)

Zephaniah significantly addresses the importance of humility and seeking the LORD when one has strayed from His commands. For an abuser, this Scripture is a direct call to recognize their wrongdoings, repent, and change. The act of seeking the LORD requires one to be introspect, to acknowledge one's sins, and to actively work toward alignment with God's commands. The phrase, "seek righteousness, seek humility," reinforces the necessity for moral uprightness and genuine humility. Doing this can lead an individual away from abusive tendencies. Zephaniah's mention of the "day of the LORD's anger" is a stark reminder of God's judgment. It emphasizes the grave consequences of persisting in sin without repentance. The verse hints at God's protective mercy and suggests that one can find refuge by seeking Him and living righteously. In a biblical counseling context, this Scripture presents a two-fold approach. First, it confronts the abuser with the weight of his/her actions while offering hope. Second, it offers a path to redemption through repentance, humility, and wholehearted pursuit of God's ways.

My child, if your heart is wise, my own heart"
also will rejoice; indeed, my inmost being
will rejoice when your lips speak what is right.
Prov 23:15-16
(for the abuser)

Solomon's wisdom highlights the joy and peace that emanate from making the right decisions and speaking about what is just. For those who have taken the path of spousal abuse, this is a direct call to acknowledge their actions, repent, and walk in the wisdom of God. A wise heart aligns with God's commands. God's commands for marriage involve love, understanding, and respect. Spousal abuse is not aligned with wisdom and thus not aligned with God's intent for marriage. This verse can be a crucial reminder for those who have chosen to harm their spouse that there is a path of righteousness that leads to inner peace. By choosing wisdom and righteousness, they bring joy to themselves and their families and communities. Recognizing the connection between wise actions and a joyful heart can motivate abusers to seek help, make amends, and strive for a marriage that embodies God's love.

> *LORD, how my foes increase! There are many who*
> *attack me. Many say about me, 'There is no help for*
> *him in God.' But you, LORD, are a shield around me,*
> *my glory, and the one who lifts up my head. I cry aloud*
> *to the LORD, and he answers me from his holy mountain.*
> *I lie down and sleep; I wake again because the LORD*
> *sustains me. I will not be afraid of thousands of people*
> *who have taken their stand against me on every side.*
> **Ps 3:1-6**
> **(for the victim)**

Many people may speak against those who accuse their loved ones of abuse. Some will even belittle them and try to talk them out of what they are doing. God sees those who have been oppressed and has compassion for them (Mal 3:5). He makes a way for them to get the relief and justice they deserve, and He will deal with the oppressor in His timing. When it seems like no one is on their side, God acts as a shield. Even though they are beaten and alone, He is protecting them from further harm or even death. Though they may be experiencing pain and suffering, He grants sleep and peace to those upon whom He has compassion. He may not act immediately, but His help is promised.

> **The LORD is close to the brokenhearted**
> **and saves those who are crushed in spirit.**
> **Psalm 34:18**
> **(for the victim)**

This word from the Psalms can be deeply comforting for victims of spousal abuse. This passage reiterates God's enduring love and commitment to hurting people and assures them of His presence during the darkest times. Even when they feel utterly alone and misunderstood, they can take solace that God sees their pain and is close to them. This verse can be a powerful affirmation in counseling, reminding victims that they are not alone in their suffering. They have a divine advocate who cares deeply about their well-being. For those feeling crushed by the weight of abuse, this psalm offers hope that healing and salvation are on the horizon. In the journey of healing from spousal abuse, this verse can serve as a beacon of hope and a testament to God's unyielding love and support for those who are brokenhearted.

> *Husbands, love your wives, just as Christ loved the*
> *church and gave himself for her to make her holy,*
> *cleansing her with the washing of water by the word.*
> *He did this to present the church to himself in splendor,*
> *without spot or wrinkle or anything like that, but holy*
> *and blameless. In the same way, husbands are to love their wives*
> *as their own bodies. He who loves his wife loves himself.*
> **Eph 5:25-28**

Paul provides valuable guidance for those dealing with spousal abuse by laying out the principles of love and respect that should govern a marriage relationship. These verses call for husbands to love their wives as Christ loved the church. His love is marked by self-sacrifice and complete regard for the well-being of the other. The text explicitly argues against harsh treatment and promotes the nurturing and cherishing of one another. In a situation of spousal abuse, these verses can serve as a reminder of God's design for marital relationships and God's high standards for love and respect. Counseling and support should align with these principles and seek to restore the relationship to mutual care and affection or provide safety when necessary. Safety and healing from the abusive situation should also be a priority. The verses provide a spiritual basis for addressing the issue and a practical framework to assess and remedy the dynamics in an abusive relationship. By returning to these foundational principles, couples and counselors can work towards a relationship that reflects the loving, sacrificial pattern outlined in the text.

> *The Lord tests the righteous and the wicked, and the*
> *one who loves violence His soul hates. Upon the wicked*
> *He will rain snares; Fire and brimstone and burning*
> *wind will be the portion of their cup*
> **Ps 11:5-6**

Spousal abuse, whether from the male to the female or vice versa, is a grave sin that God hates. Spouses are to cherish each other, not harm each other. Some individuals view the threat of harm and the actual carrying out of harm as means to control, manipulate, and/or use the spouse and family as an outlet to vent wrath. None of these actions are biblical, and thus they should be sternly rebuked and confronted by believers. God hates the one who loves violence. The figurative language of verse six displays the extreme displeasure God has towards the abuser. God's response to the abuser in this verse is one of harsh judgement. He invokes here the imagery of Sodom and Gomorrah with fire and brimstone. Beyond hating when spousal abuse occurs, churches must respond compassionately towards the victim while responding boldly and sternly towards the abuser. Grace and mercy should be expressed, but the violent must be held accountable.

> *Husbands, love your wives and don't be bitter toward them.*
> **Col 3:19**

This verse provides a concise, yet directly relevant, admonition to those dealing with spousal abuse. It commands husbands to "love your wives and do not be harsh with them." This simple directive establishes a clear guideline for how men are to treat their wives in marriage. In the context of the Bible, love often denotes selfless and nurturing affection. This verse emphasizes love while explicitly forbidding harshness. In cases of spousal abuse, this verse is a stark reminder of the expectations set for marital relationships. It can be a powerful tool in counseling, guiding individuals and couples to recognize and reject abusive behaviors. By focusing on the love that should characterize the relationship and the explicit command against harsh treatment, this verse offers both a standard and a goal for those working to overcome spousal abuse. It highlights the importance for husbands to respect and cherish their spouses and lay a foundation for healing and growth within their marriages.

> *Husbands, in the same way, live with your wives in an understanding way,*
> *as with a weaker partner, showing them honor as coheirs of the grace of life,*
> *so that your prayers will not be hindered.*
> **1 Pet 3:7**

Peter provides valuable advice for those dealing with spousal abuse by instructing husbands to live with their wives "in an understanding way, showing honor to the woman." This commandment sets forth a principle of empathy and respect within the marital relationship. By calling for understanding, it encourages spouses to be attentive to each other's needs and feelings. This promotes emotional sensitivity. The directive to show honor further underscores the inherent value and dignity of wives. This commandment contradicts any justification for abusive behavior. In the context of spousal abuse, this verse offers a corrective to behaviors that devalue or demean and points instead to a model of care and mutual respect, which can be a significant resource in counseling and recovery. This guides individuals and couples toward a relationship characterized by compassion and honor. The emphasis on understanding and honoring one's spouse serves as a clear and powerful antidote to the dynamics often found in abusive relationships.

PRACTICAL ADVICE + HOMEWORK

Confess Sin: If you abuse your spouse verbally, physically, or sexually; you are sinning against your spouse and your God. (**Homework:** If this is true in your situation, stop right now and confess the sin of abusive mistreatment of your spouse to God and to your spouse.)

Renew Your Mind through Scripture: God has designed marriage to proclaim the gospel's good news. Abuse mars His plan. (**Homework:** Read Ephesians 5:22-33 to understand how he designs marriages for this purpose. Answer these questions from the biblical text you just read: What did you learn about God? What did you learn about your responsibility in marriage? How do your thinking, feelings, and actions need to change in light of these truths?)

Obey God: Treat your spouse as Christ does the church. This instruction means husbands must love and give themselves for their wives, and that wives must respect and submit to their husbands as the church does to Christ. (**Homework:** Spend time with God in His Word each day and attend worship at your church each week. Plan and carry out regular date nights. Be consistent in expressing love through edifying communication [Eph 4:29] and through regular sexual intimacy [1 Cor 7:14].)

Perspective Change: No one deserves to be abused. Additionally, no one forces the abuser to abuse. Counselors should make sure that this perspective is clearly communicated to the victim of spousal abuse. (**Homework:** With a pastor or trusted friend, identify where you need to ask for forgiveness from the Lord. Also, identify where you are innocent by focusing on the reality that you are not responsible for the other person's sins of abuse. Let your mind dwell on the truth found in Philippians 4.)

Older and Wiser (for the abuser): With help from your pastor, find an older gentleman who is or was married for more than forty years. Meet with him and have questions about how his marriage has lasted so long and how he has consistently treated his wife. Pay special attention to how he talks about his wife and the things he does/did for her. Through this interaction, you should glean practical advice for how to move forward with reconciling with your spouse. (**Homework:** Read through Ephesians 5:25-30. Write out what Christ does for the church and how a husband should treat his wife. The purpose of this exercise is not to realize how you have failed, but rather to provide you time to reflect on the love Jesus has for people. In the next meeting with your counselor, be ready to discuss what you observed in this passage and to answer some questions about how you can apply these principles moving forward towards repentance and forgiveness.)

Avoid Harshness: Being gentle, understanding, and patient is crucial in dealing with spousal abuse. These actions reflect the biblical principles of love and kindness (Eph 4:2). They allow for open communication and trust-building, which is aligned with God's design for marriage as a place of mutual respect and compassion (1 Pet 3:7). (**Homework:** Recognize and note moments when you might have been harsh or inconsiderate. Seek ways to amend and heal.)

Seek Counsel: In abusive relationships, seeking counsel is vital because it provides victims spiritual guidance grounded in biblical truth. Biblical counsel offers hope and healing through God's love. Additionally, practical assistance from pastors and/or biblical counselors ensure safety and helps develop a plan to escape harmful situations. (**Homework:** Contact a trusted individual, pastor, or counselor to discuss any concerns in your marriage.)

Go to Church (For the Abused): If there is any place where you should be accepted and welcomed, it will be your local church. Not all churches are healthy, but a number of churches are. When the people of God listen to His voice and Word, when you enter such a fellowship you should find comfort and compassion, as well as plenty of people wanting to help you in whatever ways they can. Do not stop looking and follow the Holy Spirit's guidance to that right church. (**Homework:** Start a prayer journal. Record every prayer you pray for peace, comfort, or anything related to your abuse. At the end of every prayer, write out Matthew 11:28-30 word-for-word to remind yourself that there is rest for your anxious and weary heart. Be ready to discuss your journal at the next session.)

Discussion Starters

1. **Pursuit of Righteousness and Humility:** Reflecting on Zephaniah 2:3, how can one actively cultivate humility and righteousness daily? How does acknowledging one's wrongdoings and seeking God's ways lead to genuine transformation? For someone who has mistreated their spouse, what practical steps can they take to actively seek the Lord and change their ways?

2. **Wisdom's Role in Marital Harmony:** With Proverbs 23:15-16 in mind, think of moments where making wise decisions led to joy and peace in your relationship? How does choosing to align with God's wisdom in treating your spouse impact your marriage's overall health and well-being? What barriers or challenges hinder you from consistently making wise choices in your interactions with your spouse?

3. **Finding Protection and Hope in God's Presence:** Reflecting on Psalm 3:1-6 and Psalm 34:18, how have you personally experienced God's protection and closeness during trying times in your marriage or relationship? How can these passages serve as a source of hope and reassurance for abuse victims? How can leaning into God's promises provide strength and courage to stand against abuse and seek healing?

SUICIDAL THOUGHTS

A sense of hopelessness and despair leads individuals to contemplate ending their own lives. Such pain echoes the lives of many biblical figures like Elijah, who once prayed for his own death, saying, "It is enough! Now, O Lord, take away my life" (1 Kgs 19:4). Jonah, too, wished for death in his distress. In navigating these harrowing feelings, it is crucial to seek refuge in God's promises and the faith community's support. Remember that every life holds immense value in God's eyes.

*The Spirit of the LORD GOD is on me, because
the LORD has anointed me to bring good news to
the poor. He has sent me to heal the brokenhearted,
to proclaim liberty to the captives and freedom to the
prisoners; to proclaim the year of the LORD's favor,
and the day of our God's vengeance; to comfort all who mourn,*

to provide for those who mourn in Zion; to give
them a crown of beauty instead of ashes, festive oil
instead of mourning, and splendid clothes instead of
despair. And they will be called righteous trees, planted
by the LORD to glorify him.
Isa 61:1-3

Isaiah captures the prophetic mission of Jesus Christ the Messiah to bring restoration, healing, and hope to the broken-hearted. In the darkest recesses of the human mind where suicidal thoughts may lurk this promise stands as a beacon of hope. The passage emphasizes the divine commission to heal the brokenhearted and speaks directly to those whose spirits are shattered, weighed down by despair, or feeling trapped in their own minds. The "year of the LORD's favor" promise reassures that God's grace and mercies are ever-present and ready to envelop those who feel forsaken. Transitioning from mourning to a "crown of beauty" and from "despair" to "splendid clothes" underscores the transformative power of God's love. These contrasting images serve as vivid reminders that one's current state of anguish and suffering is not the end but can be transformed through the divine intervention of Jesus Christ. This promise extends to the notion of him/her being "righteous trees, planted by the LORD." Trees symbolize strength, growth, and longevity. This imagery suggests that an individual who leans into God's promises will find immediate solace and a long-lasting purpose deeply rooted in God's love, ready to bear fruits of righteousness. For someone battling suicidal ideations, this passage is a life-affirming testament to the love, purpose, and hope in Jesus Christ. It encourages him/her to see beyond his/her present pain to a future filled with God's favor and glory.

Therefore, since we have so great a cloud of witnesses surrounding us,
let us also lay aside every encumbrance and the sin which so easily
entangles us, and let us run with endurance the race that is set before us,
fixing our eyes on Jesus, the author and perfecter of faith, who for the joy

**set before Him endured the cross, despising the shame, and has sat down
at the right hand of the throne of God.
Heb 12:1-2**

Paul's message in this Scripture provides solace for those wrestling
with suicidal ideations. It emphasizes endurance, perseverance, and
hope amidst adversity. The "great cloud of witnesses" illustrates that
many before us faced trials yet triumphed through faith in God. This
reminds us that we are not isolated in our struggles. The verse urges
us to shed the burdens and sins ensnaring us by acknowledging the
hardships of life but emphasizing God's overarching purpose. It lik-
ens life to a marathon requiring stamina even though weariness and
doubt. The passage centers on Jesus, who despite immense suffering,
remained steadfast. He concentrated on the joy of humanity's redemption. His endurance symbolizes that hope and a divine plan persist even
in darkness. This Scripture becomes a beacon for those grappling with
despair by emphasizing the importance of anchoring oneself in the
eternal hope found in Jesus.

**The Lord is near to the brokenhearted
and saves the crushed in spirit.
Ps 34:18**

For someone grappling with suicidal thoughts, this passage can be a reminder that God is close during life's darkest moments. It reassures that
God recognizes and understands the pain. He also provides a comforting
embrace. By focusing on this verse, an individual may sense God's presence even in the deepest despair. This verse's choice helps to connect the
individual's struggles and God's constant companionship. It opens the
way for prayer and reflection through knowing he/she is not alone. It is
a vital reminder that God's love transcends the darkness, and His saving
grace is available to the one crushed in spirit. Encouraging a relationship
with God through this passage can foster a sense of security and hope.

A Biblical Handbook for Counseling Heart Issues

For I know the plans I have for you, declares the Lord,
plans for welfare and not for evil, to give you a future and a hope.
Jer 29:11

Hope can feel elusive when dealing with suicidal thoughts, but this promise from God offers a vision of a future filled with hope even when current circumstances seem unbearable. It emphasizes that God has intentional and loving plans for each person, which affirms his/her value and purpose. This passage can act as an anchor to help the individual focus on God's love and promises, which persist despite the present turmoil. It is a reassurance that the struggle is not the end of the story. God's love will guide toward healing. By contemplating this verse, the individual can begin to shift focus away from despair towards the promise of God's loving intention. It is an essential aspect of restoring hope and building resilience.

Come to me, all who labor and are
heavy laden, and I will give you rest.
Matt 11:28

Feeling overwhelmed and burdened often accompanies suicidal thoughts, which makes this invitation from Jesus particularly relevant. It offers much-needed relief and understanding by promising rest and peace in Christ. This verse was chosen because it reminds those struggling that they can turn to Christ for peace and strength, even when their own resources feel completely depleted. It provides an image of Christ waiting to embrace them, to take their burdens, and to provide solace. The choice of this verse underlines the empathy and compassion of Jesus, who intimately understands human suffering. By turning to Him, a struggling individual can find a refuge, a place to rest, and an opportunity to heal. It is a critical component in navigating the journey from despair toward restoration.

PRACTICAL ADVICE + HOMEWORK

Confess Sin: Since God is the only One who has the right to take a life, your desire to do so usurps His rightful role (1 Sam 2:6-7). Taking one's own life in death is also a desire that aligns with Satan's intent and desire for you (John 8:44). (**Homework:** If you are considering taking your life, stop right now and confess the sin of wanting to die to God.)

Renew Your Mind through Scripture: God's Word exhorts you to live life for His purposes not your own. You have no right to take your own life. (**Homework:** Read Romans 8 to understand how to deal with a desire to die. Answer these questions from the biblical text you just read: What did you learn about God? What did you learn about yourself? How do your thinking, feelings and actions need to change in light of these truths?)

Obey God: Choose to live for Him rather than according to your desires. (**Homework:** Spend time with God in His Word each day and attend worship at your church each week. Read Romans 8 every day. Ask God by His Spirit to speak to you through this section of His Word and write down each new truth that He shows you from this passage.)

Reflect on the Hope God Gave Others: It is essential to remember the works of the Lord daily so that you do not forget how faithful He has been through the centuries. (**Homework:** Turn to Hebrews 11 and select one individual per day from this list of faithful people. Go find their stories in the Old Testament and read about them. Journal about how God was faithful to them and how that same God has been faithful to you today.)

Seek God in Desperation: Reach out to God in prayer knowing He is close to the brokenhearted. This effort can provide immense comfort and guidance for you as you battle suicidal thoughts. Prayer should reinforce the belief that God is close to your broken heartedness and understands your pain. (**Homework:** Reflect on Psalm 34:18 daily. Journal your thoughts and prayers. Seek God's nearness.)

Phone Pal: Find one or more people who will listen to you when you have discouraging thoughts. Reach out to them when you feel alone, discouraged, or lonely to have a normal conversation. In the same way that God is always listening, there are people who want to know how you are doing. Since people are not always available, have multiple people willing to talk to you. (**Homework:** Read Psalm 34:17-20; Psalm 147:1-6; and Matthew 11:28-30 and write out everything you observe about God dealing with the oppressed, brokenhearted, and weary. Be ready to discuss your observations in the next meeting.)

Find Rest in Jesus: Turn to Christ when feeling overwhelmed. Seek His peace and strength. Finding rest in Jesus is helpful for those with suicidal thoughts as it offers a personal connection to Christ during overwhelming moments. It also provides a sense of peace and strength. Rely on His love and understanding rather than embracing despair. (**Homework:** Spend time in prayer. Envision yourself offloading your burdens to Jesus based on Matthew 11:28.)

Build a Support System: It is vital to have regular communication with trusted friends, family, or a biblical counselor/pastor. Those who struggle with suicidal thoughts can find hope and strength in God's truth and love by surrounding themselves with trusted friends, family, or church leaders. (**Homework:** Identify and meet with a supportive person weekly. Share your feelings and allow them to encourage and pray with you. Work with a counselor or pastor to create a safety plan with actionable steps if suicidal thoughts intensify.

DISCUSSION STARTERS

1. **Embracing the Messiah's Mission:** Isaiah 61:1-3 paints a vivid picture of Jesus Christ's mission to heal and restore the brokenhearted. Reflect on a time in your life when you felt Christ's transformative power move you from a place of despair to a state of

hope and joy? How can you remind yourself daily of God's promises, especially when facing challenges or despair?

2. **Running the Divine Race:** Hebrews 12:1-2 encourages you to persevere and fix your eyes on Jesus. How do you envision the race that God has set before you? What encumbrances or sins do you feel are hindering you from running this race with endurance? In moments of weariness, how can you better fix your eyes on Jesus and draw strength from His example and the hope He offers?

3. **God's Nearness in Despair:** Multiple verses, such as Psalm 34:18 and Matthew 11:28 emphasize God's closeness and the rest He provides to those in despair. How do you experience God's nearness in your moments of pain or brokenness? How can you cultivate a deeper relationship with Him to ensure you always feel His comforting presence, especially when burdened or overwhelmed?

TIME USAGE

Believers are to serve God as they fulfill their God-assigned responsibilities one of which is making the best use of their time for the glory of God. Time is a divine gift entrusted to God's people and requires intentional stewardship rooted in a deep understanding of God's purpose. While the world races against the clock, believers are called to serve God even in the most mundane tasks thus radiating His Spirit through their attitudes and actions. Daily responsibilities might limit available moments, but even the briefest periods become sanctified by infusing each second with the intent to honor God. Managing time is not solely about the quantity but the quality of moments spent in genuine service to the Lord, which transforms fleeting instants into eternal investments.

Come now, you who say, "Today or tomorrow we will go to such and such a city and spend a year there and engage in business and make a profit." Yet you do not know what your life will be like tomorrow. You are just a vapor that appears for a little while and then vanishes away. Instead, you ought to say, "If the Lord wills, we will live and also do this or that."
James 4:13-15

Making the most of the time God gave us is important because time is a finite quantity we can neither increase or decrease. James tells us to make the most of every day because we are not promised tomorrow. We should make plans, have goals, and work hard doing all with the truth in mind that God's will may look different from ours. From a practical point of view, those who procrastinate, are unorganized, are undisciplined, or are just lazy need to realize that tomorrow may not come. Things that we wanted to do in the future may never happen. We must use our time wisely, making plans to honor the Lord as we recognize that there is no better time than the present to be obedient and take care of what God would have us do.

> *Do not weary yourself to gain wealth,*
> *cease from your consideration of it.*
> **Prov 23:4**

Solomon makes a very clear and important point in that we should not wear ourselves out trying to make an abundance of wealth. He writes about working hard and doing our best, even storing up grain for the winter months, in other passages. Here it discusses excessive wealth and the unhealthy devotion to its gain. Sometimes our health and spiritual status can weary us because we have been doing and pursuing much more than God had designed or purposed us for financially. Biblical counselors could take the principles in this passage a step further to apply to any pursuit or work. Believers will wear themselves out and become weary of life when they are not operating in God's will and instead are trying to do too much.

> *Pay careful attention, then, to how you*
> *walk—not as unwise people but as*
> *wise—making the most of the time,*
> *because the days are evil*
> **Eph 5:15-16**

Paul encourages readers to make the most of their time and live wisely. This message resonates with those struggling with time usage, prompting them to consider how they spend their hours and days. The warning to live not as unwise but as wise points to the importance of intentional planning and prioritization. It inspires reflection on what truly matters and encourages thoughtful time alignment with values and goals. Furthermore, the encouragement to redeem the time emphasizes our time's precious and finite nature. This advocates for purposeful engagement rather than wasteful or aimless drifting. The verse can serve as a reminder that every moment is a gift and an opportunity. This urges individuals to choose their activities carefully. Ultimately, the teachings in Ephesians 5:15-16 offer a framework for understanding time as a valuable resource that can be used effectively to grow, serve others, and fulfill one's potential.

> *Teach us to number our days carefully*
> *so that we may develop wisdom in our hearts.*
> **Ps 90:12**

The psalmist emphasizes the importance of gaining wisdom by numbering our days. This concept directly applies to those of us who struggle with time usage. By asking for wisdom in numbering our days, the passage prompts readers to recognize the finite nature of life and the need for intentional time management. The concept of numbering our days can be seen as a metaphor for making mindful decisions about spending our time. It encourages a reflective approach to considering the value and meaning of our daily activities and priorities. In the broader context of life's fleeting nature, this plea for wisdom serves as a reminder to live purposefully every day. The wisdom to number our days is about making conscious choices that align our values and goals with what truly matters. Ultimately, Psalm 90:12 provides an insightful perspective that can guide those struggling with time usage to live more intentionally and thoughtfully.

> *Act wisely toward outsiders, making the most of the time.*
> **Col 4:5**

Colossians 4:5 urges Christians to "walk in wisdom toward outsiders, making the best use of the time." Doing so provides valuable wisdom for those struggling with time usage. The directive emphasizes the importance of wise living and the efficient, effective utilization of time. People who find it challenging to manage their time can find insight into making choices that reflect wisdom and intentionality. The reference to outsiders adds a social dimension, which reminds believers that their time management affects not only themselves, but also how others perceive them. The way they handle their time can become a testimony to their values and faith. Ultimately, the instruction in this verse encourages Christians to be diligent and purposeful in their daily lives by ensuring that our time is spent in a manner that aligns with our beliefs and responsibilities. It is a call to conscious living where time is neither wasted nor taken for granted but used as a valuable resource for meaningful engagement with the world.

PRACTICAL ADVICE + HOMEWORK

Confess Sin: Time is a gift from God, and mismanaging it can be considered negligence or disobedience to God's purposes for our lives. If you recognize that you have been careless with your time by not using it for God's glory or the betterment of those around you, you need to confess your behavior to the Lord. (**Homework:** Reflect on areas where you have been wasting time or not prioritizing activities that honor God and benefit others. Write these down and confess each to God. Asking for His guidance and strength to better use your time.)

Renew Your Mind through Scripture: God's Word provides wisdom on the value and use of time. Understanding and internalizing these truths allows you to navigate life with a perspective that honors God. (**Homework:** Dive into the following verses: James 4:13-15; Proverbs 23:4; Ephesians 5:15-16; Psalm 90:12; and Colossians 4:5. For each passage, note the main message about time usage and how it speaks to your current situation.)

Obey God: Acknowledging God's truths about time is vital, but obedience to those truths is the practical outworking of our faith. God calls us to act wisely, purposefully, and with intention in how we use our time. (**Homework:** Begin each day this week by seeking God's guidance on how to spend your time. Write a plan for the day to ensure it aligns with biblical principles. Review your activities at the end of each day and assess where you used time wisely and where improvements can be made. Commit to using your time in ways that glorify God, serve others, and fulfill the purposes God has for your life.)

Self-Reflection: Reflect on how you currently spend your time. Are your activities aligned with God's purpose for your life? (**Homework:** Keep a time log of your activities for three days. Review and identify any time-wasters or habits you want to change.)

Evaluate Your Work: Ask yourself and others, "Am I trying to do too much?" By way of prayer and accountability partners, identify where you need to stay engaged along with areas where you need to step away. (**Homework:** Make a list of your obligations, jobs, and tasks to get done this week and month. Let an accountability partner evaluate with you whether you need to slow down.)

Prioritize Wisely: Understand that time is limited and precious. Prioritize what is essential based on what is eternally significant. (**Homework:** List your top five priorities in life and compare your current time usage against them. Adjust your schedule accordingly.)

Set a Schedule: Both structure and order can help with time usage, especially when tracking the time you spend doing various things. (**Homework:** Use a daily calendar to track your time usage and prepare for the following day each week. Track your time this week to see where you can improve.)

DISCUSSION STARTERS

1. **Divine Perspective on Planning:** Reflecting on James 4:13-15, how do you plan for your future? How do you see God's will play a role in those plans? Have there been instances where your plans

diverged from what eventually happened? How did you perceive God's hand in those moments? How can embracing an "if the Lord wills" mindset help you navigate uncertainties and unforeseen changes in your plans?

2. **Balancing Ambition and Contentment:** Proverbs 23:4 warns against the exhausting pursuit of wealth. How do you balance pursuing success and not becoming consumed by it? How does recognizing the transient nature of wealth and success influence your priorities and daily decisions? In what ways can aligning your ambitions with God's purposes lead to a more fulfilling and content life?

3. **Intentionality in Daily Living:** Ephesians 5:15-16 and Colossians 4:5 emphasize the importance of walking wisely and maximizing our time. How do you ensure that your daily actions and decisions are purposeful and aligned with God's will? Can you identify areas where time might be wasted or not used optimally? How can focusing on God's wisdom guide you in better using your time?

WEARY

Weariness is a state of physical, emotional, and sometimes spiritual exhaustion. It emerges not just from daily struggles but also from the burdens of life's relentless demands. Weariness, while a product of a fallen nature and world, becomes an invitation to find rest and rejuvenation in God's presence. This encapsulates the divine promise of refreshment and renewal for the soul.

> *"Come to me, all of you who are weary and burdened,*
> *and I will give you rest. Take up my yoke and learn from me,*
> *because I am lowly and humble in heart, and you will find rest*
> *for your souls. For my yoke is easy and my burden is light."*
> **Matt 11:28-30**

Jesus' words in Matthew 11:28-30 are particularly relevant for those feeling weary, burdened, or overwhelmed. In these verses, Jesus extends an invitation to all who are laboring under heavy burdens to come to Him for rest. This invitation recognizes the human condition of fatigue and offers a remedy through a relationship with Christ. He promises to provide rest and peace by portraying a yoke that is easy and a burden that is light. This metaphor signifies a shared burden and underscores Christ's gentle and humble nature. For those feeling weighed down by life's demands, these verses provide assurance that they do not have to carry their burdens alone. This teaching encourages trust in Jesus, who provides relief and renewal as He transforming weariness into strength through His grace and understanding.

> *"I will always obey your instruction, forever and ever.*
> *I will walk freely in an open place because I study your precepts.*
> *I will speak of your decrees before kings and not be ashamed.*
> *I delight in your commands, which I love. I will life my hands*
> *up to your commands, which I love, and will meditate on your statutes."*
> **Ps 119:44-48**

In Psalm 119, there is a distinct lack of fatigue and weariness because of the study of the Word of God. Later in that chapter, the writer says, "Your statutes are the theme of my song during my earthly life" (119:54). Life is complicated and will constantly throw difficulties toward us. When we set ourselves in the Word of God, then we have the strength to walk freely and stand before kings without shame. When we neglect God and His Word, we lose these blessings. When we take Him seriously and dedicate time to know more about Him, He will give us the strength we need.

> *Let us not get tired of doing good, for we will reap at*
> *the proper time if we don't give up. Therefore, as we have opportunity,*
> *let us work for the good of all, especially for those who belong*
> *to the household of faith.*
> **Gal 6:9-10**

Paul speaks directly to those who feel weary, especially to those who either are weary in doing good deeds or pursuing a righteous path. The passage encourages believers not to lose heart or grow tired in their pursuit of doing good for they will reap a harvest if they do not give up. This promise offers hope and a sense of purpose to those who may feel overwhelmed or disheartened. It stresses the importance of perseverance by reminding the readers that their efforts are not in vain. By framing it in the context of sowing and reaping, the passage connects today's effort with the future's potential rewards. It encourages a broad view of the community by urging believers to do good to all and particularly those in the faith community. It balances personal, spiritual encouragement and communal, social responsibility, which makes for a powerful antidote to feelings of weariness.

Youths may become faint and weary, and young men stumble and fall, but those who trust in the Lord will renew their strength; they will soar on wings like eagles; they will run and not become weary, they will walk and not faint.
Isa 40:30-31

This verse is an encouragement for those who feel weary or overwhelmed. It recognizes that even the young may grow tired and weary and thus validates people's exhaustion. It does contrasts human weakness with the everlasting strength of the Lord which providing hope and reassurance to the weary. According to the text, those who hope in the Lord will find new strength and soar on wings like eagles. This metaphor vividly depicts rising above difficulties and being rejuvenated by faith through trust in God's power. The promise is a sustained renewal that enables one to run without growing weary and to walk without growing faint. It is a message of enduring strength and support for all who are struggling with feeling weighed down. This verse offers a spiritual solution to physical and emotional fatigue.

PRACTICAL ADVICE + HOMEWORK

Confess Sin: If you try to serve God in your strength, you will find how weak you are. God's people can only do what He asks when they do so in His strength. Suppose you have tried to serve God independently of Him. In that case, this sin must be confessed to God. (**Homework:** If this is true in your situation, stop right now and confess to God the sin of independence within your heart and the outward striving and exhaustion it has produced).

Renew Your Mind through Scripture: God's Word exhorts us to be renewed in Him. (**Homework:** Read the following biblical texts to understand how to deal with weariness (Isa 40:28-31 and Matt 11:28-30). Answer these questions from the biblical text you just read: What did you learn about God? What did you learn about your need for Him? How do your thinking, feelings, and actions need to change in light of these truths?)

Obey God: Practice obedience by putting your hope in Him knowing He will renew your strength when you do so. (**Homework:** Spend time with God in His Word each day, and attend worship at your church each week. Memorize Matthew 11:28-30 to help you remember that God is the source of your strength).

Seek Christ's Rest: Recognize that true rest for the soul and body comes from Jesus. Lean into His promises and find comfort. He offers a deep, lasting peace that transcends human understanding. Trusting in His promises provides a temporary respite and a spiritual rejuvenation by grounding the weary soul in faith and hope. (**Homework:** Spend ten minutes each evening this week meditating on Matthew 11:28. Visualize handing over your burdens to Christ.)

Stop and Fill: Find or create a playlist of your favorite worship songs and hymns on a streaming platform. Listen to it when you feel tired. Instead of taking a nap or relaxing mindlessly, fill your heart with songs that point you toward God. If you can avoid doing anything for a few minutes, hear praises towards the mighty God of all power and set your mind on Him for a few moments. Doing this will give you something to keep your attention and set that attention on God where it needs to be. (**Homework:** Write a schedule of everything you do every day. This exercise is not to overwhelm you with the number of things you do but to show you that some things may not be as important as you think. In the next meeting, be ready to discuss your schedule and decide if there needs to be any change. Ask for help in certain areas or possibly drop events altogether. Schedule daily moments to read Scripture or a theological work consistently to rejuvenate your soul.)

Persevere in Goodness: Even in seasons of weariness, holding fast to God's promises demonstrates genuine faith. This perseverance can bring hope and strength in challenging times and reinforce the belief that God's plan includes faithfully blessing those who serve others. (**Homework:** Identify one act of kindness you can perform this week and commit to do it regardless of how you feel.)

Hope and Renewal: Focus on God when tiredness sets in. When weariness starts to overwhelm you, focusing on God offers a source of hope and assurance grounded in His promise as seen in Isaiah 40:31. (**Homework:** Whenever you feel weary this week, recite Isaiah 40:31 to yourself and visualize the renewal it promises.)

DISCUSSION STARTERS

1. **Embracing Christ's Invitation to Rest:** Reflecting on Matthew 11:28-30 where Jesus invites those weary and burdened to find rest in Him, how have you experienced or sought relief from your burdens recently? Do you often try to bear your burdens alone, or do you turn to Christ? How can accepting Christ's invitation to take on His yoke bring peace and rest into your life, especially in times of overwhelming weariness?

2. **Finding Strength in God's Word:** Drawing from Psalm 119:44-48, how do you find strength and solace in God's Word when faced with life's complexities and challenges? Have there been instances where immersing yourself in the Scriptures has renewed your energy and perspective? How can dedicating consistent time to study and meditate on God's Word transform feelings of exhaustion into feelings of empowerment?

3. **Persevering through Weariness:** Considering Galatians 6:9-10, have there been moments where you felt weary in doing good or

felt discouraged in your righteous pursuits? How do you find motivation to continue even when it seems challenging? How can keeping in mind the promise of reaping the rewards at the proper time inspire you to persist in your good works, especially when serving others in faith.

SUBJECT-SCRIPTURE INDEX

PER PDI TOPIC

Adultery: Exodus 20:14; 1 Peter 1:14-16; Proverbs 6:32; Proverbs 28:13; Matthew 5:27-28.

Anger: Ephesians 4:26-27; James 1:19-20; Proverbs 15:1-3; Proverbs 19:11-12

Anorexia and Bulimia: 1 Corinthians 6:19-20; Romans 12:1-2; Psalm 139:14; 1 Peter 5:7; Jeremiah 50:18-20; 1 Samuel 16:7

Anxiety/Worry: Psalm 139:23-24; Philippians 4:6-7; Proverbs 3:5-8; Isaiah 26:3, Philippians 4:8; Psalm 4:4-5; Philippians 4:9

Apathy: Colossians 3:17; Isaiah 49:4, Zephaniah 1:12-13; Colossians 3:23-24; Proverbs 22:3

Bitterness: Ephesians 4:31; Romans 8:31-34; Lamentations 3:5; 3:22; Acts 8:23; Hebrews 12:15

Children: Ephesians 6:1-4; Proverbs 22:6; Proverbs 29:17; Deuteronomy 6:5-7

A Biblical Handbook for Counseling Heart Issues

Childhood Sexual Abuse: Psalm 147:3, Isaiah 1:16-17; Psalm 18:2; Psalm 56:8; Romans 8:28-29

Communication: Proverbs 15:1; James 1:19; Ephesians 4:29; Proverbs 25:11

Conflict (Fights): Matthew 18:15-16; James 4:1-3; Romans 12:18; Proverbs 15:18; 1 Peter 4:8

Control: Romans 6:11-13; Proverbs 16:9; Exodus 14:14; Jeremiah 10:23; Isaiah 41:10

Critical Spirit: Job 42:7; Romans 2:1-3; Matthew 7:1; 1 Peter 4:8

Deception: Proverbs 12:22; Ephesians 4:25; Nehemiah 6:8-9; Colossians 3:9

Decision Making: Proverbs 3:5-6; Exodus 33:13a; James 1:5, Philippians 4:6

Depression: Psalm 34:17-18, Psalm 42:11; Matthew 11:28; Lamentations 3:18; 3:24

Disciplined Living: Proverbs 25:28; Proverbs 21:5; 1 Corinthians 9:24-27; 2 Timothy 1:7

Disorganization: 1 Corinthians 14:40; 1 Corinthians 14:33; Proverbs 21:5; 24:30-34

Discouraged/Downcast: Joshua 1:9; Psalm 63:6-8; Psalm 34:17-18; 2 Corinthians 4:8-9

Drunkenness: Ephesians 5:18; Proverbs 31:6-7; Proverbs 20:1; 1 Corinthians 6:10

Dysfunctional Family: Exodus 20:12; Proverbs 15:1; Colossians 3:13; Ephesians 6:1-4

Envy: Proverbs 14:30; Philippians 4:11; James 3:16; Galatians 5:26; Proverbs 23:17

Fear: Isaiah 41:10; Proverbs 28:1; 2 Timothy 1:7; Psalm 23:4; Psalm 27:1; Matthew 6:34

Finances: Proverbs 22:7; Matthew 6:24; 1 Timothy 6:10; Matthew 25:26-27; Proverbs 13:11; 21:5

Gluttony: Proverbs 23:20-21; 1 Peter 4:3-5; Philippians 3:19; Proverbs 25:16; Proverbs 23:20-21; 1 Corinthians 6:13

Grief: Isaiah 53:3; Psalm 147:3; Revelation 21:4; Matthew 5:4; Romans 8:18; 1 Peter 5:7

Guilt: Job 10:7; John 3:17; Psalm 32:5; 1 John 1:9; Romans 8:1; James 5:16; Hebrews 8:12

Health: 3 John 1:2; Proverbs 17:22; 1 Corinthians 6:19-20; Jeremiah 17:14; Romans 12:1; Jeremiah 33:6; Matthew 11:28

Impotence: Romans 4:19-25; Psalm 113:9; Proverbs 3:5-6; Ephesians 6:10; Romans 8:28

In-Laws: Genesis 29:25-26; Matthew 19:4-6; Ruth 1:16-17; Genesis 2:24; Ephesians 4:2-3

Laziness: Proverbs 6:6-8; Proverbs 20:4, 2; Thessalonians 3:10; Genesis 2:15; Proverbs 24:33-34; Colossians 3:23

A Biblical Handbook for Counseling Heart Issues

Loneliness: Psalm 68:6; Isaiah 41:10; Psalm 27:10; Matthew 28:18-20; Proverbs 17:17; Ecclesiastes 4:9-10

Lust: Matthew 5:28; Job 31:1; 1 Corinthians 6:18-20; Ephesians 2:3-7; Proverbs 4:23; Proverbs 5:18-19

Marriage: Ephesians 5:25; Proverbs 18:22; 1 Corinthians 13:4-7; Proverbs 5:18-20; Mark 10:9

Moodiness: Psalm 42:11; 1 Corinthians 13:11; 2 Corinthians 4:7-9; Isaiah 26:3; Psalm 23:1-3

Overwhelmed/Stress: Psalm 61:2; 1 Kings 19:4-8; Matthew 11:28-30; 2 Corinthians 4:8-9; Psalm 34:18

Perfectionism: Matthew 5:48; Philippians 3:12-14; Mark 10:20-22, 26-27; 2 Corinthians 12:9; Ephesians 5:27

Pornography: Proverbs 31:30; Matthew 5:28; 1 Corinthians 6:18-20; 1 Corinthians 10:13; Job 31:1

Procrastination: Ecclesiastes 11:4; Proverbs 20:4; Proverbs 13:4; Ephesians 5:15-16; Proverbs 6:10-11; Proverbs 27:1

PTSD–Post-Traumatic Stress Disorder: Psalm 23:1-3; Psalm 73:16, 26; Isaiah 26:3, 1 Peter 5:6-8; Psalm 147:3, Isaiah 41:10

Rebellion: 1 Samuel 15:23; Hebrews 13:17; Proverbs 17:11; Titus 3:1-2

Rejection: Psalm 71:9; Isaiah 43:1; Psalm 94:14; Psalm 55:22; Ephesians 4:31-32; Romans 14:23

Relational Idolatry: Proverbs 18:1; Philippians 2:3-4; Exodus 20:3; Matthew 10:37; Philippians 3:8

Sexual Immorality: 1 Corinthians 6:18-20; Romans 13:13-14; 1 Thessalonians 4:3-5; Hebrews 13:4; Matthew 15:19; Matthew 5:28

Sleep/Insomnia: Mark 6:31; Psalm 127:2; Proverbs 3:24; Ecclesiastes 5:12; Psalm 127:2; Psalm 4:8; Psalm 56:3

Spouse Abuse: Zephaniah 2:3 (for the abuser); Proverbs 23:15-16 (for the abuser); Psalm 3:1-6 (for the victim); Psalm 34:18 (for the victim); Ephesians 5:25-28; Psalm 11:5-6; Colossians 3:19; 1 Peter 3:7

Suicidal Thoughts: Isaiah 61:1-3; Hebrews 12:1-2; Psalm 34:18; Jeremiah 29:11; Matthew 11:28

Time Usage: James 4:13-15; Proverbs 23:4; Ephesians 5:15-16; Psalm 90:12; Colossians 4:5

Weary: Matthew 11:28-30; Psalm 119:44-48; Galatians 6:9-10; Isaiah 40:30-31

OLD TESTAMENT

Genesis

Exodus

A Biblical Handbook for Counseling Heart Issues

Deuteronomy
> 6:5-7 – See Children

Joshua
> 1:9 – Discouraged/Downcast

Ruth
> 1:16-17 – See In-Laws

1 Samuel
> 15:23 – See Rebellion
> 16:7 - See Anorexia/Bulimia

1 Kings
> 19:4-8 – See Overwhelmed/Stressed

Nehemiah
> 6:8-9 – See Deception

Job
> 10:7 – See Guilt
> 31:1 – See Lust, Pornography
> 42:7 – See Critical Spirit

Psalms
> 3:1-6 – See Spouse Abuse
> 4:4-5 – See Anxiety/Worry
> 4:8 – See Sleep/Insomnia
> 11:5-6 – See Spouse Abuse
> 18:2 – See Childhood Sexual Abuse
> 23:1-4 – See Fear, Moodiness, PTSD
> 27:1 – See Fear
> 27:10 – See Loneliness
> 32:5 – See Guilt

34:17-18 – See Depression, Discouraged/Downcast, Overwhelmed/
Stressed, Spouse Abuse, Suicidal Thoughts
42:11 – See Depression, Moodiness
55:22 – See Rejection
56:3 – See Sleep/Insomnia
56:8 – See Childhood Sexual Abuse
61:2 – See Overwhelmed/Stressed
63:6-8 – Discouraged/Downcast
68:6 – See Loneliness
71:9 – See Rejection
73:16-26 – See PTSD
90:12 – See Time Usage
94:14 – See Rejection
113:9 – See Impotence/Sexual Dysfunction
119:44-48 – See Weary
127:2 – See Sleep/Insomnia
139:14 - See Anorexia/Bulimia
139:23-24 – See Anxiety/Worry
147:3 – See Childhood Sexual Abuse, Grief, PTSD

Proverbs

3:5-8 – See Anxiety/Worry, Decision Making, Impotence/Sexual
Dysfunction
3:24 – See Sleep/Insomnia
4:23 – See Lust
5:18-20 – See Marriage, Lust
6:6-8 – See Laziness
6:10-11 – See Procrastination
6:32 – See Adultery
12:22 – See Deception
13:4 – See Procrastination
13:11 – See Finances
14:30 – See Envy
15:1-3 – See Anger, Communication, Dysfunctional Family

15:18 – See Conflict (Fights)

16:9 – See Control

17:11 – See Rebellion

17:17 – See Loneliness

17:22 – See Health

18:1 – See Relational Idolatry

18:22 – See Marriage

19:11-12 – See Anger

20:1 – Drunkenness

20:4 – See Laziness, Procrastination

21:5 – Disciplined Living, Disorganization, Finances

22:3 – See Apathy

22:6 – See Children

22:7 – See Finances

23:4 – See Time Usage

23:15-16 – See Spouse Abuse

23:17 – See Envy

23:20-21 – See Gluttony

24:30-34 – Disorganization, Laziness

25:11 – See Communication

25:16 – See Gluttony

25:28 – Disciplined Living

27:1 – See Procrastination

28:1 – See Fear

28:13 – See Adultery

29:17 – See Children

31:6-7 – Drunkenness

31:30 – See Pornography

Ecclesiastes

4:9-10 – See Loneliness

5:12 – See Sleep/Insomnia

11:4 – See Procrastination

10:37 – See Relational Idolatry

11:28-30 – See Depression, Health, Overwhelmed/Stressed, Suicidal Thoughts, Weary

15:19 – See Sexual Immorality

18:15-16 – See Conflict (Fights)

19:4-6 – See In-Laws

25:26-27 – See Finances

28:18-20 – See Loneliness

Mark

6:31 – See Sleep/Insomnia

10:9 – See Marriage

10:20-27 – See Perfectionism

John

3:17 – See Guilt

Acts

8:23 – See Bitterness

Romans

2:1-3 – See Critical Spirit

4:19-25 – See Impotence/Sexual Dysfunction

6:11-13 – See Control

8:1 – See Guilt

8:18 – See Grief

8:28-29 – See Childhood Sexual Abuse, Impotence

8:31-34 – See Bitterness

12:1-2 – See Anorexia/Bulimia, Health

12:18 – See Conflict (Fights)

13:13-14 – See Sexual Immorality

14:23 – See Rejection

Subject-Scripture Index

1 Corinthians

6:10 – Drunkenness

6:13 – See Gluttony

6:18-20 – See Anorexia/Bulimia, Health, Lust, Pornography, Sexual Immorality

9:24-27 – Disciplined Living

10:13 – See Pornography

13:4-7 – See Marriage

13:11 – See Moodiness

14:33-40 – Disorganization

2 Corinthians

4:7-9 – Discouraged/Downcast, Moodiness, Overwhelmed, Stressed

12:9 – See Perfectionism

Galatians

5:26 – See Envy

6:9-10 – See Weary

Ephesians

2:3-7 – See Lust

4:2-3 – See In-laws

4:25 – See Deception

4:26-27 – See Anger

4:29 – See Communication

4:31-32 – See Bitterness, Rejection

5:15-16 – See Procrastination, Time Usage

5:18 – Drunkenness

5:25-28 – See Marriage, Perfectionism, Spouse Abuse

6:1-4 – See Children, Dysfunctional Family

6:10 – See Impotence/Sexual Dysfunction

A Biblical Handbook for Counseling Heart Issues

Philippians
>2:3-4 – See Relational Idolatry
>3:8 – See Relational Idolatry
>3:12-14 – See Perfectionism
>3:19 – See Gluttony
>4:6-11 – See Anxiety/Worry, Decision Making, Envy

Colossians
>3:9 – See Deception
>3:13 – Dysfunctional Family
>3:17 – See Apathy
>3:19 – See Spouse Abuse
>3:23-24 – See Apathy, Laziness
>4:5 – See Time Usage

1 Thessalonians
>4:3-5 – See Sexual Immorality

2 Thessalonians
>3:10 – See Laziness

1 Timothy
>6:10 – See Finances

2 Timothy
>1:7 – Disciplined Living, Fear

Titus
>3:1-2 – See Rebellion

Hebrews
>8:12 – See Guilt
>12:1-2 – See Suicidal Thoughts
>12:15 – See Bitterness

ABOUT THE AUTHOR

Jonathan Okinaga, Ph.D.

Dr. Okinaga (Dr. O to his students) is the Director of the Biblical Counseling Certificate Program, Assistant Professor of Biblical Counseling, and Hope for the Heart Chair of Biblical Counseling in the Jack D. Terry School of Educational Ministries at Southwestern Baptist Theological Seminary in Fort Worth, Texas. He is a Certified Biblical Counselor with the Association of Certified Biblical Counselors (ACBC). Having over fifteen years of counseling experience, he has served in various ministries and treatment facilities specializing in addiction and substance abuse. He has written multiple books including: *How God Sanitized My Soul, My Loved One Is an Addict, Now What?,* and *From Sin to Disease: The Medicalization of Addiction and Its Influence on How the Southern Baptist Convention Approaches Ministering to Those Who Struggle with Mind Altering Substances.*

Dr. O often covers topics such as "A Biblical Approach to Addiction Counseling," "Depression and Anxiety," and "Discipleship & Biblical Counseling." He has made presentations in locations as varied as Tokyo, Japan; Vidalia, Georgia; Honolulu, Hawaii; various locations in the state of Texas; and online. He has been a part of the Southwestern Baptist Theological Seminary community since 2014 in the roles of Teaching Assistant, Adjunct Professor, and his current roles. Dr. O is married to Nicole, and they are parents to James.

ABOUT THE CONTRIBUTORS

Cheryl Bell, Ph.D.

Dr. Bell is an Adjunct Professor at Southwestern Baptist Theological Seminary in the Jack D. Terry School of Educational Ministries where she teaches Biblical Counseling to degree-seeking ladies in the school's Women's Studies program. She has served in this role since 2016. In 2021, she accepted the role of an Adjunct Professor at Midwestern Baptist Theological Seminary where she currently teaches and supervises students in the Biblical Counseling program. With eleven years of biblical counseling experience, Dr. Bell regularly counsels women in the seminary community, her church, and in national and international contexts through online platforms. She is married to Rex, with whom she has four adult children—Anna, Austin, Lauren, and Emily—who have families of their own.

Derrick Bledsoe, Th.M.

Derrick serves as the Senior Pastor of City on a Hill church in Fort Worth, TX. He has served in teaching and preaching ministries for over a decade. He is a contributing author and speaker of Mockingbird Ministries, as well as having spoken at various ministerial and theological conferences. Derrick earned a Bachelor of Arts in Linguistics from the University of Texas at Arlington with an emphasis in syntax; both a Master of Divinity and a Master of Theology from Southwestern Baptist Theological Seminary. He is currently working on a Ph.D. in Systematic Theology at Southwestern Baptist Theological Seminary. His research focuses on how Christ's incarnation impacts anthropology, ecclesiology, and pneumatology. Derrick grew up in an extremely broken and non-Christian home. As a result, he has a heart for seeing the Word of God applied to brokenness, addiction, abuse, and other maladies wrought by sin.

John Hofecker, Ph.D.

Dr. Hofecker is an Adjunct Professor of Biblical Counseling at Southwestern Baptist Theological Seminary, Mid-America Baptist Theological Seminary, and Luther Rice University and Seminary. Certified by the Association of Certified Biblical Counselors (ACBC), he provides counsel to those within his local church community. Dr. Hofecker assists individuals in delving into the depths of Scripture and applying its teachings to their daily lives through biblical counseling. He frequently works alongside his wife, Stacey, to offer guidance to couples.

Gady Youmans, D.Ed.Min.

Dr. Youmans, lead pastor at Word of Life Baptist Church in Vidalia, GA, has devoted two decades to ministry. His dedication extends beyond the church doors as he champions biblical teaching and training at the Sweet Onion Christian Learning Center (SOCLC). Since founding the ministry in 2014, he has served as the Executive Director and Lead Teacher, guiding public school students through Bible courses. He pursued and earned two bachelor degrees from Brewton-Parker College in 2011. He later graduated with two Master of Arts degrees in 2020 and a Doctor of Educational Ministry in 2022 from Southwestern Baptist Theological Seminary. His love for spreading the gospel has taken him across the globe on mission trips that have sown seeds of the gospel in diverse cultures. His beloved wife, Lauren, and their two children, Samuel and Naomi, anchor his life. Dr. Youmans' vision is to witness lives uplifted through the truth of Scripture.

www.ingramcontent.com/pod-product-compliance
Lightning Source LLC
Chambersburg PA
CBHW070051030426
42335CB00016B/1853